A NATION IN THE RED

The Government Debt Crisis and
What We Can Do About It

MURRAY HOLLAND

New York   Chicago   San Francisco   Athens   London
Madrid   Mexico City   Milan   New Delhi
Singapore   Sydney   Toronto

1 2 3 4 5 6 7 8 9 0 DOC/DOC 1 9 8 7 6 5 4 3

ISBN   978-0-07-182979-3
MHID   0-07-182979-2

e-ISBN   978-0-07-182980-9
e-MHID   0-07-182980-6

Library of Congress Cataloging-in-Publication Data

Holland, Murray.
  A nation in the red : the government debt crisis and what we can do about it / by Murray Holland.
      pages cm
  Includes bibliographical references and index.
  ISBN 978-0-07-182979-3 (alk. paper)–ISBN 0-07-182979-2 (alk. paper)
  1. Debts, Public–United States.   2. Government spending policy–United States.   3. Financial crises–United States.   4. United States–Economic conditions–2009   5. United States–Economic policy–2009   I. Title.
  HJ8119.H65 2014
  336.3'40973—dc23   2013027445

Dedicated to my wife, Kim,
the love of my life.

CONTENTS

CHAPTER
4 THE FINANCIAL CAUSES OF THE DEBT TRAP 101

CHAPTER
5 PSYCHOLOGICAL CAUSES OF THE DEBT TRAP 127

CHAPTER 9

WHAT DOES ALL THIS MEAN TO YOU, AND HOW CAN YOU HELP?   245

PREFACE

The federal government debt and deficit problem has been in the news over the last few years and has reached a fever pitch. There is no doubt the United States is in serious financial trouble. This book presents all the information necessary for you to understand how the country got here, how bad things are, and what can be done about it. As I listened to all the news over the last five years, I realized that I didn't have enough information to determine if the nation really was at risk or whether the media was exaggerating. Sound bites could not give me enough information to make a decision about whether or not the U.S. government would collapse from its own debt or whether all the news was just sensationalism and the government was really financially solvent. I decided to find out for myself all the information necessary to make a decision about my own investments and assets in the long term, whether to cut and run (sell everything and move to Singapore), or keep all my assets in the United States denominated in dollars. I also thought about what I should do about my family and living in a world after an economic collapse, if that was even going to happen.

In early 2011, I started studying all the information I could get my hands on to make an informed decision. My financial background, analyzing hundreds of companies and running a few, was the perfect background to plow through the literally thousands of pages of government financial information; hundreds of thousands of pages of reporting on the European problems, currency issues, and economic issues; and millions of pages of blogs, academic viewpoints, and public opinions. I was determined to figure out what was going to happen in the United States so that I could decide what to do with my family and assets. I have reviewed detailed government budgets since the country was founded as well as prepared analyses by multitudes of government and banking agencies, including the Treasury, Federal Reserve, Congressional Budget Office, Bureau of Economic Analysis, Census Bureau, Office of Management and Budget, and independently produced analyses and opinion.

It never occurred to me to write a book about the problem until I started having discussions with friends who are themselves financial professionals. Many of them asked me to share my work, as they had not done the work themselves. They wanted to see my analysis. When I realized that many of my very smart colleagues were not fully informed, I decided it was time to convert my work into a book that everyone can understand and from which everyone can benefit. In this book, I have set out all the information necessary for an understanding of how and why the country has gotten to this point. There is a debt crisis in the immediate future that will cripple the United States; there is no doubt about that. Anyone who reads this book should be able to take the information and determine on her or his own what is getting ready to happen and what the U.S. government should do at this point. How it affects each person is a separate issue, since everyone has a unique financial, family, and psychological situation.

In this book, I have set forth the steps necessary to save the nation from collapse and the government actions necessary to get us there. Whether Congress and the Obama administration over the next few years can make the necessary changes to save everybody from the Debt Trap is something that is purely speculative. I have set forth the options (five of them) now that the country is caught in the Debt Trap. If you are a prepper (the modern version of survivalist), you will find all the evidence you need in this book to conclude there will be an economic collapse. If you are an eternal optimist, you probably will not be after reading this book. If you believe the government will always be there to take care of you, you will not think that after reading this book. I have endeavored to provide actual government data in a form that will be understandable to most people so that you will have the resources you need to decide whether to start taking action to protect yourself and your family.

A NATION IN THE RED

To contract new debts is not the way to
pay old ones.

—George Washington

The United States through reckless management and spending by Congress has become *A Nation in the Red,* joining a large group of countries suffering through depressions caused by irresponsible governments. The use of debt by governments is a politically easy way out of increasing taxes that people do not want to pay. It is also a good mechanism to make the economy appear as though it is growing fast when, in fact, it is not. When government borrowing is accompanied by borrowing by the private sector, a robust economy can develop that includes housing and stock market price increases, income increases, tax receipt increases, and so on. This phenomenon is known as a bubble and is a great experience for everyone...until it bursts. During the buildup of the bubble, banks appear more stable and profitable as their underlying portfolio is performing well and profits look strong. The downside of these buildups is the bust: we have had two since 2000. The first being the dot-com bust that started in 2000, and the second the housing bust that started in 2008. Every time there is a bubble there is a bust or a recession ... and the bust always is more painful than the bubble was fun. The United States of America has borrowed too much money. It is now *A Nation in the Red*, and nothing good will come of it.

Sovereign debt defaults and crises in the economy, currency, and banking are all interrelated. Sovereign debt crises occur when a nation in the red determines not to pay interest and principal on its debts. Investors stop lending to that government, and the entire economy of that country goes into depression. Economic crises happen when investment and business activity slow down in a country. When businesses slow down expansion or actually downsize, they fire employees who in turn cannot pay their mortgages or eat out at restaurants; if the downturn is large scale, it can cause banks and other businesses to fail. Currency crises are triggered when the international demand for a currency shrinks or the amount of the currency available increases as a host country prints more of its currency. The value of the currency then falls quickly and deeply, which in turn can hurt the host economy. Banking crises occur when a large number of banks become insolvent. Banks become insolvent when the value of their loans drops significantly due to a fall of economic activity, such as we have experienced since 2008. When people are unable to pay their mortgages and businesses cannot pay their loans, banks that have made these loans may end up repossessing assets that are not worth the loan value. At this point, banks will fail, causing more problems to the economy. To make things worse, these crises usually happen all together, and central banks like the Federal Reserve Bank have to keep it all together by throwing money at the problems.

In their paper entitled "This Time is Different: A Panoramic View of Eight Centuries of Financial Crises," Carmen Reinhart and Kenneth Rogoff reviewed 800 years of sovereign defaults, how they were created, and the devastation left in their wakes. Their work is not unique but is often cited as an excellent compendium of defaults that are readily accessible. Hundreds of historians throughout time have written about sovereign defaults; the point to glean from this historical review is how easy it is to walk into the trap created by sovereign debt. Most countries as they are developing have many debt defaults as well as high inflation, currency crises, and banking crises. Reinhart and Rogoff also point out that debt defaults happen in cycles, which in turn are followed by a "lull" in defaults.

Importantly, Reinhart and Rogoff have charted all countries that have defaulted on their debt throughout history and not surprisingly there is a cycle of defaults. (This is a worldwide phenomenon because the world is connected economically.) The first such cycle happened during the Napoleonic wars. The second was from 1820 to 1840, when almost half the countries in the world were in default, including all of Latin America. The third was from 1870 to 1890. The fourth covered the years 1930 to 1950, which included the Great Depression and the Second World War, when again nearly half of all countries defaulted. There was another default cycle in the 1980s and 1990s due to defaults in emerging market debts. Their analysis goes one step further in combining each country's gross domestic product (GDP) to find out what percentage of global GDP was in default. What they found was that after World War II, countries making up nearly 40 percent of global GDP were in default. This is eerily similar to the world today.

A default is simply the inability to pay a debt when it becomes due, a definition used to judge whether a company, an individual, a country, or an institution is bankrupt. This is the core tenant of the bankruptcy laws in the United States. It is this simple definition that has come to haunt many countries over time and will be the ultimate issue that the U.S. Congress will face soon.

All defaults are not the same. One is an outright repudiation where a country says it will not pay creditors. There is no doubt this is a default. Another is a country saying it is reducing the current interest rate or will simply suspend interest payments for a period of time. Yet another is a country saying it is extending the period of time to repay the principal. Some countries like the United States originally agreed to repay in gold but instead repaid in dollars. Other countries inflate their currencies by printing more to pay the debt. These various "gimmicks" are really one and the same form of default.

In 377 BC, ten out of thirteen Greek municipalities (cities) defaulted on their debt to the Delos Temple.[1] (The Temple of Delos, or Delos Temple, was a religious temple that had made loans to a number of cities around Greece.) This is the first recorded government default on debt borrowed from others. Since then, hundreds of defaults of debt by countries, states, and municipalities have occurred and will undoubtedly continue to happen forever. Greece has defaulted five times since 1800; England three times before 1600; France eight times between 1558 and 1788; China in 1929 and 1939; Nigeria five times since 1960; Russia in 1839, 1917, and again in 1998; and Argentina three times since 1980. The all-time leader in serial defaults is Spain, having defaulted seven times in the nineteenth century alone, and that is after defaulting six times in the previous three centuries. This is just to name a few. How and why does this happen? Can it actually happen to the U.S. federal government? What happens to the U.S. dollar? How does it affect the economy? How does it affect each of us? If you are not asking these questions, you need to read this book.

Table 1.1 is a representative listing of defaults by countries in recent history.

Table 1.1 Selected Sovereign Defaults or Restructurings[2]

EUROPE							
Austria	1868	1914	1932				
Bulgaria	1915	1932					
Germany	1932						
Greece	1824	1843	1860	1893	current crisis		
Hungary	1932						
Italy	1940						
Moldova	2002						
Poland	1936	1981					
Portugal	1834	1892	current crisis				
Romania	1915	1933	1981				
Russia	1839	1917	1998				
Serbia/ Yugoslavia	1895	1933	1983				
Spain	1820	1831	1851	1867	1886	1899	1944
Turkey	1876	1915	1940	1978			
Ukraine	1998	2000					
AMERICAS							
Argentina	1830	1890	1915	1930	1982	2001	
Bolivia	1874	1931	1980				
Brazil	1826	1898	1914	1931	1983		
Chile	1826	1880	1931	1983			
Colombia	1826	1879	1900	1932			
Costa Rica	1827	1874	1895	1937	1983		
Cuba	1933	1982					
Dominica	2003						
Dominican Republic	1869	1899	1931	1982			
Ecuador	1832	1868	1911	1914	1931	1982	1999
El Salvador	1827	1921	1931				
Grenada	2004						

AMERICAS (*continued*)							
Guatemala	1828	1876	1894	1933			
Honduras	1827	1873	1914	1981			
Mexico	1827	1859	1867	1914	1982		
Nicaragua	1828	1894	1911	1932	1980		
Panama	1932	1982					
Paraguay	1827	1874	1892	1920	1932	1986	2003
Peru	1826	1876	1931	1978	1983		
Uruguay	1876	1891	1915	1933	1983	2003	
Venezuela	1832	1847	1864	1878	1892	1898	1982

In addition to these defaults, and in order to make observations without having to walk through every detail, there have been dozens of other sovereign defaults. Many African countries, such as Angola, Cameroon, Congo, Egypt, Gabon, Liberia, Nigeria, Madagascar, Malawi, Côte d'Ivoire, Morocco, Mozambique, Niger, Senegal, Seychelles, Sierra Leone, South Africa, Sudan, Tanzania, Togo, Uganda, Zaire, and Zambia, have defaulted on their sovereign debt. Many Asian and Middle East countries, such as Indonesia, Jordan, Philippines, Pakistan, and Vietnam, have defaulted. Iceland defaulted. The current European situation, where we have seen defaults by Greece, Cyprus, Portugal, Ireland, and potentially Spain and Italy, are red flags to the situation facing the United States today.[3] These countries are simply countries that have borrowed too much money.

All these listed defaults are by a country to outside, third-party lenders and do not include what are probably hundreds of defaults that never make headlines, such as sovereign debt to citizens or financial institutions within a country. These are often renegotiated and restructured inside the complex relationship of a government, its central bank, and the institution. For example, Argentina, during its many years of debt problems, would close banks, take gold and dollars held in safety deposit boxes and accounts, and replace them with pesos. This was not considered a default to third-party lenders but was considered outright theft by citizens.

There is no sense in trying to describe each default by each country, or even to list all the defaults by each country. Defaults, it turns out, come in many forms from simple technical glitches in the payment process, which cause a delay in payment (as has happened with U.S. government debt payments), to outright repudiations of debt (as has happened thousands of times throughout history). Particularly interesting examples include the default during the Bolshevik Revolution in Russia in 1917; a default in 1867 when Mexico repudiated the debt incurred by Emperor Maximilian (installed by the French) and again in 1911 after a revolution; and a default in 2012 with a negotiated repudiation of debt that was owed by Greece. This does not include hundreds of other forms of defaults by countries facing the "Debt Trap" (as explained in Chapter 3), which have dug themselves out of a hole by modifying the terms by lowering interest rates or extending the due dates of principal and interest payments. This, of course, is still a default since investors did not receive payment when or as promised. A default list also cannot cover all the instances where countries issued newly printed currency to lenders, particularly lenders within their own borders. This technique, of course, really doesn't solve anything, as the value of the currency falls so fast that the same effect as a default occurs for lenders and the general population. Attempting to classify a sovereign default is a tricky matter, since the actions of the debtor government can turn a default into a forced restructuring of the debt, recession, depression, or currency crisis. It all depends on what actions the government decides to take.

The unavoidable conclusion is that sovereign debt default is almost a common occurrence, and the size of the government has nothing to do with a default. Every country that has become a Nation in the Red faces the pain of the markets and payment of interest on the national debt becomes a significant burden. Until the recent default situation with Greece, Argentina held the record for the largest default at $89 billion. At that point in time, the total debt to GDP was only 48 percent, but the interest rate environment was considerably higher than it is today. The burden of interest expense was too great to keep paying it. We will get into this issue in a later chapter.

Economists love to delve into the details of each default and compare clusters of defaults, countries that continue to default, and countries that have learned better. To me, this is an interesting academic exercise, but the details of it are not going to help me with planning for what is facing everybody in the United States over the next few years and possibly decades. The conclusion I am drawing from all this is that politicians, who of course are the people who borrow all this money, are capable of driving the bus over a cliff all around the world. I do, however, know a lot of smart people who actually think it cannot and will not happen in the United States.

U.S. DEFAULTS

Surely the United States and the individual states have never defaulted on their debt; that would be unthinkable. But they have. Four times in U.S. history the federal and state governments have turned to default to get out of financial trouble. During the Revolutionary War, the states ran up a significant amount of debt to support the war effort. It became clear that they would not be able to pay it back, and the value of the debt dropped significantly, being traded among investors at pennies on the dollar. In 1790, Congress passed a law assuming all the states' debts, amounting to $21 million. Interest on the debt was deferred to 1801, and payment of the principal was extended. This was actually a change in terms of the bonds, a "default," as the original bonds could not have been repaid by the states. After the legislation was signed by President Washington, the value of the bonds skyrocketed, as investors now had a chance of getting their money back. Other "defaults" were timing issues, except for the one in the 1930s, when the U.S. government refused to pay in gold as promised.

THIS TIME IT IS DIFFERENT

There is a mantra in political circles that goes like this: "This time it is different" (which also is the title to the Reinhart and Rogoff book). The view is that both countries and creditors have learned from history how to stay out of the Debt Trap. The assumption is that macroeconomic policies and smarter lending practices will prevent the United States from another wave of defaults. More governments are relying on domestic financing. Reinhart and Rogoff conclude that this thinking is delusional, and I concur. This thinking, I am afraid, is one of the causes of the Debt Trap.

WHY GOVERNMENTS DEFAULT

So why does a government default? The simple answer is that it does not have the cash to pay the principal and interest on money it borrowed when it becomes due. But why? A government has to pay its debts when they become due, just as any company or individual does. It has to pay those bonds with cash. It really doesn't matter where a government gets its cash so long as it pays the bonds according to the terms of the bond. The two primary sources of cash to a government are taxing and borrowing. We all know what taxing is, as all of us pay lots of taxes that come in all shapes and sizes. If a government spends more than it takes in through taxes, it must either borrow the difference or issue new currency. The act of spending more than you take in is called "deficit spending." This deficit has to come from somewhere, so governments have been borrowing it from investors for years. So, who loans them all this money?

Borrowing is managed through well-developed global debt markets. In ancient times, there was no developed market for government bonds, and when individuals loaned money to a government, the government would pay them back. Today, however, the worldwide market for government bonds is enormous: around $49 trillion.[4] These bonds are traded freely and electronically and make up around 60 percent of all debt securities traded around the world. Of the countries with the top 20 economies in the world today, all of them have a significant amount of sovereign debt outstanding. The bonds are bought by banks, pension funds, insurance companies, other governments, companies, and individuals. Government bonds are generally viewed as low-risk investments that can always be counted on to pay on the date promised. But as we know from the previous list of defaults, this is not always true.

So why can't a country simply borrow more from the market to pay the debt that is coming due? Well, this is exactly what countries do, including the United States. Few countries actually have the cash from taxes to pay back their bonds, so they borrow more money to pay back the money they previously borrowed. Not only are they borrowing money to pay the amount that is coming due, they are borrowing additional money to spend. So let's say the U.S. government has a $50 billion bond coming due this Friday. The government will issue $50 billion of new bonds Friday morning and take the proceeds and pay off the bonds falling due. Then it will also issue another $20 billion to get new cash to pay government bills. The markets seem to always loan governments more than they can pay back, and this situation has been true for some time.

To bring the economic analysis a little closer to home, we all know people who have overborrowed on their mortgage, credit cards, cars, and so on. Their income is not sufficient to pay the mortgage, car payment, baby sitters, electric bill, water bill, and food bill. So they start cutting back. They eat at home, don't buy steaks, cut coupons, turn off lights when not in use, use only one water heater, and so on. This clearly saves cash, and they need to do it. They get an offer to roll over credit card debt to a new credit card, which is nothing but reborrowing: if you borrow $10,000 to pay off a $10,000 debt, maybe even at a lower interest rate, in the end you will still owe $10,000. The problem they have is that the mortgage payment cannot be reduced; neither can the car payment and the credit card payments. These fixed-debt payments are just that: fixed. They have to be made regardless of the amount of income one has coming in. So the debtors are enslaved to lives of figuring out how to make each payment each month to keep the whole thing together another month. They may "borrow" from friends and family, or perhaps they'll pawn rings and anything of value. The extent to which these people will go is impressive, but these are just "games" to keep the ultimate crash from actually happening, although everyone knows the crash is going to happen.

This game is played until one day there are no more rings to pawn or no more friends from whom they can borrow, and the mortgage, car, and credit card payments are past due. This is the end for these people. There is no cash and no more ability to keep it going any longer. They are about to experience a train wreck of their own making. If only they had not started borrowing on their credit card in the first place. If only they had bought a cheaper house. If only they had bought a used car. If only …

These people are financially irresponsible and are now financially devastated. It is fun to borrow so you can lead a better lifestyle, but each of us is responsible for our own financial planning, and debt commitments need to be well thought out and planned to make sure our own debts can be paid. Your own financial planning needs to include what happens to you in a recession if you lose your job, if you get divorced, if you can't sell your old house, and so on. The blame for poor financial planning lies squarely on your shoulders. No one else is going to help you. It is clear that the markets (banks and credit card companies) are willing to loan you more money than you are capable of repaying so you cannot rely on the banks, credit card companies, or car finance companies to do your homework for you. You have to do it for yourself. What is amazing to me is that so many people go through their own personally created Debt Trap many times, declaring bankruptcy several times in their lives.

It would be terrifying to be in the position of these people. Their lives will spiral down to a meager existence that is hard to imagine. Needless to say, you do not have to have an actual "crash" to experience the effects of overborrowing, but the day comes when you have to pay it back, and that is when you wish you had never borrowed it in the first place. When you borrow for the first time, it feels like you are spending Other People's Money because you have not yet faced paying it back. The payback is always difficult, and once you are within the jaws of the Debt Trap, payback is impossible. Financial ruin is the remedy.

Governments are no different than individuals. The economics are the same, although they have more games they can play to keep the whole thing together longer. Reborrowing works for a long time, but one day it will stop. What makes it stop? For governments, the market makes it stop. Just as there comes a time in the lives of people who are overextended when no bank will loan them any more money, such is the case with governments. At first, the markets will increase the loan interest rate because they know the government is borrowing too much and they perceive there is some risk in being repaid. Then, when a government gets in real trouble, the market interest rates skyrocket. In the case of Greece, interest rates ballooned to 50 percent before the actual default. As I was researching the issue of how a debt or currency crisis starts, I was surprised at how it is triggered and how fast it proceeds.

Investors in the bond market are not stupid. They study risk and options, and at some point they realize that a government is too much in debt and is never really going to be able to repay the money it has borrowed nor be able to reborrow money to pay the debt that is becoming due. But why are there so many defaults if investors are so smart? Throughout history, this has happened hundreds of times, if not thousands. It is at this point that the market refuses to lend any more money unless the loan is at higher interest rates. This market reaction is the beginning of the end for the creditor nation. Historically, this happens after the point in time where a country can correct the situation. In the case of Greece, this point occurred when its national debt hit 160 percent of its GDP. Why didn't the market rebel when Greece's debt hit 70 percent, 80 percent, 90 percent, or 100 percent of GDP? When investors start to rebel, it is generally too late for a country to save itself without some form of debt restructuring. The situation in Europe today should be considered a blessing to countries like Italy and France, for the problems with Greece have put a spotlight on all of Europe as well as the United States. Some countries have acted swiftly and decisively when the markets focused on them, as was the case with England and Ireland. But more about Europe later, for it is clear that without market reaction, governments would borrow an infinite amount of money until a final implosion. Why do the markets keep lending to a Nation in the Red, a country that is clearly in financial trouble?

The Western Europe debt crisis occurring under our noses is a live study that is well documented and analyzed. The data coming out of the mess is endless, with thousands of charts, microeconomic analysis, currency exchange issues, and the like. The economists' views of the debacle are excruciatingly detailed and mind-numbingly complex. Luckily for me and you, while the myriad of economic details are interesting to read and absorb, the crux of the problem and the solution to the problem boil down to a few, easy-to-understand concepts that we use in our everyday lives.

The reasons investors continue lending to countries that are clearly and highly leveraged are many. The first is due to credit default swaps (CDSs). A credit default swap is simply an insurance contract between the issuer (usually an insurance company, bank, or hedge fund) and the purchaser, say, the owner of a government bond. Suppose, for example, that Bank A wanted to buy a bond issued by the government of Italy. Bank A could purchase a credit default swap on the bond from an insurance company or hedge fund. The credit default swap would guarantee Bank A that in the event the government of Italy defaulted on its debt held by Bank A the issuer of the credit default swap would pay interest and principal on the bond. Bank A does not even have to own a bond to buy a credit default swap. The bank can simply enter into a contract with a hedge fund referencing the government of Italy and a specific bond, pay a fee for the "insurance," and get paid in the event of a default. These instruments, similar to mortgage guaranties, are now a multitrillion-dollar global phenomenon and are used and traded in totally unregulated markets. Most sovereign debt today is supported by credit default swaps. (This type of contract was mentioned often during the economic crisis of 2008–2009; in fact, it was the instrument that brought down AIG, the largest insurance company in the world at that time.)

There are no exchanges for credit default swaps; they are not registered anywhere; they are not subject to state insurance regulations; and they are not all structured the same. Moreover, the higher the risk of the credit, the higher the premium for the CDS and the more money a CDS issuer makes. For instance, a CDS on Italy's five-year bonds would cost around 4 percent in 2012. A purchaser of

$10 million of Italy's bonds would pay $400,000 to get insurance. The issuer of the CDS just made $400,000 for writing the contract, and if Italy does not default, the issuer gets to keep the entire $400,000. It's very easy money, so long as there is no default, which is why hedge funds and insurance companies like it. The higher risk they take, the more money they make. Issuers love credit default swaps because there is such a large market and trillions of dollars of potential profit. If there were no credit default swaps and investors had to actually take the credit risk, the market probably would never loan as much to countries with credit risk. George Soros, one of the leading currency traders, estimates that there are $45 trillion of credit default swaps issued. The U.S. Comptroller of the Currency thinks there are over $200 trillion of credit default swaps just with U.S. banks.

A second reason that investors continue lending into the market even if a country's debt exceeds 100 percent of GDP is because there is a highly liquid market into which they can sell in a matter of seconds. If you own $1 billion of federal government Treasury securities, you can track the market value of those securities every second. If you decide to sell, you can do that in a matter of seconds. So long as investors feel that there is an easy, fast out, they do not look to the long-term fundamentals of the underlying securities; they look only at the current market. Were investors required to hold all government securities until maturity, let's say 10 years, without the ability to sell into the market before maturity, they would be more concerned with the underlying credit of the United States. Clearly the U.S. federal government is taking advantage of this market as do all governments and larger corporations issuing debt. Because the Treasuries (or corporate bonds, for that matter) are "liquid," they are cheaper to sell into the market than to sell to someone (a bank, for instance) that would hold the bond in a portfolio until maturity.

When a company's financial performance is analyzed, three primary financial statements provide a good picture of that company's historical financial performance and a good background for assessing its future. These statements are a balance sheet, results of operations (an income statement), and a cash flow statement. The balance sheet discloses a company's assets and liabilities. It gives a snapshot at a certain date of the amount of liabilities. For the U.S. government, we know what the current snapshot of liabilities looks like. As of March 31, 2013, the government owes $16.8 trillion in "gross debt." Realistically, there is no need to look at assets, since it is not foreseeable (although possible) that the government would sell assets to pay off debts. The next analysis is results of operations, or how much net income or loss a company has had in the preceding period, say a year. We know the federal government lost $1.1 trillion during 2012 and is projected to lose $642 billion in 2013. We also know that the cash it burned was around this amount.

Studying historical financial statements is step one in looking at a government's financial condition. The next step is to make projections of future results of operations and cash flow. This is a complicated task for many companies, but with respect to our federal government these numbers are readily available. The Office of Management and Budget, Federal Reserve, Congressional Budget Office, and many banks, investment banks, financial data providers, university economists, and others provide all the projections anyone could possibly review. While there are many nuances throughout all these different projections, we have reached the point where micrometering is a meaningless exercise. The numbers are simply astounding.

Table 1.2 shows the United States actual operating numbers for the last 10 years (fiscal year October 1 to September 30).

Table 1.2 Operating Expenditures of U.S. Government, 2002–2013[5]

	2002	2003	2004	2005	2006	2007	2008	2009	2010	2011	2012
Receipts ($ trillion)	1.9	1.8	1.9	2.2	2.4	2.6	2.5	2.1	2.2	2.2	2.5
Outlays ($ trillion)	2.0	2.2	2.3	2.5	2.7	2.7	3.0	3.5	3.5	3.8	3.6
Deficit ($ trillion)	0.1	0.4	0.4	0.3	0.3	0.1	0.5	1.4	1.3	1.6	1.1

The total of all federal government expenses (outlays) and programs that exist today, according to the budget released by the Obama administration in March 2013, are projected to grow as shown in Table 1.3.

Federal government tax receipts are a wild card. The entire budget starts with one primary assumption on which all revenue is based: growth in GDP. The assumption for fiscal 2012 was 4.5 percent GDP growth. Historically, GDP growth has been 3.3 percent over the last 80 years. Nevertheless, Table 1.4 shows what federal receipts looks like using Obama's GDP growth rate assumptions in the 2012 budget.

These projections were released in February 2012, half way through the fiscal year. The assumption of 4.5 percent growth did not happen. It was close to 2 percent. When these numbers were released, the Treasury Department and the Obama administration knew that GDP could not possibly hit 4.5 percent growth, as they had numbers for six months of 2012 and knew the rest of the year would not be great. Their release of this assumption strains credibility. The government has been so bad at projecting numbers that it can never be trusted, as has been the case with most administrations as well as with the Congressional Budget

Table 1.3 Projected Growth Rate of U.S. Government, 2013–2022[6]

	2012	2013	2014	2015	2016	2017	2018	2019	2020	2021	2022
Expenses ($ trillion)	3.5	3.7	3.8	3.9	4.1	4.2	4.4	4.7	5.0	5.2	5.5

Table 1.4 Projected U.S. Government Receipts, 2013–2022[7]

Revenue	2012	2013	2014	2015	2016	2017	2018	2019	2020	2021	2022
GDP Growth Assumption (%)	4.5	4.7	5.3	6.0	5.9	5.7	5.0	4.5	4.4	4.3	4.3
Federal Revenue ($ trillion)	2.5	2.9	3.2	3.5	3.7	3.9	4.2	4.4	4.6	4.9	5.1

Office (CBO). Was the White House trying to deceive the public? Is it just wishful thinking on their part? When we look at future numbers, the Obama budget expects the economy to grow by 4 to 6 percent each year over the next decade, despite the fact that the average growth over the last 50 years has been around 3.25 percent. The government's numbers are flawed and should not be trusted. The same analysis is true with respect to expenses. Things are worse than the government admits or publishes.

The delta between revenue and expense is the deficit. As you can see, it really doesn't matter what revenue case is used, the country is facing mammoth deficits. At some time in the near future, the markets are going to price federal debt at higher and higher interest rates. As this happens, a larger and larger percentage of government expenses will go to pay for that interest. It will reach the point where the government will decide to default rather than pay the interest because too much of its receipts will be used to cover interest expense instead of government programs.

Here is how it will work.

In early 2013, the United States was sitting at $16.8 trillion in debt and receiving $2.7 trillion in tax revenue. The U.S. interest expense for 2013 will be around $360 billion.[8] This is an abnormally low number for three reasons. First, due to the Great Recession that started in 2008, interest rates have fallen to their lowest levels in modern history. Secondly, during 2012 the U.S. Treasury undertook the issue of mostly short-term debt to lower the country's interest expense. Third, the Federal Reserve has kept interest rates artificially low to encourage GDP growth. All this will change. The average interest rate on all Treasuries, which has averaged around 6 percent over the last 40 years, is now less than 2.2 percent.

The government reports a "net interest" expense, which subtracts the interest income it receives from many sources like student loans, from the interest expense on government debt, even though the two are unrelated. This makes bureaucrats in Washington, D.C., feel better for some reason, but the expense of $360 billion on the outstanding U.S. national debt is still there and will grow substantially as the economy recovers or the market starts risk-adjusting the country's debt. This expense is equal to almost half the U.S. military budget and more than half the size of Medicare or Medicaid. Neither the government nor any citizen gets any benefit from this expense. When interest rates rise back to a normal rate environment of 6 percent average for all outstanding Treasury debt, the interest expense will be around $720 billion a year (on just the debt to third parties), or almost 25 percent of the current federal tax revenue.

Interest rates can rise due to economic expansion and growth or perceived risk in the federal debt. In the case of Greece, interest rates reached over 50 percent before the European Central Bank stepped in to resolve the debt crisis. In Italy, interest rates reached 7.5 percent before government action to stop the deficit spending and statements by the European Central Bank quelled the market turmoil, at least temporarily. Spain saw interest rates of 8 percent, Ireland 9 percent, and Portugal 11 percent. All this is to say that none of these governments that were deficit spending were politically capable of balancing their budgets until market interest rates forced them to do so by requiring higher interest rates. Unfortunately, Congress is doing exactly what all these other countries have done, and the United States will find itself in their shoes as soon as interest rates return to normal. It is simply mathematical.

Once a country issues enough debt to make the market lose confidence, interest on its debt soars very quickly. Chapter 6 explains how this happens, and countries such as Cyprus, Greece, Portugal, Ireland, Iceland, Spain, and Italy know how this works very well. This high interest rate forces the government of a country to balance its budget by cutting expenses, increasing taxes, or both. High interest expense takes up so much of a government's budget that there is not enough left for essential services. In addition, the market refuses to loan any more money to the government, so it has no choice but to balance its budget. Either increasing taxes or decreasing expenditures takes money out of the economy, causing an immediate recession or depression and corresponding reduction in tax revenue. The downward spiral of higher interest rates and shrinking economy make the government deficit worse, and the spiral perpetuates itself. Such a government is not capable of paying its debt as it becomes due, has no cash for essential services (such as feeding its people or providing healthcare for its people), and must choose between paying for essential services or paying interest on its debt. When governments get to this point, they are caught in the "Debt Trap" and have always chosen to stop paying on their debt.

So politicians look at their options and first try some "gimmicks," such as manipulating their country's currency or implementing exchange controls, to try to escape the Debt Trap, but once the jaws of the trap are set, there is no real escape. The economy fails and joblessness skyrockets as more and more businesses fail. The government is powerless because either it has no money to distribute or it distributes money that is valueless. After all, the real power of government is economic; it has the ability to take money from people via taxation and redistribute it to other people in the way it sees fit. Without this ability, government is powerless. This is what the United States is facing: its citizens are about to become a victim of the government's foolish and irresponsible behavior.

A Nation in the Red is a nation plagued with poor leadership.

CHAPTER 2

REAL NUMBERS

The men and women of this country who toil are the ones who bear the cost of the Government. Every dollar that we carelessly waste means that their life will be so much the more meager.

—Calvin Coolidge, 1925

We do not have to look very far to see a clear picture of exactly what is going on with government finances. There is good financial data dating back to the beginning of the United States that we can view and analyze. This financial history is useful because we can see "real" numbers—what actually happened. As you will see, there is a large gulf between what people were told by the government would happen and what actually happened. Some of this was outside government control or projection, such as the events of 9/11 and Hurricane Katrina, but most, in my view, is simply inexperienced optimism by various government entities who want to sell a line to the American voters. These people are no different from the millions of entrepreneurs who show up projecting high returns from a great new product they are developing. It is very easy to make a great-looking PowerPoint presentation, but it is a different story converting that to reality, as we shall see.

GROWTH OF GOVERNMENT

The primary growth of government has been the federal government, but even state and local governments have contributed to a massive buildup in the government participation in the lives of the people and in GDP. Figure 2.1 shows federal, state, and local government growth as a percentage of GDP.

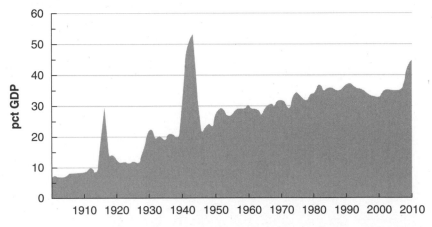

Figure 2.1 Government spending as a percentage of GDP.[1]

These are "real" numbers because they are historical and provided by the Office of Management and Budget (OMB) and the
U.S. Census. Many other sources, such as the Organization for
Economic Cooperation and Development (OECD), believe the
numbers are higher. The OECD, for example, shows U.S. federal,
state, and local outlays as 42 percent of GDP.[2] The U.S. Census
Bureau shows a total of 89,000 governments in the United States,
including federal, state, county, city, municipal utility districts,
and school districts.[3] All these spend money, and no one can actually tally the spending from all these entities. The obvious fact on
display is that government has grown steadily as a percentage of
GDP since 1929. During the 1790–1920 period, federal government spending averaged only 2.5 percent of GDP.[4] In 1930, total
government expenditures were under 3.4 percent of GDP.[5] Had the
government kept total expenditures there, the country would not
find itself in the current financial crisis.

Government programs enacted throughout history have managed to keep getting funding despite the obvious lack of need for a
large percentage of them. Ronald Reagan said, "The nearest thing
to eternal life we will ever see on this earth is a government program." This is the creeping nature of the growth of government.
Everyone elected to Congress thinks he or she has been elected to
spend taxpayer money. Congressmen and congresswomen want to
leave their mark on the world by sponsoring a program that will
do something and live forever, and that is what they do. So after
each program is enacted, it adds to the overall expenditures already
in place, and the slow escalation of government continues. The
only good news about this phenomenon is that they will have to
stop once they reach 100 percent and control every single penny
of spending!

Outside the spending during World War II, total government
spending rose considerably during times of economic downturns:
1929–1933 and 2007–2009. These two periods when government
spending rose dramatically as a percentage of GDP were primarily caused by the decline in GDP and by an increase in actual

spending by governments. During the period 1993–2001, total spending declined as a percentage of GDP primarily due to the "peace dividend"—there were no wars, and defense spending was cut significantly.

Almost all spending continues to rise in nominal dollars as the country experiences inflation. So, in nominal dollars the entire government budget is increasing. The only good method for analyzing the budget over time is to compare it to GDP so we can get an estimate of the relative size of expenditures. Comparing all government expenditures to GDP in Figure 2.1, we get a good assessment of what is actually happening. While most government expenditures have declined or stayed flat as a percentage of GDP over time, "social" programs have grown dramatically. Figure 2.2 shows the growth in social programs that is principally made up of social security, Medicare, and Medicaid, and much smaller components of welfare, housing, and recreation.

These are also "real" numbers. They tell the story of where the money is going. Social security is different from the medical and

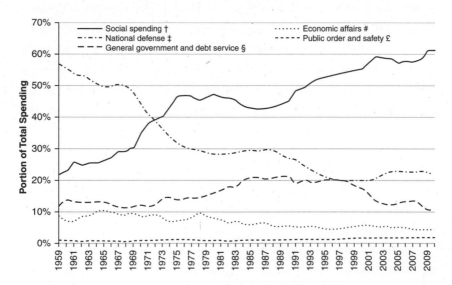

Figure 2.2   Federal government current expenditures by function, 1959–2010.[6]

welfare social programs in that social security was designed to be a mandatory savings account for all citizens. Since people paid into their accounts all the years they worked, the program should pay them back after retirement, just as a savings account in a bank must pay you back for savings contributions. This program, unlike all the other social programs that are flat-out handouts, is not really causing the deficit spending. It needs to be adjusted to reflect longer life expectations and changing demographics as the baby boomers are retiring, but I cannot place blame on it. The budget item that is really causing most of the pain is healthcare spending and various welfare programs.

Defense spending as a percentage of both GDP and the federal budget is going down. In fact, other than social program spending, all other components of the federal budget are either shrinking or are so small they are not causing any of our major financial problems. The cause of the higher spending, and hence deficit spending, is singularly social programs, namely Medicare, Medicaid, welfare, housing, education, and the like.

When John F. Kennedy was president, only about 25 percent of federal spending went to various entitlement programs, including social security, that covered 21 million Americans. Today, 61 percent of the federal spending goes to entitlements (including social security) covering 67 million recipients, or roughly 20 percent of the population. Today, the average American family of four that relies on federal assistance can receive $32,748 in benefits. This number is greater than the national average disposable income of $32,446.[7]

Table 2.1 shows the major transfer payments of the federal government that fall under social programs and "transfer payments," meaning they are taking money from people who made it and giving it to others.

The inescapable conclusion of the numbers in Table 2.1 is that almost two-thirds of the federal government is nothing more than a money collection and distribution machine. The federal government itself is not providing any service other than collecting and distributing cash as it sees fit.

Table 2.1 Major Social Programs and Transfer Payments of the U.S. Federal Government, 2011–2013[8]

($ billions)	2011	2012	2013 (est.)
Social security	$707	$755	$801
Medicare	$564	$554	$607
Unemployment	$117	$107	$77
Veterans benefits	$64	$63	$75
Railroad retirement	$11	$12	$12
Military medical	$11	$12	$12
Food stamps	$72	$78	$76
Black lung benefits	$1	$1	$1
Supplemental security income	$46	$49	$53
Refundable tax credits	$99	$83	$84
All other	$69	$66	$67
To the rest of the world	$18	$19	$20
Grants to states (Medicaid, other health and income security)	$518	$512	$524
Total transfer payments ($ trillion)	$2.3	$2.4	$2.0
Total government spending	$3.8	$3.9	$4.0
Percentage of total spending	61%	62%	62%
Percentage of GDP	15%	15%	15%

ARE BUDGET FORECAST NUMBERS "REAL"?

The Congressional Budget Office (CBO) prepares projections based on current laws and its expected GDP growth assumptions. These projections do provide the financial basis of congressional actions (except with respect to the Patient Protection and Affordable Care Act, commonly known as "Obamacare," which was passed without CBO projections) and give some guidance to Congress and administrations as to the impact of legislation. The only problem with their approach is that it is consistently wrong—and not by a little. Take, for instance, the CBO projections made in 2000. These projections are shown in Table 2.2.

Table 2.2 Projections by the Congressional Budget Offices of GDP Growth, 2000–2010[9]

	2000	2001	2002	2003	2004	2005	2006	2007	2008	2009	2010
Surplus ($ trillion)	0.115	0.137	0.194	0.194	0.219	0.241	0.292	0.32	0.342	0.369	
Public debt ($ trillion)		3.5	3.4	3.2	3.0	2.8	2.5	2.2	2.9	1.6	1.2

In 2000, the CBO projected that the federal government would have paid back essentially all debt held by the public by 2010, and this despite the fact that the government had been running deficits for almost 40 years. It did not project the dot-com bust, the Bush tax cuts, Hurricane Katrina, the housing bust that started in December 2007, or a host of other spending programs created during that decade. In 2000, when these projections were made, the CBO was unaware that the events of September 11, 2001 would occur, along with the economic devastation that it caused. It also did not plan for the Iraq and Afghanistan wars, which have cost over $1 trillion. Of course, by the end of 2010, the national debt was not $1.2 trillion, but a whopping $10.1 trillion. When Medicare was enacted in 1965, CBO projected Medicare expense would reach $10 billion a year by 1990. The actual number was $90 billion. In January 2012, the CBO projected that the federal deficit for 2012 would be $1.1 trillion. Two months later, it revised the deficit to $1.193 trillion. In just two short months the CBO increased the loss by $93 billion, or 7.6 percent. It actually came in at $1.09 trillion. This is how wrong the CBO and many government projections are, and no one should be assuming these projections are accurate, particularly projections of more than one year. In January 2012, the CBO projected that over the next 10 years the country will always have a healthy, growing economy and that all government programs will stay on a conservative projected slow-growth path. It is now May 2013 and we know that assumption to be wrong, dead wrong.

RECEIPTS

Receipts to the government are all the various ways it receives cash, including taxes of various types, interest income, penalties, services, and so on. All this together is the government's total cash inflow from every source except borrowing. A useful measure of receipts is not raw dollars but instead the percentage of GDP, so as the economy grows and the percentage stays the same, total receipts in dollar terms will also grow. The same is true for outlays (expense) analysis. As the GDP grows, outlays will also grow, if their percentage of GDP remains the same. Using the percentage of GDP analysis for both receipts and outlays allows us to compare numbers from various periods of time more easily than using dollar figures because inflation over time changes numbers so dramatically that they are no longer comparable. Over the last 30 years, the average federal receipts have hovered around 18 percent of GDP, peaking at 20.9 percent in 2000. This percentage fell dramatically after the start of the 2008 fiscal year. Federal receipts fell to 14.4 percent of GDP; they have been slowly rebounding since then. Because GDP has fallen as a result of the recession and the percentage of GDP being paid to the government as receipts has dropped while spending has increased, the deficit has soared. This percentage drop is the reason the government has spent trillions of dollars trying to stimulate economic growth and get receipts back to 18 percent of GDP (more on this spending in Chapter 3). If receipts as a percentage of GDP had remained at 18 percent during the 2008–2011 fiscal years, the federal government would have had additional receipts, as shown in Table 2.3.

Table 2.3 Additional Receipts the U.S. Federal Government Would Have Had If the Receipts Remained at 18 Percent of GDP, 2008–2012

	2008	2009	2010	2011	2012
Additional receipts ($ billions)	140	495	508	602	424

The total of these numbers is $2.2 trillion. In other words, had receipts stayed at 18 percent of GDP throughout the recession, there would be $2.2 trillion less government debt. But of course that did not happen, and the United States does suffer under that debt. Also during this period unemployment programs, food stamps, and many other programs experienced automatic increases in expenses. This amounted to several hundred billion dollars. (The CBO uses an analysis called "automatic stabilizers" to incorporate both loss of receipts and increase of expenses that happen automatically during a recession. Its calculation for 2008–2012 is $1.6 trillion.)[10] During the first four years of the Obama administration the federal government borrowed around $6 trillion. The $3.5 trillion to $4.1 trillion of additional deficits were principally spent on stimulus-related expenses, including add-on expenditures to agricultural and housing, Obama's $860 billion stimulus plan, bailouts of the Federal Home Mortgage Corporation ("Freddie Mac") and the Federal National Mortgage Association ("Fannie Mae"), the Troubled Asset Relief Program, the tax rebate in 2008, cash for clunkers, mortgage relief, and green energy. All this money spent is at the center of the debate as to whether government expenditures actually had any effect on the economy.

Federal government receipts as a percentage of GDP have become the government's focus as the recession has made the percentage plunge. Table 2.4 shows the federal government's actual receipts from 2008 through 2012 and projected 2013 through 2018.

Table 2.4 2012 CBO Budget Projections[11]

	2008	2009	2010	2011	2012	2013	2014	2015	2016	2017	2018
GDP ($ trillion)	14.4	14.1	14.5	15.1	15.6	16.8	17.8	18.8	19.8	20.8	21.9
Percentage of GDP	17.5	14.9	14.9	14.4	15.7	17.9	18.7	19.1	19.3	20.2	20.0
Receipts ($ trillion)	2.5	2.1	2.2	2.5	2.5	3.0	3.3	3.6	3.8	4.1	4.3

Table 2.5 2013 CBO Budget Projections[12]

	2008	2009	2010	2011	2012	2013	2014	2015	2016	2017	2018
GDP ($ trillion)	14.4	14.1	14.5	15.1	15.6	16.0	16.6	17.6	18.8	20.0	20.9
Percentage of GDP	17.5	14.9	14.9	14.4	15.8	16.9	18.0	19.1	19.1	18.9	18.8
Receipts ($ trillion)	2.5	2.1	2.2	2.5	2.5	2.7	3.0	3.4	3.6	3.8	3.9

In February 2013, one year later, the CBO prepared projections on receipts, which have changed dramatically as a result of permanent extension of most of the Bush era tax cuts (see Table 2.5).

The total drop in receipts over the five-year period 2013–2018 totals $1.7 trillion, and over the 2013–2023 decade, more than $4 trillion. Of course this means that the budget deficit estimate as well as the amount of debt the government will have to borrow is increased by this amount. In May 2013 the CBO revised the projections that it had made just three months earlier. As a result of businesses and individuals contemplating a tax increase in January 2013, many transactions happened at the end of 2012 so that a lower tax would have to be paid. This increased tax receipts by $100 billion. In addition, Fannie Mae and Freddie Mac, the two largest home mortgage companies in the world and essentially owned by the federal government, reduced their expected losses by almost $100 billion. As a result of these changes, the CBO forecast a deficit of $640 billion for fiscal 2013, $200 billion below the estimate made just three months before. While positive, these changes are more examples of how projections can change and why we should not rely on them.

The new Obama administration 2014 budget prepared by the Office of Management and Budget has GDP growing at over 5 percent and receipts increasing to around 19 percent of GDP for the next five years. Due to all the new taxes in Obamacare, receipts will rise above the historical average of 18 percent, and receipts may top 19 percent of GDP. The numbers in the 2014 budget from the Obama White House show receipts reaching 20 percent of GDP in 2023. Both CBO and the

White House budgets *assume* that GDP will grow at 4 to 5.2 percent over the period and that government revenue will reach 19 percent of GDP. Neither *assumes* a recession, nor a war, nor natural disasters (greater than $41 billion per year). They both *assume* healthcare expenses will rise at 4 to 5 percent. They also *assume* very low interest rates on the national debt. They also *assume* that there will be no new spending legislation, which is being considered on a daily basis in Congress. Generally, they *assume* that nothing will go wrong during the next decade and that all economic indicators will stay strong and never waiver. The CBO and OMB mandate is to present these types of projections, but those of us who live in the real world don't have to believe them or rely on them.

In the investment banking world, I see hundreds of projections prepared by companies. The stories are always rosy, and the numbers always look great. After all, who would invest in a company that projects numbers that show losses forever? When companies make projections, they are made from a set of assumptions that have to be realistic; otherwise, no investor would invest. The CBO and OMB projections are patently unrealistic because the assumptions are unbelievable. No one can make long-term financial decisions based on the numbers prepared by the federal government.

To be fair to the CBO, it readily admits that its forecasts are very sensitive to small changes in GDP growth, tax rates, changes in tax law, wealth distribution, wars, recessions, new spending by Congress, and a myriad of other variables that affect revenue and expenses. It also admits that it has projected no recessions, wars, recessions, or other cataclysmic events. The CBO is required to prepare projections for only the legislation that is in existence and cannot assume new spending programs.

REAL NUMBERS

In order to bring some reality to government projections, we need to make some more realistic projections. Starting with the receipts line items, a serious financial analysis has to adjust the CBO and White

House numbers, as tax receipts are highly dependent on assumptions of growth in GDP. For a number of reasons, economic growth will be less dramatic than the historical 3.3 percent experienced over the last 50 years. The first reason for this is that the U.S. national debt will hinder economic growth. The added burden of the high level of interest expense incurred will usurp billions of dollars that would otherwise be invested in businesses that grow the GDP. The CBO concurs with this analysis:

> Debt that is high by historical standards and heading higher will have significant consequences for the budget and the economy: National savings will be held down, leading to more borrowing from abroad and less domestic investment, which in turn will decrease income in the United States relative to what it would be otherwise.[13]

Many economists espouse that too much debt causes slower GDP growth, but I know all too well what too much debt does. You don't have to be a full-time economist to figure this one out. The "overhead" burden of interest on the national debt (along with every other outlay of government) to every taxpayer and business is economically equivalent to corporate overhead allocated to operating units of a company. In the case of a business, "overhead" is the cost for "administrative" expenses, including top management, finance, accounting, legal, sales, and marketing. While all these functions are necessary for the operation of a business, excess of any of these functions kills a business. For instance, if interest expense is too high, a business does not have the money to invest in new computers, a new manufacturing plant, more salespeople, more sales materials, more advertising, and so on, and slowly, or quickly, it declines. The drain caused by excess overhead will kill a business just as it is killing all taxpayers to have too much government "overhead." I have personal experience in businesses with too much overhead; when the overhead exceeds an efficient amount, the business is hurt.

So if GDP growth and job growth are important to the government, government needs to lower the overhead burden it is placing on the economy. This overhead on society is represented by government spending because spending always equals tax (overhead) on society. As government spending grows, there are more burdens placed on all taxpayers.

The fact that the United States has such a heavy government debt load will make its economy grow more slowly than it would without the debt load. A number of economists around the world, as well as analyses by the European Central Bank and Bank for International Settlements, have studied this phenomenon using 50 years of data from the OECD and the International Monetary Fund (IMF). Many conclude that once you get to 90 percent debt-to-GDP an economy suffers. Others believe that each small increase in debt hurts economic growth.[14] But this is not rocket science. Thomas Jefferson figured this out in 1797 after studying governments and economies around Europe. "Most bad government has grown out of too much government," he said. This is also true when private debt (debt owed by individuals and businesses) exceeds reasonable amounts. Currently in the United States private debt is at 260 percent of GDP and clearly above reasonable amounts.

GDP is expressed in terms of "real" and "nominal" growth. Real GDP growth is the actual increase of goods and services performed in the United States. Nominal GDP growth is equal to real GDP growth plus any inflation or deflation. To confound everyone even more, the federal government recently announced a new calculation for GDP that will increase the GDP by about 3 percent.[15] This change will make the U.S. debt-to-GDP ratio decline overnight; will make the U.S. calculations different than the rest of the world's, so comparisons will be skewed; and will include items that are not products and should not be included in any event. However, this is to be expected, as every administration changes the definition of *unemployment* to make that number look better. Why not change calculations of GDP to make it look better? So starting in July 2013 all economists around the world need to adjust down U.S. GDP by 3 percent to get an apples-to-apples comparison.

The Federal Reserve's control of money supply through interest-rate control and actual money in circulation has traditionally worked well to control both real and nominal GDP growth. The Fed has done this by increasing cash in the system when GDP slows and decreasing cash in the system when GDP grows too fast (above 4 to 5 percent). Since 2008 these actions have not had the economic effects they have had in the past. So the Federal Reserve has had to resort to extreme money supply increases and interest-rate decreases in an attempt to get the economy growing. Despite extraordinary money supply increases and an interest rate environment that approaches zero, the economy has not responded as it has in the past. Many experts blame the "structural" government deficit, debt burden, and related annual interest expense as the reason. I am one of those.

Unfortunately, the United States is faced with not only too much government overhead but also a demographic problem that will slow GDP growth. People over the age of 55 slow their personal spending, and as the average population age increases, primarily due to the baby boomers aging, the growth of GDP will also slow because of this phenomenon. Because of slower economies in Europe and almost everywhere in the world, globalization growth from businesses has slowed. All these factors mean that the new "normal" GDP growth will probably be around 1 to 2 percent rather than the historical 3.3 percent. This has very significant implications for long-term government operations as well as for any recovery from excessive government debt. Bill Gross, managing director of PIMCO, the investment firm with the largest exposure to government debt, concurs with these expectations. In a letter to investors in December 2012, he outlines some of these same issues. Even Ben Bernanke confirmed slower growth in the United States "at least for a time" in a speech to the New York Economic Club in November 2012. The Congressional Budget Office also concurs with a slow-growth future: "Potential GDP is projected to grow at an average annual rate of 2.3 percent between 2019 and 2023, substantially below the average rate since 1950 of 3.3 percent. ... That estimate is mainly a result of slower projected growth in the potential labor force."[16] This is because of slower expected growth in the labor force from both the retirement of the baby-boom generation and an end to the longstanding increase in the labor force participation of women. This is exactly the situation in Japan for the last 20 years and one reason that country's GDP growth rate has remained flat. The new Japanese prime minister Shinzō Abe is determined to change this and is starting to print lots of money to weaken the yen and stimulate the economy. We will see what happens in Japan.

To figure out what more realistic federal government projections should look like, "normal" GDP growth should be around 2.0 percent, not the 4 to 5 percent used by the White House and earlier CBO projections. In addition, if the United States has a recession, let's say in 2017–2018, tax receipts as a percent of GDP will decline to 17.5 percent for those years. That leaves us with the revenue assumptions shown in Table 2.6.

For just the six years from 2013 to 2018, the difference in tax receipts from my case compared with the cases from the White House and CBO is $2.3 trillion. I believe their GDP growth assumptions as well as their lack of planning for a recession are not realistic; consequently, U.S. government tax receipts are not realistic. The difference

Table 2.6 Revised 2012–2022 Revenue Assumptions with GDP Growth at 2.5 Percent

	2012	2013	2014	2015	2016	2017	2018	2019	2020	2021	2022
GDP ($ trillion)	15.6	16.0	16.4	16.8	17.0	17.0	17.0	17.6	18.1	18.5	19.0
Percentage of GDP	15.7	16.9	18.0	19.1	19.1	17.5	17.5	18.0	18.6	19.0	19.5
Receipts ($ trillion)	2.5	2.7	3.0	3.2	3.2	3.0	3.0	3.2	3.4	3.5	3.7

in receipts for a simple and probable recession (maybe not in those years) is by itself $2 trillion. That means that compared to the CBO and Obama administration budget, a simple recession, which happens on average every 7 to 8 years, would set the government back another $2 trillion. Neither Congress nor the Obama administration has a plan for the recession scenario: they both project that GDP will grow at 4 to 5.2 percent for 10 straight years. Just on the revenue side, I believe the CBO and White House projections will be wrong by $2.3 trillion over the next 6 years and almost $5 trillion over the next 10 years. We now know that the GDP assumption of $15.8 trillion in the 2012 CBO and White House projections is wrong as was the percentage of GDP the federal government received in taxes in 2012. Those numbers are $15.6 trillion in GDP, 15.7 percent of GDP in receipts, and $2.45 trillion in cash receipts.

Now, let's look at the outlays issues. Table 2.7 shows the OMB 2014 budget outlays (spending) projections for 2013 through 2023.

These are the outlays projections from the government that have been wrong by almost $9 trillion in the last 10 years. We know that initial Obamacare cost projections were wholly inadequate at $100 billion per year and now look more like $260 billion per year. But again, this is still just a projection, and if there is any lesson in projecting healthcare costs, we know they are historically very wrong. What could possibly go wrong with their numbers for the next decade?

If I were putting my name on a set of projections for the next decade, I would assume that Congress will enact some more spending on some new programs and that there will be a war with Iran or North Korea in 2014 lasting four years, costing $200 billion a year; an increase of medical costs of Obamacare, Medicare, and Medicaid of 8 percent per year, or 3 percent above CBO and OMB estimates;

Table 2.7 OMB 2014 Budget Outlays Projections, 2013–2023[17]

	2013	2014	2015	2016	2017	2018	2019	2020	2021	2022	2023
Spending ($ trillion)	3.7	3.8	3.9	4.1	4.2	4.4	4.7	5.0	5.2	5.5	5.7

a large hurricane or other natural disaster every three years; and an interest-rate increase to an average rate of 6.5 percent on federal debt starting in year 2015. After all, even the CBO acknowledges that the market will be charging the government higher interest rates as a result of the risk of default:

> If the amount of debt held by the public remains so large, federal spending on interest payments will increase substantially when interest rates rise to more normal levels. Because federal borrowing generally reduces national saving, the stock of capital assets, such as equipment and structures, will be smaller and aggregate wages will be less than if the debt were lower. In addition, lawmakers will have less flexibility than they ordinarily might to use tax and spending policies to respond to unanticipated challenges. Moreover, such a large debt poses an increased risk of precipitating a fiscal crisis, during which investors would lose so much confidence in the government's ability to manage its budget that the government would be unable to borrow at affordable rates.[18]

Interestingly, the Congressional Budget Office released an analysis of various interest-rate assumptions that are greater than those used by CBO and OMB, reflecting much higher interest rates along the lines of my expectations. The analysis shows an interest expense increase of $1.6 to $6.2 trillion from 2014 to 2023.[19] As a side note, the U.S. Treasury is now issuing mostly very short-term Treasury bills (T-bills), which have an interest rate of almost zero. This is to keep the interest expense investors and borrowers have to pay today very low. This is being done for political purposes. Smart businesses are taking advantage of the lowest interest rates in history to issue long-term debt, thus assuring that interest expense for them will be low for 20 to 30 years. This is exactly what folks in government should be doing, but they are not smart financial people ... they are politicians. When interest rates turn, everybody will suffer from this short-term decision.

These are outlay estimates I can believe in. Now, let's take a look at our new assumptions (see Table 2.8).

Table 2.8 Federal Government Outlays Projections by Murray Holland

($ billions)	2012	2013	2014	2015	2016	2017	2018	2019	2020	2021	2022
Spending	3,627	3,685	3,778	3,908	4,090	4,247	4,449	4,724	4,967	5,209	5,470
War cost			200	200	200	200					
Healthcare rise			70	70	70	70	70	70	70	70	70
Interest increase				525	577	601	640	680	720	760	800
Natural disaster					60			60			60
New programs			50	100	150	200	250	300	350	400	450
Realistic total	3,627	3,685	4,098	4,803	5,147	5,318	5,409	5,834	6,107	6,439	6,850

Table 2.9 Federal Government Budget Projections by Murray Holland

($ trillions)	2012	2013	2014	2015	2016	2017	2018	2019	2020	2021	2022
Receipts	2.5	2.7	3.0	3.2	3.2	3.0	3.0	3.2	3.4	3.5	3.7
Outlays	3.6	3.7	4.1	4.8	5.1	5.3	5.4	5.8	6.1	6.4	6.9
Deficit	(1.1)	(1.0)	(1.1)	(1.6)	(1.9)	(2.3)	(2.4)	(2.6)	(2.7)	(2.9)	(3.2)
Public debt	11.6	12.7	13.7	14.8	16.4	18.3	20.6	23.0	25.6	28.3	31.2
GDP	15.6	15.9	16.2	16.6	16.9	16.8	16.8	17.1	17.5	17.8	18.2
Debt to GDP (%)	74	80	85	89	97	109	123	135	146	159	171

Let's now put our more realistic receipts projections together with more realistic outlays projections and see what the whole picture looks like. See Table 2.9.

This amount of debt is, of course, not possible because no one will loan the government that much. In Chapter 3, I show what happens to governments that escalate their debt above 90 percent of GDP, and in Chapter 6 I show it actually occurring to large economies. The markets would charge such enormous interest rates that the government would be forced to default or shut down most other government functions. The government could just do a wealth confiscation by taxing everyone, but this would put the economy in a recession or depression, as I talk about in Chapter 3. A default by the U.S. government is a terrifying prospect, as it would trigger a global financial disaster. The United States is too big to fail, or is it? I am reminded of a story I heard: When Ross Perot sold Electronic Data Systems (EDS) to General Motors in 1984, the shareholders of EDS were issued a special stock in General Motors, termed "GME." That stock came with a note by General Motors guaranteeing a rate of return on the GME. The story goes that one of Perot's daughters said, "What if General Motors goes broke and can't pay the note?" At that point everyone had a good laugh, since there was no way General Motors could go bust. Right? Well, we all know the rest of the story. Now might be a good time to review the list in Chapter 1 of the countries that have defaulted and see how you feel.

DEBT IS DEBT, OR IS IT?

The debt owed to the public is easy to understand. It is simply the amount borrowed in cash from the public in exchange for a bill, note, or bond. It has to be paid back at some future date designated on the bill, note, or bond. The $5 trillion the government owes to itself is a more complicated matter. The government borrows from itself by taking cash paid into "trust funds," in particular social security, Medicare, highway and airport trust funds, some military retirement funds, and so on. It works like this: as social security payments are received by the government, the cash payments go into a trust fund, and the cash in the fund is used to pay current social security beneficiaries. Any excess cash not paid out of the trust fund is loaned to the federal government, and the trust fund receives a note from the government for the loan. Putting reality glasses on, there is no trust fund and no "lending" going on. All cash from FICA (the Federal Insurance Contributions Act—i.e., social security) taxes goes straight into the federal government's general fund, and the "borrowing" activity is nothing but some accounting entries that are merely a paper or electronic fantasy. Only the government can borrow from a trust fund it manages, as this would be a violation of a "real" trustee's fiduciary duty.

The politicians and CBO consider this debt to be what the government owes to itself, so they eliminate it and say that it just doesn't exist. Their argument is that the concept that it is "debt" is meaningless and that the only real effect is the future cash that will be required to pay the beneficiaries. This cash must come from the general fund. That may be, but if you subscribe to that argument, then all "public debt" is not "debt" but just some sort of future commitment to pay cash from the general fund. If instead of the social security payments going to the federal government they went into a bank account somewhere and were borrowed by the government, that would be debt, clear and simple. It is true that had the legislation setting up these trust funds used the term "tax," then it would not have been debt. No matter what you consider it to be, debt or nondebt, there is a future obligation to pay it just as there is a future obligation to pay Medicare and Medicaid expenses. Therein lies the problem.

My conclusion about these various "trust" funds and all the debt the government owes to them is that everything about borrowing from them can be disregarded and that the obligations under these various programs should be considered a general liability of the federal government. The treatment of them as somehow separate from the government's general fund is an accounting fiction. In other words, the $5 trillion in government-issued debt is a meaningless concept, but the future negative cash flow of these programs is real. In my view, the federal government has severe cash flow problems, and the negative cash flow from these programs has to be addressed immediately. The failure to realize and address the negative cash flow will hurt the entire economy, as we shall see in Chapter 3.

INTEREST IS INTEREST

The numbers being generated by the White House and Congressional Budget Office do not tell the story of what is really going on inside the government budget. There are thousands of twists and turns to understanding what is actually happening, and every number is spun politically. People at the Congressional Budget Office, for instance, are required to prepare budgets and forecasts that reflect current laws and regulations, and the assumptions they use for forecasts are rarely realized. Consequently, they are never "right" and rarely even close once they project more than one year. I don't really blame them, but I do differ with them regarding a number of items. For instance, they are not required to follow generally accepted accounting principles (GAAP), as all publicly traded United States companies do.

Another concept that is important to understand in order to make sense of government financial statements is interest expense. Today, the United States spends around $220 billion a year on "net" interest expense. What this number doesn't tell you is the government has interest income from a number of sources that offsets the raw interest expense of federal debt. Interest income from all these sources, such as interest and penalties on tax receipts and interest income on student loans, ranges from $140 billion to $200 billion a year. Actual interest on the federal debt in 2011 was $400 billion and in 2012 was $360 billion. Although the United States had borrowed more money in 2012 than in 2011, interest rates were lower than in 2012 and a program by the Treasury to reduce interest expense by issuing mostly short-term treasuries had the effect of lowering rates. Another factor to lower interest rates has been the large purchases of federal debt by the Federal Reserve. Since the profits of the Fed belong to the federal government, there is effectively no interest on the Treasuries owned by the Federal Reserve. Of course, the Federal Reserve buys these Treasuries with newly printed money, so the United States will have an inflation problem down the road.

Had Congress not deficit spent during the 1970s, 1980s, 1990s, and 2000s, the federal government would not have this expense, and the government would be a lot closer to balancing the budget today. Also note that all these interest expense numbers are generated with an interest rate on short-term debt of around .2 percent (one-fifth of 1 percent) and long-term rates of under 3.0 percent. In a healthy economy, we commonly see short-term interest rates of 4 to 5 percent, or 20 to 30 times the interest rate in today's environment. So far, the markets have not started pricing up these rates, factoring in a risk of a U.S. default. These interest rates are the result of supply and demand for Treasury bills and notes as well as some tinkering by the Fed and the U.S. government. The United States is experiencing a very low interest rate environment because of the slow economy, Federal Reserve actions, and high demand for what is perceived to be risk-free federal government debt. If and when the economy picks up, interest rates will return to a normal level that is experienced in a healthy economy. Assuming there is no fear of default by the U.S. government, normal interest rates are about 4 to 5 percent for short-term bills (under one year) and 6 to 8 percent for long bonds. If the United States returns to normal economic activity, say 4 to 5 percent growth in GDP in 2013 and thereafter, the Obama administration projects the government will continue the deficit spending and have national debt and interest expense on that debt as shown in Table 2.10.

Note that the Obama administration budget projects that by 2022 the U.S. government will be paying $1.115 trillion in net interest expense, which means that the total interest expense on outstanding Treasuries will be somewhere near $1.4 trillion. This amount is greater than the military budget, the Obamacare budget, social

Table 2.10 Projected National Debt and Interest Expense, 2013–2022[20]

	2013	2014	2015	2016	2017	2018	2019	2020	2021	2022
Gross debt ($ trillion)	17.3	18.2	19.1	20.0	20.9	21.7	22.5	23.2	23.9	25.4
Interest rate (%)	3.5	3.8	4.1	4.5	4.9	5.2	5.4	5.5	5.6	5.7
Interest ($ billion)	446	505	584	680	770	845	916	982	1,046	1,115

security, Medicare, or Medicaid. It is the single largest budget item and drains the life out of every other government program. This, of course, is irresponsible management of the financial affairs of the government. About one-third of the annual budget would be used to pay interest expense. Since there is no way the money borrowed could ever be repaid, this would be placing a burden on ourselves, our children, and our grandchildren forever. The government would be spending $1.4 trillion a year, $14 trillion each decade, and $140 trillion every century forever, and the money borrowed would have been spent on nonessentials.

This interest expense would be more than sufficient to balance the budget had the government never started borrowing in the first place. These projections are also *assuming* that the economy will grow at 4 to 5 percent and there will not be a recession any time in the next 10 years. This of course is also patently wrong. These projections are also *assuming* that the debt markets will not penalize the U.S. government for risk of default. This of course is also absurd, particularly if we see budget deficits as outlined in the more realistic case above. This behavior is that of an irresponsible person borrowing up to his limits to keep the whole thing going and then spending everything he earns to pay interest on his debt. Just think of the programs that could be financed, the hungry people who could be fed, and the sick that could get medical care with that money. Above all, imagine if these trillions of dollars of capital had been invested in the economy instead of wasted by Congress. This money would have been available in the market in the form of capital to build businesses and hire people. Just think.

LONG-TERM OUTLOOK

Financial projections after 2014 are an exercise in considerable speculation but are worth undertaking nonetheless. Since the U.S. economy is sputtering now and federal debt will burden the economy forever, it is hard to think that things could get much better. I don't think they will get better, and neither does the CBO. The federal government should spend a lot of energy making sure that it does not put the country's citizens in the same position as Greece, Spain, Portugal, and Ireland have put theirs. Over the last 40 years, elected officials have been borrowing money to spend on programs that are meaningless today. Today, however, is when we have to pay for their borrowing. Every Congress has participated in this, and they are the ones to blame (along with the presidents who did not fight the borrowing).

The projections for the upcoming decade set forth are disastrous, but the outlook after 2022 is even worse. The demographic phenomena of things like the impending retirement of the baby-boom generation portend even larger demands on healthcare and social security. The obesity problem is also a looming disaster for healthcare. Looking back over the last 20 years at the rate of healthcare per capita, we have learned that the cost of healthcare has increased far faster than the rate of inflation. This is due, in my opinion, to a number of things: (1) the amount of money being poured into the healthcare system from the government, (2) obvious problems associated with having the person receiving the service not being the one paying for it (it's easy to spend Other People's Money), (3) new technologies and drugs that people want to make their lives better, and (4) out-of-control litigation.

We may not know the magnitude of the increases, but it will almost certainly be greater than the inflation rate. Today, the federal government spending on healthcare is about 6 percent of GDP, and the CBO expects that to rise to 9 percent over the next quarter of a century and continue to rise thereafter. Spending on social security will also rise from about 5 percent of GDP today to 6 percent by 2035, according to the CBO. I believe that Obamacare will contribute another 2 to 3 percent to these numbers over the same period. The combined two budget items of healthcare and social security will make up almost 18 percent of GDP. Looking back over the last several decades, the entire federal budget has averaged a little over 18 percent, and this includes the military, all government operations including all administrative functions, interest on federal debt, and so on. If the U.S. government continues down this path, it will certainly fail.

The Office of Management and Budget has prepared a graph representing two scenarios of federal government operations (see Figure 2.3). One has Bush era tax cuts expiring and tax rates skyrocketing, including the nearly $1 trillion of new taxes in Obamacare. The "extended baseline scenario" would grow federal revenues to 23 percent of GDP by 2035 and continue growing thereafter. Defense spending as a percentage of GDP would decline to the smallest percentage in a hundred years. Federal debt as a percentage of GDP would continue to rise as well as the interest expense on it. The "alternative fiscal scenario" assumes that the Bush era tax cuts are adopted for the next 10 years. In addition, things such as payment rate declines in various healthcare laws will not be implemented and spending on things like military will not fall so fast (as a percentage of GDP). Under this scenario, federal debt held by the public to GDP would hit 100 percent by 2020 and 190 percent by 2035. Gross debt would be far greater.

The extended alternative fiscal scenario would of course never work because the capital markets would stop lending to the U.S. government. We now know that Congress has made permanent most of the Bush era tax cuts and the United States is faced with a deficit and debt scenario approaching the "extended alternative fiscal scenario." What's shown in Figure 2.3 is overpowering, particularly in light of its assumptions. There are no plans for a natural disaster, another 9/11 type event, a war, a recession or depression, high-interest-rate environment, and so on. The projection is a constant 4 to 5 percent

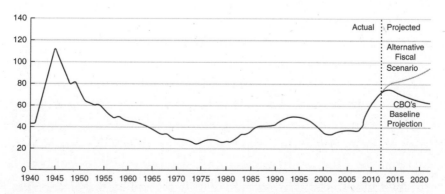

Figure 2.3 Federal debt held by the public, 1940–2020 (projected).[21]

GDP growth with nothing bad ever happening. This, of course, is a fantasy but it points out Congress's outrageous conduct for putting U.S. citizens in this position even if nothing bad happens. The budget deficit over the next 50 years exceeds $60 trillion by some estimates and $100 trillion by others. I would assume several wars during this time, several large natural disasters, several recessions, and some other bad things that have never happened in the past, such as bankruptcies of states and large cities. To be conservative, I would venture to project an aggregate deficit of $125 to $150 trillion over this time period, unless some major changes happen to healthcare, social security, pensions, and so on.

But wait, all is not lost. It seems the country has been saved by Congress. In February 2013, Congress kept in place a reduction of growth in government spending of $85 billion, meaning that planned increases this year have to be scaled back $85 billion. This so-called sequester was the result of legislation in 2011 aimed at reaching a balanced budget. To put this in perspective, we can take eight zeros off the federal government numbers and make them more like a typical household budget. We now have a household with income of $27,000 a year (up from $24,500 last year) and planning to spend $35,500. The $85 billion reduction in government spending correlates to a household spending reduction of $850 a year in our example, so we will spend only $34,650. The CBO has also made everybody feel better with updated projections showing strong (25 percent) growth in tax receipts in the next two years, 5 to 6 percent economic growth through 2018, unemployment dropping to 5.5 percent, and interest rates below 4.5 percent. Figure 2.4 is the same graph seven months after the first.

Now I feel so much better that we will only have debt held by the public of just under 80 percent of GDP. The problem in Figures 2.3 and 2.4 is fairly obvious. Not much really changed with Congress and spending, but the assumptions used did change. Receipts are now projected higher and expenses lower. While CBO can be very accurate for a 12-month period, they are not so over a 10-year period because of the assumptions used. These assumptions are very optimistic. I don't believe the GDP growth rates used, that the federal

(Percentage of gross domestic product)

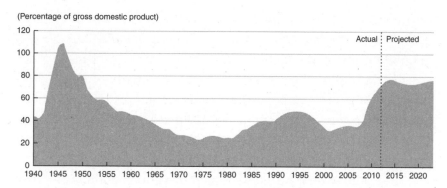

Figure 2.4 Federal debt held by the public, 1940–2020 (revised)[22]

government will receive the growth in tax receipts, and certainly not that interest rates will be as low as projected.

TWO TYPES OF DEBT

The gross debt of the U.S. government is actually made up of two types: debt owed to the public and debt owed to government entities. Currently, the debt owed to the public is around $11.9 trillion (adding almost $100 billion per month), and the debt owed to government entities is around $5 trillion. Debt owed to the public is simply the amount of cash the government has borrowed from people, other governments, pension funds, banks, the Federal Reserve, and any other entity that wants to loan it money. There is no doubt that this is "debt." The federal government also borrows money from government-run trust funds that have excess cash, including social security and the Civil Service Retirement and Disability Fund. By taking the cash out of these trust funds and using it for general government purposes, the government is essentially violating the independence of the funds. But where else could this amount of money go? It was determined when these funds were set up that they would buy Treasury securities. But if you follow the cash, these entities might as well be straight government programs with no "trust" fund involved at all. Social security and other payments should be termed a "tax" and not contributions.

The issue with this type of debt is whether or not it is "debt" that should be dealt with as true government debt. It is debt for money borrowed, but the deficits for the payments owed in the future essentially are coming straight out of the budget. Politicians are very comfortable using the "debt to the public number" since it is much smaller than gross debt, which includes both types of debt. There is no doubt it is debt, but for purposes of interest payments and actual cash payments to beneficiaries of these trust funds, the interest expense is eliminated when the books of the government are consolidated with the books of the trust funds.

The national debt numbers touted by various politicians rarely take into account money borrowed from these trust funds. For instance, liberals love to claim that during the Clinton administration the government ran a "surplus." They point to a decline in "debt to the public" of roughly $430 billion. The problem with their analysis is they forgot to add that during the Clinton administration the government borrowed $1.3 trillion from social security and other trust funds.[23] If the government wants to disregard these trust funds, it should just collapse them into the government and disregard the separate "trust" nature of each, which is essentially how these funds are operated today. Figure 2.5 shows all the trust funds from which the federal government borrows.

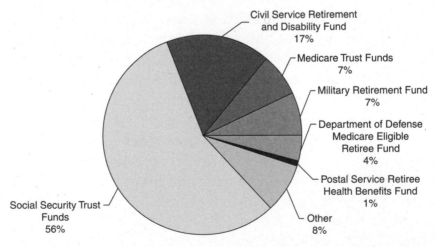

Figure 2.5 Trust funds from which the U.S. government borrows.[24]

SOCIAL SECURITY

Most people do not know how social security works. When you and your employer pay FICA taxes into social security, you are not paying money into any fund for yourself. This money goes into the general government account, just as all other taxes do, and an accounting entry is made for social security. There is really no "money" for you invested anywhere. There never will be. When you make your payments for FICA taxes, that money is used to pay for people already retired. When you retire, current workers will be paying FICA taxes that will be used to pay your social security benefits. Hence, the concept of "borrowing" from the social security trust fund is nothing more than accounting fiction; since the fund is run by the government, this practice is legal. This is why accounting for the federal debt that includes the debt owed to these trust funds is nothing more than an accounting fiction. The concept of "trust fund" used for social security has nothing whatsoever to do with a "trust fund" in the real world. You do not have any money socked away as you would in an Individual Retirement Account (IRA) or pension plan, and your social security benefits to be paid after you retire are subject to Congress changing the plan to reduce or increase benefits.

The major problem with the social security scheme is a change in demographics. People are living longer, and the baby boomers are retiring in droves. When social security was created in 1935, the average life expectancy was around 60 whereas today it is around 78.[25] Further, as the baby boomers continue retirement, by 2040, there will only be 2.1 working contributors to social security for each 1 person receiving benefits (2.1-to-1 ratio)[26] compared to 16.5 to 1 in 1950, 3.7 to 1 in 1970, 3.4 to 1 in 1990, and 2.9 to 1 in 2010.[27] These demographic changes are indisputable and are the reason social security is running a deficit today and will run deficits for the foreseeable future unless the program is modified.

INTEREST RATES

Greece saw interest-rate increases when its debt-to-GDP ratio hit 150 percent, France 100 percent, Italy 110 percent, Spain 120 percent, and Ireland 120 percent. The benchmark interest rate in Europe is German government debt. It has remained at lower levels throughout the crisis facing these other countries because its debt-to-GDP ratio remains relatively low.

Let's do a bit of simple arithmetic applying the outstanding federal debt, blended for short-term to long-term debt as currently outstanding. For purposes of this exercise, we will use the average blended interest rate on government securities from 1982 to 2008. Figure 2.6 shows the average interest rate on all government debt over the period, which is over 6 percent.

If the United States returns to normal economic times, we should see the interest rates from Figure 2.6. If the government is downgraded by the market and its bonds are viewed as risky, yields could go much higher. But for purposes of this exercise, let's assume

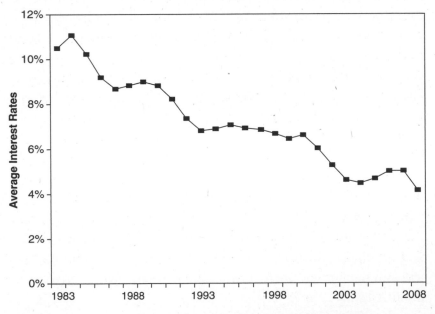

Figure 2.6 Average interest rates of federal debt outstanding.[28]

they return to the average 6 percent. The calculation is simple: $11.9 trillion in debt times 6 percent equals $714 billion per year in interest expense. That makes interest expense one of the largest single outlays of the federal government. These interest rates are going to happen if the country returns to economic growth, and we will see interest expense at these levels. Another reason we will see these rates is the market response to assuming more risk of the United States defaulting. This will certainly happen in the next few years if the government continues deficit spending. Internally, the government will not recognize interest expense on $5 trillion of bonds it issues to itself. What makes this number so bad is that the federal budget is already operating at a deficit of $600+ billion and an interest expense increase of $300 to $400 billion would push our deficit to $1 trillion.

As you can see, with even a normal interest-rate environment, interest expense spirals out of control and there is nothing the government can do about it. If the average interest rate hits 10 percent, that would make interest expense $1.2 trillion on "debt to the public." This represents about 44 percent of all receipts of the federal government and will represent the largest single category of expense: bigger than the defense budget, the social security budget, and Medicare. This scenario will be a disaster to the United States. I do not think the country will hit that inter-est rate within a year, but the market is certainly capable of risk-adjusting the rate to this level, as we saw with Greek debt. Faced with this exact scenario, Greece, Italy, France, and Ireland have all cut expenses and raised taxes dramatically. The larger economies of France and Italy have not had that far to go to balance their budgets. In 2011 they are deficit spending at around 7 percent and 4 percent, respectively. In 2012, that number will be around 4 per-cent and 2.5 percent, respectively. In other words, to balance their budgets, they would have to cut 4 percent and 2.5 percent of GDP in expenses from government budgets. The United States, on the other hand, has been deficit spending around 7 to 8 percent of GDP, and 2013 should be around 4 percent of GDP. In order to balance its budget, the country would have to suffer an economic decline of 4 percent of GDP—that is, enter into a severe recession, which would have the potential to spiral into a depression. This cannot be done, unless of course the market ceases to lend to the United States. This type of depression would push unemployment over 20 percent and have so many bad effects that I do not even care to describe them for fear of being branded a doomsayer.

The concept to grasp in looking at how precarious U.S. finances are is how much debt the country has compared to GDP and how soon the government can balance its budget so it can afford to pay the interest expense. The closer it is to balancing the budget, the more comfortable its citizens should feel they can survive without a market rebellion. The lower the debt to GDP, the more the government can absorb deficits. In both these tests, the United States is a failure, and the markets will quickly turn on the country. U.S. debt is accumulating at the fastest pace in its history, and the deficit of 4 to 6 percent of GDP is extremely difficult to turn around. As you have seen from the previous analyses, and particularly the Obama administration budget, the numbers generated by the government are simply not going to be accepted by the market.

CAN MATTERS GET ANY WORSE?

Matters can certainly get worse, if all countries release what they claim to be their outstanding debt to GDP. For instance, France claims its debt to GDP is equal to 86 percent, as shown in Figure 2.7.

What Figure 2.7 does not fully disclose is that France has many other commitments for cash that are financial in nature and will require cash payments in the future. Table 2.11 is a short list of commitments for France.

In addition to the debt shown in Table 2.11, France has also guaranteed the debt of its large banks, which totals $672 billion. Guarantees do not mean that France will ever have to pay the debt back, but it creates a risk of having to do so. If you include all the guaranties along with the debt, France debt to GDP is 146 percent.

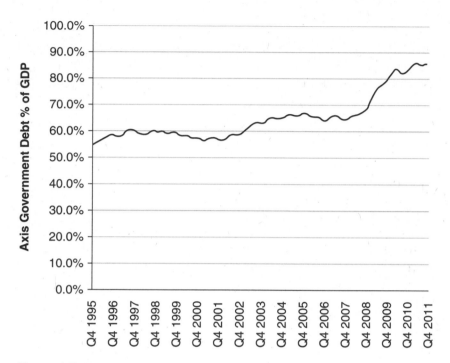

Figure 2.7 National debt of France, 1995–2011.[29]

Table 2.11 France's Financial Commitments (2012)[30]

Gross domestic product	$2,774 billion
Admitted sovereign debt	$2,261 billion
Loans to the "nation"	$215 billion
Total national debt	$2,476 billion
Liabilities to ECB	$569 billion
France cost to EU budget	$23 billion
Liabilities-stabilization funds	$110 billion
Liabilities macro financial asst.	$203 billion
Total European debt	$905 billion
France total national and European debt	$3,381 billion
France official debt to GDP	86%
France real debt to GDP	121%

When we undertake this same exercise with the U.S. government, the list of additional liabilities gets very long. Figure 2.8 shows the gross U.S. debt-to-GDP ratio.

Following the same exercise we just completed with France, we need to make adjustments to U.S. debt; see Table 2.12.

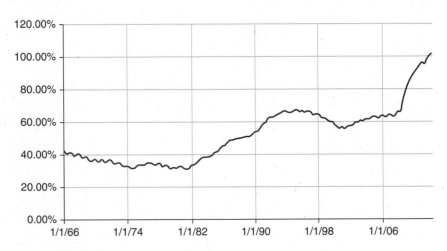

Figure 2.8 U.S. debt-to-GDP ratio.[31]

Table 2.12 Adjustments to U.S. Debt*[32]

Gross domestic product	$15,811 billion
Gross debt	$16,800 billion
Debt to public	$11,900 billion
Insurance and guaranty liabilities	$228 billion
Pension and postemployment health	$7,300 billion
Environmental disposal	$324 billion
"Other" liabilities	$484 billion
Total liabilities	$19,836 billion
Official gross debt to GDP	100%
Real debt to GDP	125%

*The data is from the OMB, a White House–controlled agency; the number of $6,200 billion is actually far less than the number of $7,300 billion that the trustees of the pension reported. See *Fiscal Year 2011 Financial Report of the United States Government* (Washington, DC: U.S. Department of the Treasury, December 2012).

The pension and postemployment health figure in Table 2.12 is the present value of all future obligations and includes costs for personnel that have not yet retired and personnel that have not yet been hired. This item of expense is unlike most of the government's social expenses, since pensioners receiving these benefits have or will have contributed years of employment to earn their pensions whereas most social expenses of the government are not earned by the recipient. Pensioners' end of the bargain will have been met, and I consider the obligation of the federal government to these people to be the same as debt. These numbers, by the way, are "booked" liabilities that are required to be recognized and reported by companies under GAAP. They do not include obligations under so-called social programs such as social security and healthcare.

HAVE WE HIT ROCK BOTTOM YET?

It is much worse than all of the above. The first liability number in Table 2.12 is the federal debt, which stands at $16.8 trillion ($11.9 trillion owed to the public), costing $360 billion in cash a year in interest expense; it is easy to understand because it is the same type of debt you incur with a bank or credit card company. The fourth is federal employee retirement and veterans' benefits, which total $6.3 trillion according to the Department of the Treasury.[33] This number is disputed by the trustees themselves: they put the unfunded liability at $7,300 billion.

In the business world, companies must report all liabilities, including debt, pension liabilities, lease obligations, and other obligations for money to be paid in the future. Generally accepted accounting principles require this disclosure to allow investors to see a clearer picture of a company's financial position and, in particular, its liabilities. This is not the case with the federal government. There is no reporting requirement that makes the government disclose all liabilities.

In order to see a clear picture of all liabilities of the federal government, we need to look at all commitments the government has made for future payments. The national debt is a liability of the government. It consists of agreements to pay money in the future, and it is the primary focus of public debate today. As large as it is and as harmful as it is to the economy, it is not the only liability. As a matter of fact, it is really a small problem (costing the U.S. government only $360 billion a year) compared to the other liabilities the federal government signed up for. There are many contingent liabilities such as guarantees of Freddie Mac and Fannie Mae, two multitrillion-dollar lending institutions that own home mortgages. The federal government can lose a lot of money from loan defaults. There are also huge potential losses in the federal student loan program. But rather than get into the hundreds of potential liabilities the government has, it will suffice to focus on the few very large liabilities.

There are two more numbers that are not included in the previous calculations because they are not liabilities that have been agreed to. They are funding under so-called social programs that exceed the amount of revenue from those programs. The first is the underfunding of the social security system, which totals $20.5 trillion. This amount is the excess of commitments to beneficiaries over the funds in social security and the projected contributions to social security, discounted to a present value.[34] The second is commitments under Medicare Parts A, B, and D that are underfunded for a total of $24.5 trillion (present value).[35]

These numbers are the present value of future obligations, so the actual numbers are far greater than these numbers indicate. To grasp the magnitude of these commitments, U.S. combined liabilities total $68 trillion, an amount greater than the net worth of every single person in the United States combined.[36] That is before the realities of the statements from social security and Medicare trustees set in. There are "significant uncertainties" surrounding our "best estimates" of future obligations. Medicare's numbers are currently scheduled to be modified by Obamacare, which eventually reduces "Medicare prices for hospital, skilled nursing facility, home health, hospice, ambulatory surgical center, diagnostic laboratory, and many other services [to] less than half of their level under the prior law. ... Well before that point, Congress would have to intervene to prevent the withdrawal of providers from the Medicare market and the severe problems with benefi-ciary access to care that would result. ... [This] would lead to far higher costs for Medicare in the long range than those projected under current law."[37]

The two principle financial ratios used to measure the financial performance and risk of default by any country are: (1) the negative cash flow the country is facing and (2) the amount of debt outstand-ing. These two measures, along with the projections for these two measures, determine the risk of default by a country. The analysis, by the way, is the same a bank uses on an individual or a business. The first measure is used to determine the financial health of a country's operating budget. If a country is operating at a negative cash flow, this is not good: the same goes for any business. The second measure is used to determine the amount of debt you have against your ability to pay it.

Investors look to the ability of a country to repay its debts by looking at the amount of debt compared to the size of its economy (see Figure 2.8): this is the primary factor determining its risk. The treaty establishing the European Community (EC) adopted the concept of "convergence" criteria (also known as "Maastricht criteria") for member countries that wanted to enter the third stage of the Economic and Monetary Union. These criteria lim-ited maximum debt to GDP to a ratio of no more than 60 percent and limited government deficits of no more than 3 percent. These targets were meant to put all member countries on stable financial footing so that there would not be a financial problem with one member country that could hurt the other members. These two criteria are the determinants of the financial stability of a country and the two analyses in which investors are most interested. These two criteria interact with each other in that if a country's debt to

(Percentage of gross domestic product)

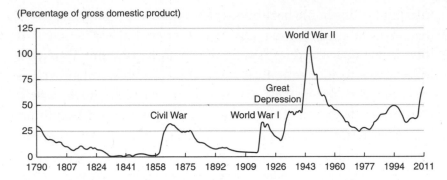

Figure 2.9 Federal debt held by the public, 1790 to 2011.[38]

GDP is low, it is acceptable to run deficits for periods of economic slowdown. Conversely, if a country has a high debt-to-GDP ratio of, say 60 percent, it has reached its safe maximum borrowing capacity and cannot run a deficit. In the event a country has debt to GDP above 60 percent and a deficit above 3 percent, it has an unacceptable financial position and must implement austerity measures. The United States is far past the safe level of debt and deficit.

The reader should now be sufficiently terrified. The data in Figure 2.9 reflects debt to the public and does not reflect debt the federal government owes to trust funds it manages. Currently, this ratio of debt to trust funds equals about $5 trillion.

In addition to all this mess, the federal government has essentially taken over Fannie Mae and Freddie Mac, the two quasi-governmental institutions that are the principal source of funding for home mortgages in the United States. They have a total of $5 trillion of debt, so if there is another wave of defaults, the federal government will suffer another round of multitrillion-dollar expenses. Certainly, if the country suffers an economic collapse, this will simply heap another few trillion dollars of debt on the government. Similarly, the federal student loan program has about $1 trillion in outstanding loans. Defaults and "forgiveness" will be losses, and during a collapse these will add another massive amount to the U.S. debt.

CONCLUSIONS

The United States is in very deep trouble. First, the concept of repaying $16.7 trillion in debt is not even a remote possibility over the next 100 years, even if the government had small surpluses. Then, because the country is running such large deficits, the national debt is increasing and getting worse ... much worse. In addition, the government has approximately $70 trillion in unfunded liabilities that have to be resolved. This means it needs either to decrease the benefits, primarily under Medicare and social security, or to increase taxes, or both. Pray that the market for the national debt remains open so the United States can keep borrowing to repay the money it previously borrowed and then will have to reborrow to repay the money it just borrowed. There is no chance the market will not change its demeanor over the next 100 years. It will certainly go through periods of higher interest rates. It will also go through times of lack of demand due to economic pressures and events around the world. Even under the Obama administration budget, interest expense will grow to over $1 trillion a year by 2022.

The scenario of worse-than-projected tax receipts for the government along with considerably higher than disclosed liabilities is a recipe for disaster in the United States. The effects of the financial system collapse witnessed in Greece will be the same with the collapse of the U.S. financial system because the laws of economics are the same everywhere and cannot be changed by the government. They are as powerful as the laws of nature. In Chapter 3, I will explain how the market creates a trap that the U.S. government is already in and what happens when the trap closes on a country. In Chapter 6, I will show the effects of the Debt Trap closing on a number of countries, which is exactly the road the United States is facing. If you are not terrified at the thought of the collapse of the United States, you should be. Almost everyone in the world will be negatively affected, particularly the poor.

With all the smart people in power in the United States, it should terrify every citizen to know that we now have the ninth worst debt/GDP ratio in the world.

CHAPTER 3

THE DEBT TRAP

"How did you go bankrupt?"
"Two ways. Gradually, then suddenly."
—Ernest Hemingway, *The Sun Also Rises*

The Debt Trap is the trap a country gets into with a weak economy and deficit borrowing that in the view of the market exceeds its capacity to service the debt. A country enters the Debt Trap early on when its government starts borrowing even during good economic times and years before it has borrowed too much debt. The trap is set when the market demands higher interest rates on debt issued by the country. This is the first jaw in the trap. The trap closes when a government is forced by the market to reduce borrowings or face quickly escalating interest rates. Soon after a dramatic rise in interest rates of a country's debt because of the market assessment of risk, the market will completely stop loaning a country any more money. At this point, the only options are to stop deficit spending by cutting expenses or raising taxes, both of which will kill an economy. There are other gimmicks such as exchange controls, printing money, artificially lowering interest rates, increasing money supply, and so on, but they do nothing to forestall the Debt Trap. At this point, a country enters a depression and then has to deal with its debt from an extremely weak position.

All this of course is being orchestrated behind the scenes by economists. They are an interesting breed. They are mostly academicians who stay well protected in their academic environments. Most are not rewarded for their successes, nor are they punished for their failures: they do not live in the real business world and seem to always have a reason their prognostications do not pan out. As we saw in Chapter 2, most of the economists in the various administrations as well as the CBO have been dead flat wrong for a long time. They spend their days analyzing data, arguing theory, debating central bank decisions, and generally being armchair quarterbacks. Their job is to be opinionated.

In the investment banking business, we all had our own economists who we would bring along to larger clients to talk about macroeconomic topics. Everyone seems interested in listening to economists talk. The interesting thing to me about them is their total disagreement with one another about economic theory. They all look at the same data and come to polar opposite conclusions.

They disagree about whether deficit spending in a recession is good or bad, whether higher tax rates slow growth in GDP, whether debt issued by a government harms the citizens, and what is the economic cost of regulation. Their profession is clearly not a science where theory and experimentation ultimately bring everyone to a consensus. It is more like a philosophy: liberals will argue liberal positions and conservatives, conservative positions.

Before the reader gets too wrapped up in what economists have to say about the future, they should note that there are thousands of them, and each one likes to make predictions about the future. As a result, there are thousands of predictions, and some of them are actually right, but there is no way to predict which predictions will be. For instance, in late 2000, I had a portfolio of stocks that I watched weekly, all managed by one of the top investment banking firms in the world. There was not one word of advice to get out before the dot-com crash—not from the broker, not from their economists or ones from other major firms, and not from the "market gurus" (although I am sure some economist somewhere said to get out). By September 2001, the market was down over 20 percent. The same was true in 2008, but this time it involved markets around the world. Similarly, when the Queen of England visited the London School of Economics in late 2008 and asked, "How come nobody could foresee this?," no one could answer her.

In his book *The Signal and the Noise,* Nate Silver noted that since 1968 economists' GDP predictions fell outside the prediction interval almost half the time. He points out that economists are not simply unlucky: they overstate the reliability of their predictions. My view of all the forecasts coming from our government is that they are generally good over the next six months, but that is all. After that, there are too many variables that are in no one's control that can have a major, negative impact on the future.

Interestingly, a lot of people put a lot of faith in these projections, particularly from the CBO and OMB, even though they are consistently overoptimistic decade after decade. It seems as though the U.S. government should run things more conservatively than it does, because the country will probably be around a long time, and over a long period the chances government officials are taking will hit a financial snag that can sink the nation, particularly since it has used most of its borrowing capacity. But leaders do not seem to know or care. They are oblivious to the headlines about what has happened to or is happening to other nations in the red. Are they really this dumb? Winston Churchill said about Adolph Hitler: "Hitler must have been rather loosely educated, not having learned the lesson of Napoleon's autumn advance on Moscow."

THE CONCEPT OF KEYNESIAN ECONOMICS

John Maynard Keynes was a British economist who lived from 1883 until 1946. He was clearly the most influential economist of the twentieth century in that many governments, including the United States, believed in his theories and acted in belief that his theories were correct. His theories are set forth in his book *General Theory of Employment, Interest and Money* (1936). The first major tests of his theories were undertaken during the 1930s when the entire world was living through the Great Depression. Governments looked to economists to help solve the problem and get the world back to work. One major reason Keynes's theories were adopted by many economists and governments is that they are very simple.

The concepts on which Keynes founded his theories of money and the economy are that money has a circular flow through the economy. In a normal economy, people spend the money they make. That expenditure is someone else's earnings, then they spend the money they made, and the circle continues all the way back to the person who made it in the first place. When confidence is shaken, consumers save their money instead of spending it. This decision to save instead of spend causes the circle to break. For example, my decision to hoard money means that you do not have the earnings you used to have from me, making things worse for you. In reaction, you start hoarding money, which makes it worse for the next person, and the circle comes all the way back to me. There is a vicious cycle created here that causes people to save money instead of spend it, and when everyone starts doing that, the economy slows way down. The solution to this slowdown, the theory goes, is for the central bank to increase the amount of money in circulation. The thought is that by putting more money in the pockets of people their confidence will return. People would then start spending more money, the circle of money flow would start back up, and the economy would grow. This is a very simple concept.

Keynes's concept of the entire economy is an aggregation of demand for products and services, with the private sector and government sector working together at the macro level (that is, the entire economy). Thus, Keynes argued, the aggregate demand for goods and services during a major downturn (depression) in the economy can be remedied by having the government spend a lot of money to get the economy going again. According to Keynes, when a recession becomes very severe, at some point people will hoard money no matter how much the government increases money supply (like an air pocket in a pump, which prevents it from ever getting started); a depression ensues. When faced with a depression, a government should restart the spending cycle by spending vast amounts of money to "prime the pump." Keynes's theory is that if the pump gets primed, then it will start working again; money will start flowing; the circle of money flow will reestablish itself; and the economy will recover. Governments can do this by borrowing large amounts of money and throwing it at the problem.

Keynes also predicted that money "pumped" into the economy would multiply due to the circulation, so that if the government put in $1, by the time it revolved around the circle it would have created $2 in GDP. It is clear from my survey of almost 100 years of economic data that this type of government deficit spending does not stimulate the economy and does nothing but build up massive amounts of debt. This, of course, is precisely what the Obama administration and Congress have done since 2008. If this simple Keynesian concept actually worked, Cuba, the Soviet Union, North

Korea and many other purely communist countries would be the most successful economies in the world!

Keynesians also believe that during times of high unemployment (that is, bad recessions and depressions) the government can do a better job than the private sector in taking unemployed people and turning them into productive people: creating jobs and increasing GDP. When the newly employed people go to work, they add to the economy by buying goods and services that otherwise would not have been sold. They argue that this helps the economy.

Congress, just as many other governments around the world do, has been handing out other people's money as fast as it can. The senators and representatives are not doing it because they have a basic belief in Keynesian theory; they are doing it to buy votes or contributions to their campaigns. Nonetheless, they turn to Keynes any time they need any basis on which to justify their spending. Deficits, Keynes theorizes, are necessary during depressions but not during normal economic times. Keynes clearly contemplated no deficits and maybe even surpluses during times of economic growth. But again, this is just theory, and the politicians really don't care about it until they need some cover. I might point out that during the Ronald Reagan and George W. Bush administrations, the national debt grew significantly when there were good economic times as well as recessions. This was not a time to deficit spend, even according to Keynes.

Liberals believe in the government taking money from taxpayers or borrowing it and determining how to spend it and what projects to spend it on. This is precisely what has happened in the United States during the Obama administration. The government has spent trillions of dollars to keep all federal operations going, to increase "entitlement" payments, and to invest in "shovel-ready" projects (meaning that projects can immediately get underway and the money get into the economy quickly) to help out the economy and get the "pump primed." This is where liberals and conservatives have a wide difference of opinion on what stimulates the economy. Liberals cannot help their thinking that the government does a better job of investing than the private sector; they crave control over everyone's money. Over the last three years, there is no doubt that the concept of government investment in projects and in politicians' favorite new technologies such as solar energy is a miserable failure and has done nothing to "stimulate" the economy. Even the president, who initially said the government would invest in shovel-ready projects, admitted there is no such thing as shovel-ready projects. Conservatives would never trust the government to make investments for them in an attempt to stimulate the economy.

In contrast to the liberals, conservatives believe in capitalism, where individuals and companies should be the people who determine what businesses they should invest in, not the government deciding for people. Conservatives know that a bloated bureaucratic institution cannot make good investment decisions and tends to invest in political aims and not in well-run profitable businesses. Governments do not have the same mindset as investors, because making a profit is not the primary goal of the bureaucrat's investment decisions. In addition to their belief in capitalism, conservatives believe in monetarism as a control mechanism for the economy, not government spending. In the case of the United States, monetary control is in the hands of the Federal Reserve System, referred to in this book as the Federal Reserve. In the event of a major financial downturn, any stimulus of the economy should come in the form of tax rebates or dramatic tax reductions across the board to all taxpayers because all taxpayers have so-called shovel-ready projects. Increasing the amount of currency available to them would have been the most effective method of stimulating the economy over the last four years.

MONETARISM

Milton Friedman is the father of monetarism, which is an economic theory quite different from Keynesian theory. In his book *Monetary History of the United States 1867–1960* (1963) Friedman relates his study of money supply to economic activity and concludes that it is the control of money supply that drives economic activity. His theory, which has been adopted by the Federal Reserve as the everyday working model of the economy, is that when the economy slows, the Federal Reserve should increase the amount of money in circulation and lower the interest rates in the market. Conversely, when the economy is growing too fast—say, 6 percent GDP growth—the Federal Reserve should contract the money supply and raise interest rates. This theory is a large divergence from Keynesian economic theory in that the government spending in Keynesian theory plays an important role in growing the economy while in monetarism it plays no role and effectively has no impact on economic growth rates.

Underlying this theory is a simple equation: money supply (M) times money velocity (V) equals the average price of goods and services (P) times the quantity of goods and services (Q), or $MV = PQ$. The primary money supply the Federal Reserve focuses on is M2, which includes actual currency, checking deposits, saving deposits, and other time deposits. Money velocity is the number of times M2 turns over in a year. That half of the equation speaks a lot because in the measure of economic activity (GDP) dollars are the measurement. I believe it is a law of nature that GDP has to be M times V because these are the only two things that can make up GDP. Another law of nature, I think, is that if money is spent, it is spent on either goods or services. So in thinking about the entire GDP, if a certain amount of money passed through the economy, that money had to be purchasing that amount in goods and services. If that much money paid for goods and services, the function on the other side of the equation has to be the average price of goods and services times the quantity of goods and services.

There is no doubt that the equation is a law of accounting, if not of nature, but the real question is, what causes what to happen in the equation? Monetarists believe that causation starts with the money supply—half of the equation. An increase in the money supply by the Federal Reserve stimulates economic activity by either increasing prices or the quantity of goods or services. Of course there is a lag in timing, but the reaction nonetheless happens. Indeed, we have almost 100 years of Federal Reserve data to back up the theory, and I believe this theory explains economic activity far better than Keynesian concepts.

SUPPLY-SIDE ECONOMICS

Supply-side economics was adopted by Ronald Reagan and became the primary theory used by his administration. It theorizes that supporting businesses that produce goods and services by lowering taxes and regulations helps economic activity. The theory goes that if businesses stand to make more money and operate with fewer expenses imposed by the government, they will hire more employees, build more plants, and stimulate more economic activity. In addition, the economy needs a stable currency in which all participants can depend. Nobel Prize winner Robert A. Mundell and Art Laffer were the primary champions of supply-side economics. The core tenets of their theory was that during a recession or depression, a country should first lower its tax rates, and second, undertake many fiscal changes such as reducing regulation, maintaining a stable currency, supporting free trade, and maintaining spending levels.

The importance of this concept is that the government should do everything to support businesses so that they can make more money. This primarily means lower taxes as incentive for businesses to produce more goods and services, which will enable them to hire more employees. Reduced regulations (regulations being nothing more than another tax) also help businesses so they can grow more easily. All this, coupled with sound monetary policy (meaning low inflation), is the key to economic growth. If businesses are free to produce more goods and services, then the economy will grow. If the government hinders business by taxes and regulations, then they cannot produce as much, hire as many employees, or build as many plants, and the economy will suffer. This is my view of how the government should treat businesses.

CONFIDENCE

The word *confidence* has become a cornerstone of all economic theory and controls much of what we recognize as gross domestic product today. All the actors in the economy must have confidence in one another and in the system. In some areas, such as demand deposits, confidence is critical and when it wanes, depositors cash out their deposits. There is no agreed-upon definition of *confidence* among economists, but it includes consumer confidence, business confidence, government confidence, and investor confidence. Confidence is such a crucial factor in economic growth that it is measured in a number of ways, such as consumer confidence. The focus of this book is confidence in the state: in this case, the United States.

The confidence in Greece was lost in October 2009 when government officials announced that the country's debt and deficit problems were much worse than they had been portraying to the public and investor community. Not only was Greece's deficit three times greater than officials had been reporting, but the level of its debt had been underreported, apparently by use of derivatives. At this point, the country started its economic train wreck as investors started requiring higher interest rates on Greek debt and soon thereafter stopped lending to the Greek government at all. The Greek government had to turn to the "Troika"—the European Union (EU), the European Central Bank (ECB), and the International Monetary Fund (IMF). Investors had lost confidence that the Greek government would repay its debts, and the consequences were that no one in the financial markets would loan the government any more money.

The concept of *confidence* is well understood by everyone even though there is no real agreed-upon definition of the word. When the head of state, such as the president of the United States, speaks publicly, he (or she) is generally managing "confidence." He wants the audience to feel confident in him and in the country. For example, today one of the primary jobs of the U.S. president is to assure investors that the country will be able to repay its debts, because a loss of confidence *is* what triggers financial and currency crises.

In his paper "The Role of Confidence in the European Debt Crisis," Richard Swedberg of Cornell University talks about historical financial crises being started by heretofore undisclosed financial losses in a bank or in many banks. Investors immediately react to any such news by taking their money out of the banks (and the system as a whole) and selling their government bonds, which, of course, creates a large crash in the value of their debt on markets, which sends yields soaring. This is precisely what happened to Greece; of course, most financial professionals can calculate the cash needs of a government and its debt burden and quickly discern that it will be unable to make debt payments.

Others, such as Niall Ferguson at Harvard University, focus on numbers and conclude that the fundamental change must be made in the United States and many other countries is a dramatic reversal of deficit spending that politically will most likely not happen. His analysis, which is correct in my opinion, is that the numbers are so bad that no investor should believe that this country can actually turn things around because countries do not like to cut entitlements. In their paper "Currency Crises," Reuven Glick of the Federal Reserve Bank of San Francisco and Michael Hutchinson of the University of California, Santa Cruz, reviewed statistical analyses of currency crises and what triggers them. They believe that when a country exceeds a set of parameters it will be hit with a currency crisis in which investors no longer believe in the currency and the value of the currency falls dramatically (at least 30 percent) against more stable currencies. The causes of the crisis are "inconsistencies between domestic macroeconomic policies, such as an exchange rate commitment and a persistent government budget deficit that eventually must be monetized. The deficit implies that the government must either deplete assets, such as foreign reserves, or borrow to finance the imbalance. However, it is infeasible for the government to deplete reserves or borrow indefinitely. Therefore, without fiscal reforms, the government must eventually finance the deficit by creating money. Since excess money creation leads to inflation, it is inconsistent with keeping the exchange rate fixed and first-generation models therefore predict that the regime inevitably must collapse." This can quickly be summarized as a loss of confidence when investors sell their bonds.

DIFFERENCES BETWEEN KEYNESIAN ECONOMICS AND MONETARISM

There are two major differences between these two schools of thought. First, liberals love Keynesian economics because it is their form of justification that the state should take people's money and the state should decide where to spend and invest it. Conservatives, on the other hand, believe the state should not be the entity that decides how to spend your money; it should be you, the person who made it. Second, under Keynesian economics, the state should borrow money during an economic downturn in order to "prime the pump" and get the economy going again. This is why the U.S. government has been deficit spending for the last four years. Monetarists, on the other hand, believe the U.S. economy will get going again if the Federal Reserve increases money supply by a method known as "quantitative easing." They believe there is no need for deficit spending. Furthermore, if the government feels a need to "prime the pump" by determining which projects to fund, such as road projects, school projects, and more social spending (food stamps), it should instead give that money back to the taxpayers; the "pump" then will be primed much faster, as Americans will dramatically step up spending.

To make the government's spending on specific projects even more obtuse, the benefit from the handouts will serve only a small niche of people in the entire economy rather than the economy as a whole. Let's say the government decided to spend all the almost $1 trillion on road and bridge repair on the interstate highway system. If you are a road contractor or worker, because of this stimulus you have a job for a while. If you are a bakery or gas station 100 miles from an interstate highway, you get no benefit at all. This, of course, is the problem with the government investing your money for you. It can invest in harebrained ideas with no chance of a return; when the investment goes bust, you are the one hurt. Conservatives believe that the person making the money should be the one who determines how it is spent and invested. Liberals believe the state should take your money and determine how it should be spent and invested.

CAUSES OF ECONOMIC DOWNTURNS

The causes of economic slowdowns are many; there are many reasons people stop spending and start saving or hoarding cash. The primary reason is loss of confidence in the economy, which is why there is so much focus on confidence measures. The loss of confidence can be from a banking crisis; housing bust; stock market bust; natural disaster such as a hurricane, drought, or crop failure; weak business sector (for example, loss of manufacturing to other countries, which creates a loss of jobs here); war; poor political decisions; too much tightening of the money supply by the Federal Reserve; too much government debt; and financial failures of businesses and local governments. The stock market crash of 1929 along with the tightening of the money supply by the Federal Reserve are the probable causes of the Great Depression. Clearly, the only event that got the United States out of the Great Depression was World War II, when the government spent a lot of money and got the economy going. Ever since then, economists have believed that wars are good for the economy. But was spending the thing that really got the United States out of the depression, or was it Federal Reserve easing along with a newly created confidence in the future?

The Great Depression started in late 1929, and GDP, then at $104 billion, did not recover to 1929 levels until 1940. During these years, the federal government deficit spending was as shown in Table 3.1.

Over the next five years, particularly during our active war years from 1942 through 1945, the United States saw massive GDP growth and deficit spending as a percentage of GDP; then, starting in 1947, the country had surpluses (see Table 3.2).

The liberal Keynesians claim victory in pointing to the war effort and massive deficit spending that occurred during the war years of 1942 to 1945. They say that this was the reason for the economic

Table 3.1 Federal Deficit Spending, 1930–1940

	1930	1931	1932	1933	1934	1935	1936	1937	1938	1939	1940
GDP ($b)	97	84	68	58	61	70	79	88	89	89	97
Federal Deficit % GDP[1]	+1	−1	−4	−5	−6	−4	−6	−3	0	−3	−3
M2 Money Supply ($b)[2]	46	43	36	32	34	39	43	46	46	49	55

Table 3.2 Federal Deficit Spending, 1941–1950

	1941	1942	1943	1944	1945	1946	1947	1948	1949	1950
GDP ($b)	114	144	180	209	221	223	233	257	271	273
Federal Deficit % GDP[1]	−4	−14	−30	−23	−21	−7	+2	+5	+0	−1
M2 Money Supply ($b)[2]	62	71	90	107	127	139	146	148	147	151

turnaround and claim that deficit spending during the 1930s was not large enough to "prime the pump." Conservatives, led by Milton Friedman, point to a failure of Keynesian economic concepts since so much deficit spending during the 1930s had no effect on GDP for over a decade. The cause of the Great Depression lasting 10 years was the Federal Reserve keeping money supply tight, which kept the economy from growing. The big turnaround year was 1941, when the economy grew 25 percent, with only 4 percent GDP in deficit spending. The United States had been deficit spending for a decade at this rate with no economic pickup. Instead, it was quantitative easing—putting more money in the economy—that turned the economy around.

Nowadays, however, the Federal Reserve has increased the "monetary base" from just over $800 billion in 2008 to $3 trillion in April 2013. The monetary base is the balance sheet of the Federal Reserve and Treasury combined, namely how much cash and government securities they own. When the Fed buys government securities with cash, that cash increases the amount of cash reserves the banks have. Since banks need to have 10 percent of total loans in reserve, that means that when the Fed buys government securities from them, they can now loan nine times that amount in the market. This multiple is called the "money multiplier"; during 2007, it stood at 9.0 times. The moves by the Fed were intended to make more money available for banks to lend, but banks are not lending because of lack of demand by businesses. So despite growing the monetary base so dramatically, the amount of funds constituting M2 has only grown erratically at around 6 percent per year since 2008. Since banks are not lending much, the money multiplier has fallen to around 3.6 times in April 2013. Historically, the actions by the Fed to increase money supply almost instantly increased GDP because there was always demand for borrowed money. Not today. Businesses are not borrowing, and this is the reason the U.S. economy has not recovered. The federal government has been borrowing for consumption, but consumption does not stimulate the economy as investment in businesses does, nor does it create a mechanism to repay the money borrowed.

The next important aspect in measuring the economy is the "velocity of money." Velocity of money is the number of times the money supply (M2) turns over in a year. The Fed has no control over velocity. In Figure 3.1 you can see that the velocity of money is at very low levels, almost as low as during the Great Depression. The reason velocity is important is that GDP is always equal to the money supply times the velocity (GDP = M × V). Velocity is affected by many factors but many economists believe the primary factor is

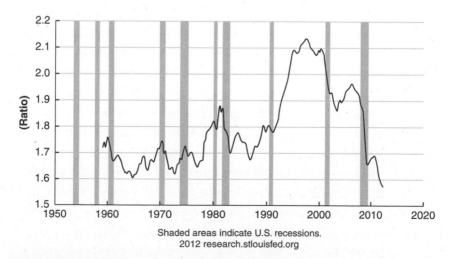

Shaded areas indicate U.S. recessions.
2012 research.stlouisfed.org

Figure 3.1 Velocity of M2 money stock (M2V).[3]

the kind of borrowing that is taking place. Borrowed money used to create income, such as a business borrowing money to build a plant, increases velocity. Over the last five years, however, most borrowing has been for consumption, particularly by the federal government, which does not increase velocity.

During the Great Depression, the United States was not inside the Debt Trap because it had plenty of borrowing capacity. The primary problem was getting the economy into growth mode. Government spending did nothing over a 10-year period to get GDP growth even though the government deficit spent. The reason, according to monetarists like Ben Bernanke, the current chairman of the Federal Reserve Bank, and Milton Friedman, was a series of bad decisions by the Federal Reserve Bank. Starting in 1928, the Federal Reserve Bank started raising federal funds rates and continued raising them through the recession of 1929 all the way through the stock market crash of October 1929. The market crash was the response of tighter money. The Dow Jones Industrial Average dropped from a high of 381 in 1929 to a low of 41 (an 89 percent drop) in 1932. This compares to a drop of 38 percent in 2000–2002 and 54 percent in 2008–2009.[4] There was a mad dash to convert dollars into gold (the dollar was backed by gold). To support the value of the dollar, the Federal Reserve raised interest rates again, effectively reducing the amount of currency available to the public. The public continued cashing out their bank accounts and the banks failed, causing panic throughout the country and the world. This, of course, caused further decreases in the supply of money. The Federal Reserve continued tight money supply during the 10-year period of the Great Depression, and solely due to their actions, the money supply decreased 30 percent. This horrific period in American history, when unemployment hit 25 percent and wages declined by over 40 percent, could have been totally avoided had people at the Federal Reserve known then what they know now. Instead of contracting money supply, they should have been increasing money supply. Fiscal deficits by the federal government had no effect on the Great Depression, just as it has had no effect on the economy in the last five years.

During the current U.S. economic crisis, which started in fiscal year 2008, the GDP and deficit spending increased as shown in Table 3.3.

Table 3.3 U.S. GDP and Deficit Spending, 2006–2012[5]

	2006	2007	2008	2009	2010	2011	2012
GDP ($T)	13.4	14.0	14.3	14.0	14.5	15.1	15.6
Federal Deficit (%GDP)	1.8	1.1	3.2	10.1	8.9	8.7	7.0

So what are we to think of all the numbers in Figure 3.1 when it comes to deciding whether government deficit spending really helps the economy? These are some pretty big deficits, but not much has happened to the economy. Possibly the only real growth has been in productivity, as there has been essentially no growth in job creation since 2007. The Keynesians (that is, the liberals) like to claim that the economy would be much worse had we not deficit spent. Monetarists disagree because the money spent went to projects favored by the Obama administration and not into the hands of the people who make business actually happen: the taxpayers. To show how ineffective government spending is in recovering from recessions, the United States has had 10 recessions since World War II, and in no other one has deficit spending exceeded 2.1 percent of GDP for only one year, except for the recession of 1974–1975, when the government deficit spending was 3.4 percent of GDP for one year.[6] In all these recessions except the 2008 one, the United States experienced GDP growth of 4 to 12 percent afterward.

This one factor is the major difference between the liberals and conservatives. Liberals want the government to decide where to spend the money: for road projects, schools, solar power, political allies, and all the other projects they are determined to invest in. Conservatives think the government is a poor decision maker and believe that if money is put back in the hands of the people who earned it in the first place, it will be spent quickly and efficiently and actually increase GDP. Wall Street investment bankers and other professional investors are very good at investment decisions and have all the tools, experience, and capital because they have been making and selling investments for a long time. No administration, senator, or congressman or congresswoman has any special knowledge, insight, or analytic capability over the professional investment community. Consequently, their investment decisions cannot be as wise as investment professionals' decisions and their investment returns cannot be as great. With regard to government spending money, one thing is very clear: there is no "multiplier" effect to the deficit federal spending as predicted by Keynes. The concept of multiplier effect is that if the government puts a dollar into the economy, that dollar will be respent by people and businesses in the economy so the economy will increase. If the increase in economic activity is $2 for the $1 contributed, the multiplier is 1 to 2. In the case of government spending during the Obama administration, all that deficit spending has done nothing to stimulate the economy and clearly has had a poor multiplier effect. The effect, if any, is low, probably around 1 to .3.

The secretary of the interior under President Obama, Tom Vilsack, has made a massive effort to increase the number of people on food stamps, claiming, "Every dollar in 'food stamps' benefit generates $1.84 in the economy in terms of economic activity."[7] This of course is preposterous on two counts. First, to take $1 of government spending and turn it into $1.84 in GDP is a better trick than turning lead into gold. Most studies, which are not exact science because there is really no way to accurately assess the multiplier, conclude the best that government deficit spending can do is 1 to 1 and it could be as low as 1 to .3. In other words, every dollar the federal government borrows and throws into the economy only picks up the economy 30 cents. Second, to peg a multiplier of 1.84 times is beyond the measuring ability of any economist because there is simply no accurate way to separate out the effect of the government stimulus from GDP in general. But Tom Vilsack claims to have miraculously done it. If government expenditures can increase the economic activity, then those countries with the most government spending as a percent of GDP would have the strongest economies. Countries like North Korea and Cuba would have the strongest economies in the world. Fidel Castro would be the world's economic hero if the multiplier would have been greater than 1 to 1, but it is not.

CRITIQUE OF KEYNESIAN ECONOMICS

Keynesian theory has been under attack since 1936, the year his book *General Theory of Employment, Interest and Money* was printed. His theories have been adopted by the liberal mind as the solution to all problems: have the government take over, and it can fix anything. Keynes even brings up Karl Marx theories in his first chapter. Keynes never meant for his theories to be extended to socialism, but clearly that is where the liberal mind has taken them. Conservatives, on the other hand, disagree with the entire set of concepts. The government should not be manipulating the economy by spending lots of taxed and borrowed money. More importantly, the economic research and data analyzed over so many years clearly debases his concepts. They were mesmerizing in their simplicity but failed in every way in actual practice.

The first concept that has completely failed is the multiplier effect of government spending. What Keynesians fail to consider is the basic concept that a dollar spent by government came from either the pocket of a taxpayer or from borrowing. When a taxpayer dollar is used, that dollar has to be subtracted from the economy at the time the government takes it, either directly as a dollar that would have been spent or indirectly as a dollar that would have been invested. With respect to a dollar borrowed by the government, that takes a dollar out of the capital markets that would otherwise have been available to private enterprise. In either case, government spending "multiplier" concepts are dead before they even start.

During the Great Depression, the U.S. government deficit spent 4 to 6 percent per year for the entire decade of the 1930s with no economic growth. This is because the Federal Reserve shrank money supply and raised interest rates. There is no doubt which of these two actions was most efficacious. Had the Federal Reserve only increased money supply and lowered interest rates, this country would never have suffered the Great Depression. Since the start of the current recession and economic slowdown, the government has been deficit spending nearly 10 percent of GDP per year, yet GDP growth has been less than 2 percent. That implies a multiplier of 1 to .2, which has been a massive waste of money. The Federal Reserve has grown money supply at around 6 percent per year, but the federal government borrowings from the market have exceeded this, emasculating Federal Reserve action.

What we are experiencing in the United States today is the same economics that Japan has experienced since the late 1980s. The Japanese government has deficit spent every year in the last 20 years and is currently deficit spending at 10 percent of GDP. Its central bank, however, has kept money supply tight and consequently all the deficit spending in the world will not help the Japanese economy. The Japanese government owes somewhere between 160 to 220 percent of GDP in debt, the highest percentage in the world. All this borrowing but no economic growth ... that is because government spending does not help the economy.

The United States has suffered 10 recessions since World War II. It has not used "fiscal policy" (spending) as a method to get out of any of the prior recessions. Automatic escalators have created deficits, which have ranged from .6 percent to 2 percent for one year during each of these recessions. During the recession of 1974, the deficit reached a peak of 3.4 percent for one year. The actions of the Federal Reserve, increasing money supply and lowering interest rates, were the method of getting the country out of all of these downturns without deficit spending. The reason the United States has a central bank and why almost every country in the world has one, is to regulate currency, money supply, interest rates, and the economy. The world knows that central bank action is the key to economic growth, and we watch central bank action every day. We also have 50 years of OECD economic data on almost 200 countries, and anyone who believes that government spending helps an economy is deluding themselves. If the Keynesians were right, there would be no need for a central bank, yet every country has a central bank that manages its money supply and economy. (The European Central Bank controls the European currency [Euro] and the economy in the participating countries.) The simple Keynesian "fix" is really not simple, nor is it a fix. Even Franklin Roosevelt thought the Keynesian fix was "too easy."

To be fair to John Keynes, his theories advocated deficit spending only in times of depressions; otherwise, the central bank can moderate economic downturns that are less severe, such as recessions, by increasing money supply. His concepts have been stretched beyond recognition by politicians and uneducated pundits. He advocated having governments run at breakeven or even surpluses during normal times and having the savings or at least borrowing capacity to deficit-spend during depressions. Few governments actually have done this, and this is a failure of the United States and many European governments. The entire matter of deficit spending is really a psychological issue that I discuss in Chapter 5.

HISTORICAL DEFICITS

In the last 82 years, since 1930, there have been 69 years of deficit spending and 13 years of surpluses. During the deficit-spending years the deficit averaged 4.1 percent of GDP, and during the surplus years the surplus averaged 1.3 percent of GDP.[8] These years include World War II and several recessions, but most of them were peacetime, strong economy years during which there was no need under Keynesian or any other economic concepts to deficit spend. So why did the government deficit spend all these years? Was it simply out of expediency, or was there a plan?

Judging from human behavior, the axiom "you can tell how someone will act in the future by how he or she acts today" is an accurate statement. If you simply reverse that, political behavior today is probably very similar to political behavior in the past. We can see that this is true in the numbers: deficit spending has been going on in years during which the government should have had surpluses. I have never seen a discussion about deficits during good economic times, because it is not a top-priority subject of politicians. I might point out here that during the eight years of the Reagan administration, national debt held by the public increased by $1.764 trillion;

during four years of the George H. W. Bush administration, debt increased $1.469 trillion; during eight years of the Clinton administration, debt increased $1.549 trillion; during the eight years of the George W. Bush administration, debt increased $4.916 trillion; and during the first four years of the Obama administration, debt increased $6 trillion.[9] There is a lot of discussion about which president borrowed how much and who was the worst for the country. This generally follows along political lines, with conservatives defending Reagan and the two Bushes, and liberals defending Clinton and Obama.

To make matters much more complicated, the numbers mentioned previously are simply the amount of outstanding debt each president accrued from the day he took office until the day he left. This, of course, is oversimplified. For instance, when each president's term starts in January in the year after he is elected, he is operating under a budget approved by the last Congress (and presumably the last president), and that budget lasts until the next October. So perhaps an analysis of budgets approved would be a better comparative analysis tool, but there are many more considerations.

Two primary factors that govern who did what to whom are the economy and which party controlled Congress. The economy is a critical factor in that it determines the amount of tax receipts paid to the government, and generally expenses rise in down economies due to unemployment. The party in control of Congress is probably more of an important determinant in who created the deficit because that is where the budget starts and is finally voted on. In addition, legislation signed after a new president takes office can affect the budget for that year. In his last four years in office, George W. Bush vetoed four spending bills that were overridden by the democratically controlled Congress. In February 2009, Congress under Obama passed two additional spending bills; one was $787 billion and the other $410 billion, which totals $1.2 trillion. The process of attaching blame is a complicated one!

The economy did not benefit from all this deficit spending, so it was for pure political expediency that Congress and the administrations did it. While George W. Bush inherited a bad recession that started when he took office in 2001 (the dot-com bust) and then presided over the recession of 2007–2009 (the housing crisis), I did not sense any angst during the middle of his term to balance the budget. Reagan dealt with a financial crisis at the beginning of his term. Clinton had no financial problems during his term, and Obama had a major financial crisis at the beginning of his term. I wish that the government, whether you blame Congress, the president, the economy, or the Federal Reserve, had never borrowed any money. The United States would not be faced with the potential ruin it is faced with today. World War II was perhaps the only justifiable national emergency when the government needed to borrow money.

I believe that the Congress and various administrations simply did not want to go through the fight to keep the budget balanced, and the easy way out was to borrow. I think it is a fair criticism of the leadership of Reagan, Bush, Clinton, Bush, and Obama that they did not fight against deficit spending. Over the 28 years of Reagan, Bush, Clinton, and Bush administration budgets, the aggregate debt borrowed was $5.1 trillion. That is approximately 32 percent of the U.S. national debt of $17 trillion. Since the country has around $400 billion ($360 billion in 2012) of interest expense a year, the government is paying around $143 billion a year on interest on the debt accumulated during those 28 years *and* it still owes the $5.1 trillion that was borrowed. U.S. citizens will be paying interest on this debt forever. As we sit here today, we can look back and say what poor financial leadership managed the country then. Americans are now paying for the deficits that were incurred over the last 100 years and should rightly ask, "What benefit was received from all this deficit spending?" Clearly, the deficits spent during World War II were worth every penny, but since then there is little justification for deficit spending. I do not like that I am helping pay for deficit spending that was used by my father's generation for something they should have paid for then. My generation is even worse; my children and grandchildren will still be paying for all these deficits long after I die.

POLITICS AND ECONOMIC THEORY

I fear that the various economic theories become just an academic discourse because I don't think politicians even know the basic constructs of economic theories or really care. Their prime focus is how to spend other people's money and create a utopian state that takes care of everyone. During all the various debates around the country about what to do during the current recession, liberals have pulled out the Keynesian theories, yet I believe they have not so much as turned a page in *General Theory of Employment, Interest and Money,* nor have they studied the history of the constant failures of the theory. What they do hang on to is the concept that government should take all the people's money and then decide how to spend and invest it. We know from 100 years of studying the results of Federal Reserve management of money supply, as well as roughly 50 years of OECD economic data, that money supply management controls the economy and that government spending ("fiscal policy") really has little if anything to do with helping the economy.

We also can see in real time that European governments with high levels of government spending have weaker economies than those governments with lower levels of government spending. Thomas Jefferson recognized this phenomenon in the 1790s after studying European governments during the years he lived in Paris, and he had almost no economic tools or education. So despite all the deficit spending in the United States during the last five years and all the borrowing of money ($6 trillion), the economy has not and will not respond to government spending. The country finds itself in this horrific financial condition, and people now realize that all this money was borrowed under the false belief that it would somehow help the economy if the government just loosely threw it around. This uneducated approach to managing the economy has crushed many countries and is now happening in the United States.

We know that a thousand dollars spent by the government on so-called social spending has a significant negative impact on the economy. Let's say the government intends to give a thousand dollars to an unemployed individual for food stamps, unemployment benefits, or other "social" needs. The first transaction is to slap a $1,000 tax on someone who did make some money: this takes a thousand dollars out of the economy, and either GDP or investment drops a thousand dollars. So we are starting with a net negative thousand dollars to the economy. The second step is to give this thousand dollars to someone who has not produced goods or services for the money. It is this step where we find the economic failure of communism and social spending by governments.

When the person receiving social benefits receives the cash from the government two negative economic events occur. First, the government social programs have significant overhead expense (an average of 15 to 20 percent), so the government is transferring only 80 to 85 percent of the original thousand dollars to the recipient. The exact overhead amount is hotly debated because the government does things very differently than private insurers do. The expense, nonetheless, is a significant one.[10] Second, a person receiving that thousand dollars given under social services programs did not produce any products or services in exchange for the money received, and therefore this transaction does not add to the economy. There is no GDP increase as a result of this transaction as there is in other transactions. From an economic perspective, this is the fatal flaw in government spending on social programs: the failure of the recipient to produce goods or services equal to or greater than the money received. This also is the fatal flaw throughout history in all communist societies and in union-based economics. We can see the economic effect clearly with current governments in Figure 3.2.

When a government operates at a deficit, it borrows money on the market and uses capital that would have been available to the private sector. This has two negative impacts on the economy. First, the government's borrowing takes capital out of the market that would otherwise have been available for private use, making the cost of capital higher for businesses and harder to find. Secondly, the nature of government deficits and ad hoc spending programs are that they are not long term in nature. Unlike a business enterprise that builds a

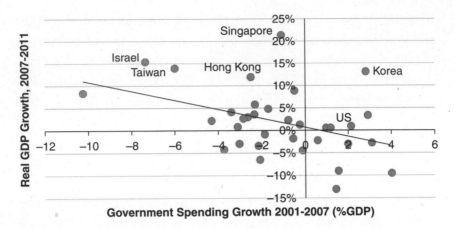

Figure 3.2 Recent GDP growth versus government growth, 2001–2011.[11]

factory or retail shop and hires employees for the long term, these short-term government deficit and spending programs do nothing to keep the economy going in the long term. For these reasons, we have seen GDP growth in the United States barely above zero, even though the government has been creating a false and temporary 7 to 9 percent GDP growth by its deficit spending. The only actions (other than reducing regulations) that have worked to stimulate the economy have been to increase the money supply and to lower interest rates. These are the only truly effective actions to reignite the economy. Further, in order to make these actions workable, they need to be done under a long-term policy, not just short-term, one-shot deals. We have seen the complete failure of deficit spending as well as short-term stimulus over the last five years, and the result of all this is a lower GDP growth.

The concept of government taking money and property so that it can determine how to spend it, by the way, is the core concept of Karl Marx and Fredrick Engels in their endearing *Manifesto of the Communist Party*. They advocate that the state should take *all* private property and control the use of all property. Many liberals also cite this work as a definitive "economic" theory. The problem is that few have ever actually read it and they do not know it contains zero theories on how the economy works, on money supply, on job creation, or any other matter involving the economy. It is only 32 pages and spends most of the time discussing the history of the "oppressed" worker and how workers should "unite" and take over all aspects of living, including all property, through government action. Later Marxist theories contain some economic thought, but it all flows from how to equalize wealth, a purely psychological construct.

We know now that not one idea put forth in Marx's writings has worked or ever will work over the long term: his ideas are based on nothing but equalizing wealth among all people. His theories, however, are still practiced by many European economists and European governments. More importantly, many European governments use these failed theories to govern their people and are advised by Marxist economists. Marx's theories were nothing more than a rehash of old theories that have been around since ancient Greece— for example, that the government should take everyone's money and spread it around evenly or that labor should get a bigger piece of the pie. Governing by these theories has resulted in only disaster most recently in Europe: it will continue to damage these countries. A primary problem with Marxism is that it completely missed monetarism. Marx really never gave a thought to money supply and interest rates: how could he? Marx's issues were psychological, not lending themselves to rational thought. Marx did casually make a comparison of labor rates in agriculture to labor rates in a gold-mining operation, but that is about as far as he went on about currency in his various theories.

The problem facing European countries that still operate under the influence of Marxist economists is they are currently facing a deflationary period and the only tools they have ever used are government redistribution of wealth. The monetary mechanisms of the European Central Bank have dramatically hurt these Marxist regimes, but the individual countries are powerless to change it because the leftist economists who control government policies basically don't want to believe in monetarism or use monetarist mechanisms to get out of trouble. Marxism has met its nemesis: economic stagnation and deflation.

The European Marxist economists have not preempted economic thought in the United States, but there are still many economists in the States who believe all this. The communist doctrines on both sides of the Atlantic are basically the same. The list of doctrines is a little scary. Today's liberals or "progressives" espouse all these basic concepts: They want the government to take as much property as it can by taxation and then distribute it as it wants (as the liberals want). We have seen this in action over the last four years as the Obama administration and a liberal Congress have passed massive spending bills like Obamacare (now estimated to cost almost $3 trillion) and massive tax increases contained in Obamacare ($1 trillion in new taxes). Liberals in Congress want to tax inheritance more than 50 percent, and had the Bush era tax cuts expired in January 2013, inheritance taxes would be there today. These taxes simply are a taking of private property on which taxes already have been paid. Liberals have also proposed taking over the Internet and regulating it, a method of putting communications in the hands of the state. So going down the list of all things Karl Marx wanted to see happen, anyone can quickly see they are happening here in the United States. This mentality that permeates American society is the primary cause of the Debt Trap.

Another significant area of impact to the economy is regulation of business by the government. Regulations are nothing more than a tax on doing business, and they often cost certain businesses their entire existence. The reason they are like a tax is that they cost a business money, like a tax, but do not help a business by providing a return on that money. One kind of regulation actually is intended to help out certain businesses, such as requiring annual prescriptions for eyeglasses or annual car inspections. In some states prescriptions for eye glasses are good for one or two years and in others they are good for five years. In Texas, the ophthalmologist can determine the prescription's length until expiration. Only 17 states require periodic safety inspections for cars, while some states require inspections only on the purchase or import of a car. These types of regulation help the beneficiaries: the optometrists and garages, who receive billions of dollars a year in revenue. But it comes at the expense of someone else, usually the public. Regulations such as this cost consumers billions of dollars a year that they would not have to spend otherwise. The regulations that cost millions of jobs and billions of dollars a year are the ones for which some special-interest group has usually lobbied. These are known as "corporate welfare" regulations because they help out some specific businesses.

THE U.S. DEBT TRAP

First Jaw

Today, the United States is in the Debt Trap. The country's economy is frail and barely hovering above recession. This, despite the federal government (as well as most state and local governments) deficit spending and throwing almost $6 trillion into the economy over the last five years. This massive deficit spending is adding very little to the economy because it is not getting a "multiplier" effect; government expenditures do not make the economy better. The liberals like to say that if the government had not deficit spent, the economy would be much worse, but there is absolutely no evidence of this; it is only supposition. If we cut deficit spending without dramatically increasing money supply and/or velocity, we will go instantly into a recession or depression. This precarious position means we are caught by the first jaw of the Debt Trap. When the economy becomes dependent on government deficit spending, it is caught in the Debt Trap. The government deficit spending is essentially a "fake" economy in that there is no real supply and demand for goods and services, but the spending is nevertheless accounted for as part of the GDP.

The implications of this fake economy are that there is no underlying economy supporting the demand for goods and services and no surviving economy when the government ceases deficit spending. It is simply the government deciding where to invest and spend money instead of the people deciding. This simple concept is really the difference in Keynesian and monetarist philosophies. Unlike the

Troubled Asset Relief Program (TARP) passed during the last days of the George W. Bush administration, the money from which was used to save our currency from collapsing by propping up banks and financial institutions, the bills passed under the Obama administration were simply "spending" bills, meaning the government decided on which projects to spend money. The claim was that it would be spent on so-called shovel-ready projects. Obama later admitted there is no such thing as a shovel-ready project, and indeed a lot of the project funding never really made it into the economy and never helped anybody. Had the Obama administration instead given a tax refund or massive tax reduction, the cash would have stayed in people's hands and in the economy. As we all know, people always have shovel-ready projects, and our economy would have recovered by now. Most of the TARP money, by the way, has been paid back, so it has cost little to the taxpayer.

The second major expense of the deficit spending boom has been the reduction of capital available to the private sector. This has enormous long-term implications to the economy. Let's say that the federal government had never borrowed any money and that all $16 trillion was now back in the hands of investors. Those investors would all be searching for a place to invest this money, and it would have ended up in the real economy, the private sector, and created real jobs: millions of them. Had this money been invested in businesses over the last 35 years, it would have been the source of the creation of thousands of businesses and millions of jobs. This lost "expense" to the U.S. economy and society can never be measured, but it is obviously several times larger than the $16 trillion number.

Second Jaw

The Second Jaw of the Debt Trap is nearly upon us: the debt markets will soon start risk-adjusting U.S. debt, and the country's interest rates will soar. The market doesn't care if a country is Keynesian or monetarist. It only cares how much debt it has and how big its deficits are. As we saw in Chapter 2, the total liabilities of the U.S. government are somewhere around $70 trillion, and there is no chance the government can ever repay even a small part of all that. Investors in our Treasury securities as well as the rating agencies go through the same exercise I have gone through in Chapter 2, and when they conclude that there is no way for the government to make it, they will stop buying U.S. debt securities, and the end will quickly be upon the country. We know the financial causes of the Debt Trap, but the question is why would any politician keep deficit spending all the way to financial collapse when all the evidence clearly indicates that that is where the country is headed? In Chapter 1, we saw that this happens all the time ... and even in current times with all the information and data we have available.

Many countries, some large, are currently in the Debt Trap (for example, Portugal, Ireland, France, Italy, Greece, Spain, Iceland, and Cyprus), and they knowingly walked right into it. These countries no longer control their destiny; the market controls them. With respect to countries such as Greece, Ireland, and Portugal, the debt markets have stopped loaning to them. The only source they have for cash is their own taxes and the Troika (described in detail in Chapter 6). When the Troika agrees to loan money, it demands austerity, meaning cutting expenses and raising taxes, or they will not loan money. These countries have lost their autonomy and can no longer make their own financial decisions. The "Golden Rule" applies always, and the market is the only person who has the "gold." The United States will quickly get to the point where the market will dictate how to run the government. Gone will be the days when the country can run a budget deficit. Interest expense will be the largest budget item, and everyone will suffer, particularly the poor.

The Second Jaw of the Debt Trap is what happens when the market finally loses confidence that a government can actually fix its financial problems. Over the last three years, we have witnessed the wrath that investors inflict on the countries that have high debt-to-GDP ratios (90 percent and higher) and are running large budget deficits (above 3 percent of GDP). In Chapter 6, I will explain why the travails of PIIGS (Portugal, Ireland, Italy, Greece, and Spain) apply to the United States and how America is facing an investor rebellion sometime soon. As discussed earlier, there is not a specific target debt-to-GDP ratio that sets off the financial crisis (although many economists have calculated "trigger" points that the country is approaching); it is the lack of confidence in the government's ability to reduce deficits sufficiently to allow a slow GDP growth rate to reduce the debt-to-GDP ratio to a manageable number (under 50 percent). Since the U.S. government is deficit spending at around 4 percent of GDP while the GDP growth rate is around 2 percent and projections for further deficit spending are staggering, investors will lose confidence and start risk-adjusting Treasuries by dramatically increasing interest rates. This is the Second Jaw of the Debt Trap, which will close around the government and press its teeth against the First Jaw of the Debt Trap. Together they will cripple the entire U.S. economy with the citizens in the middle.[12] America will follow in the footsteps of Greece (and I believe Spain) and descend into a depression (GDP decline of 10 percent or more) with unemployment of more than 25 percent. All this will be brought on voluntarily due to deficit spending by our government, as described in Chapter 4.

Figure 3.3 (a Greek tragedy) shows the recent history of interest rates on Greek 10-year bonds.

In October 2009, the investor community was shocked by Greece's disclosure that its financial situation was far worse than previously disclosed. It was also worse than the European Union

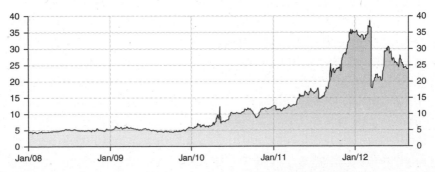

Figure 3.3 Interest rate on Greek 10-year bonds, 2008–2012.[13]

guidelines of no more than 60 percent debt to GDP and no more than 3 percent of GDP deficits. This shattered the "confidence" of investors and ran interest rates up from 4.9 percent to 41 percent in February 2012. Just for fun, let's do a calculation of 41 percent times $12 trillion (the amount of U.S. Treasuries held by third parties); that equals $4.92 trillion. This is almost twice the entire federal government receipts in 2012. This is $1.2 trillion more than the entire federal spending budget for 2012. The country of course will never get to this point because the debt markets will shut it out well before this happens.

What will happen is a substantial rise in interest rates to reflect the risk that investors undertake when buying federal debt, and this can easily run the interest rates from under 2 percent for 10-year Treasuries to say 5 to 8 percent. This is also going to happen if the economy recovers and starts consuming more cash. Today, the government is paying a blended rate of around 2.2 percent for all outstanding Treasury securities, for an annual interest expense of $360 billion. The average annual interest rate on outstanding Treasury securities over the last 40 years is around 6 percent. In the event the economy rebounds and interest rates return to normal, we can see an average interest rate on Treasury securities of 6 percent. Applying that to $12 trillion in debt to third parties, would mean an interest expense of $720 billion. If the market risk adjusts due to loss of confidence, average interest rates could easily reach 10 percent, meaning there would be an interest expense of $1.2 trillion. The Trap closes as the government needs to borrow more to keep its commitments to all other spending, spelling less market confidence and even higher interest rates. This market denial causes a default, because there is no money to pay the government debt that becomes due.

The key marker that the end has been reached is an interest rate significantly higher than a normal rate for a good credit. Once interest expense gets in this neighborhood, the game is over and the country will be caught hopelessly in the Debt Trap. The markets will require the United States to cut expenses or raise taxes to balance the budget, but in doing so, the government takes that much money out of GDP and the country falls straight into a deep recession or depression. Tax receipts will plummet, and total tax receipts could fall to, let's say, $2 trillion. That would mean that the government would be spending $1.2 trillion on interest expense, leaving only $800 billion for all other government operations. There would be no "social program" expenditures, very little military, very few other services, and so on.

The downward spiral continues with massive layoffs and business closures. There will be no money to pay unemployment, food stamps, social security, or Medicare, and the United States will devolve into a society just trying to figure out how to feed people. The federal government will be virtually helpless. This is life in the Debt Trap.

The Congressional Budget Office concurs with the assessment:

> In fiscal crises in a number of countries around the world, investors have lost confidence in governments' abilities to manage their budgets, and those governments have lost their ability to borrow at affordable rates. With U.S. government debt already at a level that is high by historical standards, and the prospect that, under current policies, federal debt would continue to grow, it is possible that interest rates might rise gradually as investors' confidence in the U.S. government's finances declined, giving legislators sufficient time to make policy choices that could avert a crisis. It is also possible, however, that investors would lose confidence abruptly and interest rates on government debt would rise sharply, as evidenced by the experiences of other countries.

Unfortunately, there is no way to predict with any confidence when such a crisis will occur in the United States. In a brief (Federal Debt and the Risk of a Financial Crisis) released July 27, 2010, CBO notes that there is no identifiable "tipping point" of debt relative to the nation's output (gross domestic product, or GDP) that would indicate that such a crisis is likely or imminent. However, in the United States, the ratio of federal debt to GDP is climbing into unfamiliar territory—and all else being equal, the higher the debt, the greater the risk of such a crisis.[14]

When Greece and Spain got caught in the Debt Trap, the only market for them became the central banks combined into the European Central Bank, the International Monetary Fund, and in reality, the governments behind them. Translated: the citizens of the solvent countries are paying for it. In order to reduce a deficit as mandated by this group of lenders, termed the Troika (EU, ECB, and IMF), the governments of Greece and Spain have to cut spending and/or increase taxes, both of which have the effect of reducing economic activity. Fragile economies, such as the ones in Greece, Spain, Italy, France, Portugal, Ireland, and the United States, will be thrown into recessions and/or depressions if government expenses are cut or there is a substantial tax increase. When the deficit is cut, this takes cash (activity) out of the GDP and worsens the tax realization by the country, increasing the deficit. And the situation continues to spiral down.

So what are the government's options at this point? The First Jaw of the Debt Trap is set, because the economy is being propped up by the federal and state government deficit spending. The Second Jaw of a higher-interest-rate environment on U.S. Treasuries will be set very soon. Once the market reacts to these high levels of federal debt, there is no backtracking. We have already seen six of eight rating agencies downgrade U.S. federal debt. The last set of downgrades indicated that further downgrades were expected. The only reason in my mind that the rating agencies have not continued to downgrade the federal debt is pressure from the government. Interestingly, after the first downgrade in history, Treasury rates declined, principally due to demand by foreigners who were fleeing European debt. Nonetheless, the rating agencies' responsibility to rate bonds fairly is their charter. If they are actually withholding further downgrades due to government pressure, they are doing the world, as well as the U.S. government, a disfavor. Once the market reacts with higher interest rates, the government will be forced to dramatically reduce the budget deficit. This has generally meant cutting expenses and increasing taxes. Both cases take large percentages of the GDP, throwing the country into a deep recession or depression. Chapter 8 explains the very painful ways of dealing with the Debt Trap.

My favorite country for studying the effects of the Debt Trap is Argentina. Argentina has been in the clutches of the Debt Trap since the 1980s and has tried every trick to get out, other than the hard way of cutting spending and slowly growing the economy out of the Debt Trap. First, it tried manipulating the currency, such as paying debt with newly issued currency, which of course trashes the currency, short-changing investors and causing rapid inflation. Germany did this in 1918–1923 and Figure 3.4 shows what happened to their currency.[15]

The carnage from this type of manipulation is extensive, and of course those hurt worst are the poor. The effects from this type of manipulation are described in Chapter 7.

Argentina tried enforcing exchange laws that limit the exchange of their peso for other currencies. This, of course, reduces foreign trade and hurts the economy even more. Argentina prohibited the

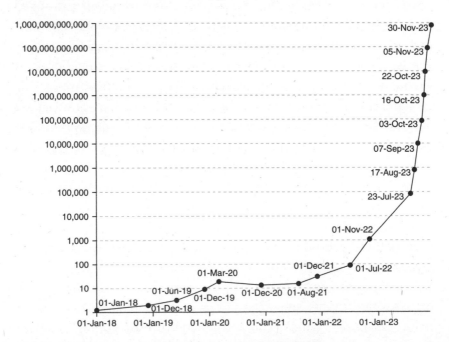

Figure 3.4 Inflation of the German mark, 1918–1923.

ownership of gold and foreign currencies and even went so far as to open safety deposit boxes and trade any gold or other currencies in the boxes for pesos. The United States also prohibited gold owner-ship during the Great Depression.

Undoubtedly, the United States will try such draconian actions when the two Jaws tighten on its neck, and citizens will suffer the consequences. Current events around Europe are directly the con-sequence of a number of countries caught in the Debt Trap. Unfor-tunately, Greece is not the only country we can study. Spain, Italy, France, Ireland and England are all caught in the Debt Trap. Their "austerity measures" are simply cutting expenses and raising taxes. To date, they have all had riots and protests, and the political leaders who have advocated "austerity" have lost support to the extent that they probably will not survive an election. Projecting forward a few years, left-wing politicians will get elected and restore spending to unions and government workers. Since there will be no capital mar-kets funding (no borrowing available), they will tax the "rich." This, of course, will not work, as England tried it during the 1970s and 1980s, and gross taxes for that group declined. The left will then be out of options and out of cash, and the society will decompose along the lines of what is transpiring in Spain, Greece, and Cyprus today.

As the United States falls deeper into the Debt Trap, it can take a page from the book of actions taken by the European governments and central banks. The actions taken are not really solving the deep-rooted problems by addressing the ultimate cause but are merely a treatment of symptoms. Deeper spending cuts and more taxes must be in the offing because these countries have already borrowed all that the market will loan them. This will treat the surface symptom of too much government debt, but it does nothing to address the true "cause" of the Debt Trap. The deeper cause and "ultimate" cause inside countries such as the United States, Greece, Spain, Ireland, Iceland, and Portugal is found in the psyche of their citizenry. I use the term "liberal mind" because psychologists and psychiatrists who have researched and written on the subject use this term. I have devoted an entire chapter to this "ultimate" causative issue: Chapter 5.

Even if the financial issues are addressed, the underlying cause, sometimes referred to as "entitlement mentality," have not been addressed and the cycle will start all over again.

WHEN WILL THE MARKET MAKE THE UNITED STATES STOP DEFICIT SPENDING?

This question is much debated among financial professionals, and unfortunately the market has demonstrated that it is not an accurate prognosticator of when a country is at the end of the road. The market completely misjudged the Greek situation, and they paid dearly for it, losing around 70 percent of their investment. The same is true for depositors in Cyprus and investors in government bonds from Ireland, Iceland, Portugal, Slovenia, and elsewhere. They were much more prescient about Spain and Italy, and the signal they gave those countries was loud and clear; they raised their interest rates so high that the governments were forced into cutting government spending and increasing taxes. That leaves us with the question of when it will happen to the United States.

Congress and the Obama administration have been warned by the Federal Reserve, Congressional Budget Office, most American economists, the governments of Germany, China, and almost every European economist about the devastation of borrowing at the current levels. The country has also been warned that taxing to balance the budget is "stupid." Yet, here we are at a breakneck pace to get caught in the jaws of the Debt Trap.

The debt markets have been burned badly in the wake of the debt problems around Europe and are extremely vigilant today. They are watching every move by Congress and the Federal Reserve. The United States has a number of very strong attributes such as a large, highly diverse economy. The dollar is the world's reserve currency and is held by many other governments and foreign banks as a capital source, and it is also the currency any foreign country or business must use to purchase much of the international trade, such as oil and gold. So let's say you are a Chilean utility and want to buy oil from Saudi Arabia; you must exchange your Chilean pesos for dollars because Saudi Arabia will only accept dollars. This creates a lot of demand for U.S. currency because the world sees it as a store of value. This is also the reason that when debt problems hit European countries the dollar strengthened against the euro because many investors decided to take their money out of Europe and run to safety—or so they thought.

My belief is that by the end of 2014, investors will make their voices heard. The first signs that the market is starting to risk adjust Treasury debt will be in long-term bonds, due in 10+ years. Since the Federal Reserve is effective in controlling short-term interest rates and the market controls long-term rates, this is where we will first see the market's statement that the United States has borrowed too much money.

THE DEBT TRAP IN A NUTSHELL

Interest rates will return to normal (considerably higher), and they will also start reflecting creditors' perceived risk in Treasuries. When interest rates rise, the federal government's interest expense will increase to an average of $700+ billion per year, making the country's deficit much worse. The government will then want to borrow more money, making the risk greater for investors, and interest rates will rise further on even more debt. The markets will finally stop lending, and the country will be faced with dramatic spending cuts and/or tax increases. This will put the economy in a severe recession or even depression.

> It is simply, and solely, the abundance of money within a state [which] makes the difference in its grandeur and power.
> —Jean Baptiste Colbert (circa 1670)

THE FINANCIAL CAUSES OF THE DEBT TRAP

My reading of history convinces me that most bad government results from too much government.

—Thomas Jefferson

The Debt Trap is caused by government spending in excess of tax receipts, period! When you focus on the money stream and follow the money, you get a much better idea of the financial causes. One of the best ways to look at government, and here I am referring to federal, state, and local governments, is as a cash collection and distribution machine. Government services, which used to be the only thing governments did, has become a small part of the federal government today. Federal and state governments actually perform services for the money they collect in taxes, but they also act as money redistribution machines.

By studying the federal machine over the last 100 years, anyone can easily see that it started as a small tax collection machine, representing around 3 percent of GDP in 1930 and provided only a few services such as national defense. It had essentially no cash redistribution operations. It has since grown to a massive, complex cash collection and distribution machine, representing over 23 percent of GDP. For every $100 spent in the United States today, $23 of that is the federal government spending. If you add state and local governments to the federal number, for every $100 spent in the United States today, over $40 is being spent by various governments: federal, state, and local. That is an unbelievable growth in the size and reach of government, particularly when you consider that people and businesses that generate GDP are being taxed at 40 percent, both directly and indirectly, so that these great money machines can perpetuate themselves. This is a hefty tax indeed.

The simple explanation for the federal government entering the Debt Trap is that expenses have exceeded receipts for most of the last 73 years (see Table 4.1).

Some people can absorb the concept better graphically; see Figure 4.1.

There are now over 89,000 governments in the United States. These include federal, state, city, and county governments and school and municipal utility districts. Someone has to pay for all this, and that someone is everyone who is alive and breathing. The size of the

Table 4.1 Receipts and Expenditures of the U.S. Federal
Government, 1930–2010.[1]

Year	Receipts (Portion of GDP)	Expenditures (Portion of GDP)
1930	3%	3%
1940	8%	8%
1950	17%	15%
1960	18%	16%
1970	18%	19%
1980	19%	21%
1990	19%	22%
2000	21%	19%
2009	16%	24%
2010	---	25%

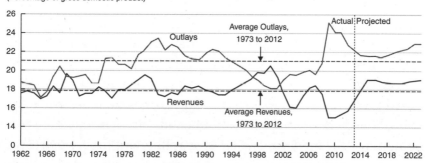

(Percentage of gross domestic product)

Figure 4.1 Total revenue and outlays as a percentage of GDP.[2]

government burden on society is "overhead" or dead expense. Most
people lead fairly frugal lives and are careful with how they spend
their salaries. Companies are likewise careful with how they spend
their money. In the business world, overhead expenses are expenses
a company must incur that do not directly benefit the business.
These expenses include accounting, legal, top management personnel, insurance, finance, and many other "administrative" expenses.
These types of expenses are disdained by managers in business

because their division is charged overhead expenses and their division earnings are reduced by this charge. This means their salaries and bonuses are correspondingly reduced. Nobody in business likes overhead, and when people say you are overhead in business, they generally mean that you are an expense they would love to eliminate; it is a derogatory term.

Government is overhead to each of us just as overhead is to insiders in a business. Government is a cost to everyone who works for a living and earns a salary. In order for us to live, have a job, and raise a family, we need government services. We need roads and bridges. In some cities, we need public transportation. We need police protection, fire protection, educators, and so on. When we are taxed, our money goes to pay for these things we frequently take for granted. Our taxes cost a lot of our earnings, and this expense is overhead to each of us. We would prefer not to be taxed at all, but we know we must have many of these items.

Another way to look at government is that it takes away market mechanisms that generate wealth, GDP, and the economy. It substitutes in its place a large mechanism of government spending that is not market based. Government spending is politically based, which is why it cannot add to the economy as a market-based transaction can. In the everyday world most of us live in, we contribute to the economy by working and getting paid. We are contributing to the economy and GDP by selling our time (services) in exchange for compensation. When we get a job, we are being hired based on an agreement with an employer who is willing to pay us an amount that is determined by the market. If you are a worker at a department store, you will be paid based on comparable pay for your position around town. This is the market for services. The employer has determined to spend its money based on market conditions.

When the government spends its money or gives it away to redistribute wealth on political grounds, it does not use any market conditions to determine how it does these things. We now know that almost two-thirds of the federal budget is nothing more than taking cash from some people and giving it to others under various so-called social programs. There is no market basis for all this ... and no market-based trade. The government gets nothing in return. The recipients of this largesse are not putting in eight hours a day nor are they selling anything to the government (although in the case of social security and Medicare, they feel as if they have paid for it; unfortunately, they have not). This entire transaction, roughly $2.2 trillion in 2013 out of a $16 trillion economy (14 percent of the entire economy), has no goods or services being sold in exchange. In all other transactions in the economy there is an exchange of goods or services that adds to the economy and GDP. Since there is no exchange and no GDP creation in the transaction, the economy does not see as much contribution as it sees with a market-based transaction. This is why countries that have a larger component of government spending have slower economies.

Even when the government spends for goods or services, I believe that it is doing so for political reasons and not true market demand reasons. Take for instance the recent display of government funding of solar power companies. The federal government invested billions of its citizens' hard-earned dollars to support development of solar panels, not because it was getting anything of value in return, but because it wanted to please some constituency. The same goes for research expenditures on snail sex, corporate welfare gifts, and so on. These transactions add to GDP, but the multiplier effect is missing. After the government expenditure in each case like this, the recipient does not continue with a business or a research project; it closes down. There are no more transactions.

Let's say you are a CEO of a large manufacturing company that makes toys for children. These can be manufactured anywhere, in any country. Countries know this and want your plant in their country so that you will hire their citizens and improve their economy. Each country can decide how much overhead it wants to place on your company by how much the government spends and, as we know, spending always equals taxation (overhead). If a government decides it wants to be a big-spending country, it has to take that money from your company and your employees as overhead. So, a prime factor that helps you decide where to locate your company is analyzing how much overhead (spending) you will have to pay in each country. There are, of course, many factors to consider, but government overhead is a big one. Government regulations are also big ones. I believe government overhead is such a major factor in deciding where to locate a factory it has a direct effect on the growth of economies. As a businessman, I know that a country with low overhead means my company can keep more of its earnings, which means I can hire more people and build more plants than a competitor in a country with higher overhead. So let's see how the major economies fare.

As you can see from Figure 4.2, the big-spending governments are the ones with economic problems—the slower economies. These countries are the ones that adopted Marxist and Keynesian economic theories, which have led them to these big-spending levels. These countries that spend over 50 percent of GDP are more socialist than capitalist. Most of Europe is socialist leaning and in a recession while

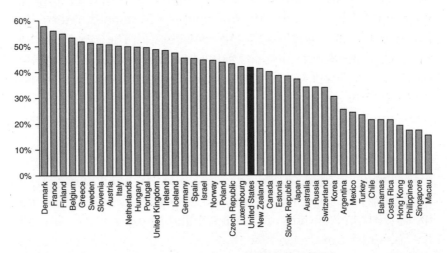

Figure 4.2 Government expenditure to GDP (%), 2011.[3]

the developing countries in Asia are growing briskly. Although each economy has its unique characteristics, the general conclusion from my perspective is that big-spending countries chase business away and consequently have worse economies. It is no secret that the United States has lost millions of jobs to countries capable of manufacturing more cheaply; most of those countries are in Asia. Notice that these are the ones with lower spending levels. By the way, governments that want their economies to prosper are making efforts to reduce this overhead by lowering taxes and reducing regulations. There is no doubt that they will be better off than those that make no effort.

As the United States has grown total government spending from under 10 percent of GDP in the early 1900s to around 42 percent today, it has handicapped the business environment. In order to remain competitive, the country will have to reduce spending to levels closer to those seen in Asia. Since this is a virtual impossibility under the current political system, I can predict the U.S. economy will be slower because of this handicap for the foreseeable future.

TAXES

We pay a myriad of taxes and fees to our various governments in so many ways—it is virtually impossible to catalog them all. There are taxes we all know, such as federal income tax and state sales and property taxes, and then there are hidden taxes such as state and local taxes on cell phone bills. These taxes alone can reach almost 25 percent of your cell phone charges and are usually hidden. The state of Texas sued Sprint because Sprint disclosed the Texas tax on a separate line item in its bills. The taxes, of course, are not the cause of the problem: taxes are simply the means of getting money to the governments. Indirect taxes are government borrowings. The cause of everyone's problems is that governments spend more than they take in as taxes. With the trillions of dollars of taxes available to these government entities, it is hard to conceive that they are incapable of balancing a budget. People do it, businesses do it, and many other governments do it.

If you are a married couple jointly making $150,000 a year and own a car and house, you can easily be spending over 50 percent of your income on taxes. In addition to all those taxes, there are a myriad of license fees for everything you can think of. Many people never stop to consider how many ways they are taxed in their everyday lives. If you are a wage-earning consumer, here is a partial list of ways you are taxed:

Accounts receivable tax
Aircraft use tax
Auctioneer tax
Automobile rental tax
Bail bonds tax
Beer tax
Bingo and charitable games tax and license fee
Boat registration tax
Boat sales tax
Building permit tax
Business district retailer's tax
Capital gains tax
Car rental tax
Cigarette tax
Coin-operated amusement device tax
Commercial driver's license tax
Corporate income tax
Court fines (indirect taxes)
Deficit spending
Dog license tax

Dry-cleaning solvent tax
Education tax
Electricity distribution and invested capital tax
Electricity excise tax
Energy assistance charges and renewable energy charges
Environmental impact fee
Federal unemployment tax (FUTA)
Fishing license tax
Food license tax
Fuel permit tax
Gasoline tax
Gift tax
Hospital tax
Hotel operator's tax
Hunting license tax
Inheritance tax
Inventory tax
IRS penalties (tax on top of tax)
Leasing tax

Liquor-by-the-drink tax
Liquor tax
Luxury taxes
Marriage license tax
Mass transit tax
Medicare tax
Mixing bar tax
Oil and gas production tax
Payroll (withholding) tax
Personal property tax
Professional privilege tax
Qualified solid waste
    disposal tax
Real estate property tax
Real estate transfer tax
Recreational vehicle tax
Rental housing tax
Road toll booth taxes
Road usage taxes (truckers)
Sales taxes
School tax
Septic permit tax
Service charge taxes
Severance tax
Soft drink tax
Sports facility and hotel tax
Stamp taxes
State unemployment tax
    (SUTA)
Telecommunications
    infrastructure
    maintenance fee
Telephone federal
    excise tax

Telephone federal, state, and
    local surcharge taxes
Telephone federal universal
    service fee tax
Telephone minimum usage
    surcharge tax
Telephone recurring and
    nonrecurring charges tax
Telephone state and
    local tax
Telephone usage charge tax
Temporary tax
Tire user fee
Tobacco tax
Toll bridge taxes
Toll tunnel taxes
Traffic fines (indirect
    taxation)
Trailer registration tax
Trash tax
Unauthorized substances
    tax
Underground storage tank
    tax and license fee
Utility taxes
Vehicle license registration
    tax
Vehicle sales tax
Vehicle use tax
Watercraft registration tax
Watercraft use tax
Water tax
Well permit tax
Worker's compensation tax

These taxes represent a partial list of taxes and license fees charged by state and local governments. The primary reason we have so many different taxes rather than one tax—for instance, one sales tax—is to keep a taxpayer rebellion at bay. Imagine a sales tax of 42 percent on all goods and services. The entire nation would riot. Indeed, there is an art to taxation well practiced for centuries by government officials. As French economist Jean-Baptiste Colbert said, "The art of taxation consists in so plucking the goose as to obtain the largest possible amount of feathers with the smallest possible amount of hissing."[4] This, of course, is exactly how federal, state, and local governments do it and for the psychological reasons discussed in Chapter 5.

Government spending is always equal to the tax on the people. This is a simple economic concept. Direct taxes are simply that: the government takes cash out of your pocket, and everyone recognizes that this is a tax. These are the taxes listed previously. The other method of paying for government spending is to borrow the money. This is also a tax, an indirect one. The money borrowed has to be paid back, and in the interim, interest must be paid on the money borrowed. The interest is real cash: cash taxes are used to pay the interest. The ultimate date that the money borrowed is paid back may never arrive because the government can (we all hope) continue rolling over its debt with fresh money borrowed. This does nothing economically except make everybody pay interest every year on the government debt forever. This is a tax that is paid by future generations, and so the spending today will be paid for in actual cash taxes charged to the next several generations. By deficit spending, we have simply moved the direct tax on ourselves to the next generation to pay. Since people in that generation are in their twenties and thirties, they have no say in whether or not they are going to have to pay our taxes later. Spending = tax = a burden on our economy. Everyone knows that putting too much burden on people kills the economy.

> An economy hampered by restrictive tax rates will never pro-
> duce enough revenue to balance our budget, just as it will
> never produce enough jobs or enough profits.
> —John F. Kennedy

By the way, many people enjoy the idea of taxing businesses because businesses make money and people believe that it is a tax on someone else. This, of course, is a political ploy and really is a tax on consumers paid indirectly. Almost all business activities and dollars that pass through the economic system ultimately come from individuals, that is, consumers. Taxes on businesses are simply passed through in the form of higher-priced products and services, and these higher prices ultimately are paid by consumers. The entire business taxation system, which is infinitely more complicated than individual taxation, is nothing more than a massive "overhead" charge that dramatically runs up the cost of products and services to the consumer.

So let's take a look at a purchase of a pair of jeans and a shirt at a retail clothing store. Each company that made a product, such as a pair of jeans or shirt, had to pay state, city, and federal income tax of 40 percent (actually higher in many states) as well as property tax, permit fees, and so on, on its business activities. In order to get the cash to pay for those taxes, the company had to price the jeans and shirt at a level high enough to cover not only its operating costs but also the taxes it paid. Let's say you just paid $100 for a pair of jeans and a shirt. Since a typical markup is 100 percent in the retail clothing business, the manufacturer would have sold the goods to the retailer for $50. The manufacturer's earnings are around 20 percent of revenue before tax, so its profit on the jeans is $10. Its taxes are $4 at least. Likewise for the income tax paid by the retailer: assuming a pretax margin of 20 percent, its tax will be $8 ($100 revenue × .20 pretax margin × .40 tax rate = $8). So before sales tax you have already paid $12 in taxes ($4 paid on your behalf by the manufacturer and $8 paid on your behalf by the retailer). These amounts are for example only but are reasonable in the industry. Actually, the number is probably higher than this because the fabric manufacturer, the fabric distributors, the farmers who grew the crop or raised the sheep, and the processors and distributors of those commodities all had to pay business income taxes and all had to add their tax costs into the final product. Now on top of all those hidden taxes you get to pay sales taxes of another 8 to 10 percent (and much higher in some cities). So, when you spend $100 at the store, the federal, state, and local taxes amount to over $12 and then you pay another $8 to $10 sales tax on that. You have just given the various governments $20 out of a $108 total bill. If you took this analysis to all the taxes paid by all suppliers to the manufacturer and retailer and if the sale happened in some cities that have sales taxes as high as 13 percent, out of $108 paid you could be paying $30 or more in total taxes. By the way, when this analysis is applied to hotel rooms and rental cars the taxes are generally more than double this amount.

The various governments do not want to aggregate all these taxes into one tax, such as a sales tax, because the tax could easily reach 50 percent. The blatant in-your-face 50 percent sales tax would create havoc with the public. Hence you see thousands of different taxes that are individually small but add up to the same amount ... and you end up paying them all when you buy something.

GOVERNMENT SPENDING

The financial causes of the Debt Trap are spending by governments in excess of their tax receipts. Since spending always equals the amount of tax, direct and indirect, the single item to focus on is spending. Taxation slows the economy; this is a well-recognized economic tenet by both the left and the right. It is also a necessary part of life that government has to provide services, including some social services, so the real issue is not to avoid all spending but rather to spend only as much as is necessary to create economic growth. Any amount above that is a hindrance to the economy.

Growth in spending by governments causes higher taxes, not the other way around. The dramatic growth in government spending at the federal level over the last 80 years was not caused by taxing people more; it was caused by the desire to spend more of the people's money. Tax increases came after the spending increased as a means of paying for it. Spending increases were for "something," and that "something" was always a new program to do "something" for people. There is a never-ending list of things politicians want to do for people. This is true in Greece and Spain today, where government spending has amounted to over 50 percent of GDP. Greece was essentially a socialist country with massive union control, higher wages and pensions, and minimal work schedules: a worker's paradise. Greek employees got to retire at 50 and live the rest of their lives on generous pensions. As we have seen, government spending and wealth redistribution do not add to GDP as a market-based transaction does. It is government's irresponsible spending of other people's money that is the financial cause of the Debt Trap.

Eighty years ago, there were few federal government programs, and the U.S. government participated very little in the economy. National defense was the primary expenditure. Today, there are over 500 federal government departments and agencies. I would love to list them all here because the sheer size of the list is daunting. At this time, if you have a computer handy, I encourage you to go to USA.gov (http://www.usa.gov/directory/federal/index.shtml) and spend a few minutes absorbing the immensity of the goliath that is our federal government.[5]

There are over 500 agencies and departments on the list, and it does not even include all the agencies and departments created in the states under grant programs from the federal government. The purpose of this list is to give the reader a sense of the magnitude of government expenditures that has led to the U.S. government getting caught in the Debt Trap. While all these agencies cost the country billions of dollars a year, the black hole of all this spending has become the so-called social programs. The list of social programs is long, but the four major categories driving America into the Debt Trap are income security (social security, welfare, and other related programs), healthcare (Medicaid, Obamacare, and Medicare), education, and housing. As John Taylor says in *First Principles: Five Keys to Restoring America's Prosperity*: "Rapid projected growth in entitlement programs such as Medicare, Medicaid, and Social Security is driving this spending."[6] These programs did not exist until after the

Great Depression when Franklin Roosevelt ushered in the "New Deal." The New Deal was actually a series of social programs never before seen in the United States and included social security, the Federal Emergency Relief Administration (running soup kitchens and dispensing walking-around money), the Wagner Act (promoting labor unions), the Works Progress Administration (making the government the largest employer in the country), the United States Housing Authority, the Farm Security Administration (FSA), and the Fair Labor Standards Act (establishing minimum wages and maximum hours worked). These social programs as well as several others created under Lyndon Johnson's "Great Society" are the financial cause of the United States entering the Debt Trap. These same types of social programs are the cause of the downfalls of Argentina, Greece, Spain, Italy, and Portugal as those governments tried to create a utopia environment for their citizens, organizing more powerful labor unions and taxing the money earners to pass around to everyone else.

Before social security, it was the individual's own responsibility to plan for his or her retirement, and most people did that. If everyone had simply made his or her own plans, there would be no need whatsoever for social security. Today, 25 percent of retirees rely on social security exclusively. So Congress in the 1930s determined to help the 25 percent of the people who were financially irresponsible by making 100 percent of us participate in the same retirement plan. For those who are financially responsible, the returns from a lifetime of social security payments are pathetic. Estimates are from 1 to 3 percent returns. No one would put their savings to work at such low rates and with the potential of losing it all if one were to die young. Social security is a really bad idea for these people. It would be far better for the government to let each person invest money in retirement plans him- or herself. The politicians, however, can't stand to think of the irresponsible 25 percent being without a safety net. While social security used to be the primary social program, today there are many.

Hopefully, you have had an opportunity to look at the long list of federal government agencies and have either been appalled at the immensity or been pleased to see that government is taking over. If you are one of the latter, you will be even happier to take a look at the *Catalog of Federal Domestic Assistance* (https://www.cfda.gov/). Here is a list of federal government programs (click the "Programs" tab at the top of the page) that are aimed at taking care of almost every aspect of life in the United States. There are over 2,200 such programs. Just to list all the programs would take 55 pages of this book. Each program has an administration full of bureaucrats to manage it, and millions of citizens are the beneficiaries.[7] All these programs did not happen overnight; they were passed by each Congress, one after the other, so that almost every congressman and senator could call a program his own, taking credit for a good deed.

The list of federal aid programs does not include state and local programs. How much money does it take to pay for all this? A lot. How many employees does it take to manage all this? A lot. Prior to Franklin Roosevelt, these activities were paid for directly by people and businesses. If someone wanted a grant for some program, she had to sell it to someone with money to give or invest. This process weeded out most of the dumb ideas, but not today.

Clearly, social spending is out of control and is singularly the financial cause of the United States entering the Debt Trap. The historic rise in spending on social programs, however, is dwarfed by the exponential rise the country will see in the future due to simple demographic changes and rising healthcare costs. Prior to 1936, there were no social programs being financed by the federal government to speak of. There were, of course, many social needs and plenty of poverty to deal with. This was all handled locally by family, friends, churches, and local governments. By 1960, social programs totaled over 20 percent of the federal government's budget; now they account for more than 60 percent. Healthcare benefits probably will continue to climb far faster than GDP growth, as they have over the last 20 years, but in any event, these costs are not easy to predict and can be grossly underestimated. The Congressional Budget Office concurs with this large uncertainty and caveats their budget predictions appropriately.[8]

To understand how out of control Congress has become with spending on social programs, we can compare healthcare spending with the other developed countries around the world. Figure 4.3 is a chart of aggregate healthcare spending as a percentage of GDP in various countries.

There is more to this graph than meets the eye. There are three types of government-sponsored systems: a single-payer system (meaning the government pays for everything), a multipayer system, and an insurance support system. All the countries listed other than the United States have some form of these, and they spend far less than America spends. I have read volumes about all the major issues in healthcare finance and management, and

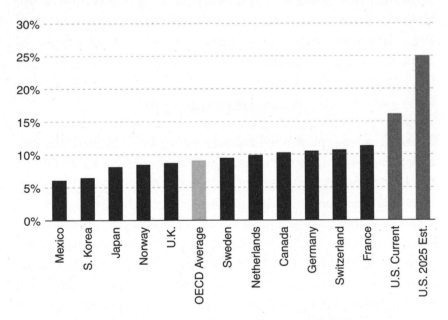

Figure 4.3 Healthcare spending as a percentage of GDP among countries, 2012.[9]

to me it boils down to a violation of the fourth law of thermodynamics, which states: a large organization cannot be managed centrally. This is actually not the fourth law, but I believe it is a law of business management. I've seen it in my businesses and even more so in larger businesses. To management professionals, centralized management of large organizations such as our government's healthcare systems is doomed from the beginning.

Healthcare in itself is *the* major financial problem facing the U.S. government. It is an area where the people paying for it do not get to decide how the money is spent. The people receiving and giving care get to decide how to spend Other People's Money. Our current predicament can be seen in Figure 4.3. Without the meteoric rise in healthcare costs, the government would be spending far less on social programs. While every dollar spent for any program has a negative impact on the deficit and national debt, the clear runaway winner in the overspending race is healthcare. As we saw in Chapter 3, spending by the federal government has all but taken over the economy. Spending is the reason the United States has debt problems, and that is where the country needs to focus its attention.

GOVERNMENT DEBT

There is no doubt that when members of the press cover the collapsing economies around the world and the serious problems the United States is facing today, they are referring to the symptom of governments running out of money, spending too much on interest expense, being unable to find someone to loan them any more money, and so on. Such is the level of understanding of most pundits ... and no doubt that they are correct in their assessment that this is the problem facing all the governments that have entered the Debt Trap. Interestingly, all these governments have gotten into the same trap in different ways. It has not been a war that drained the coffers; it has been banking failures (in the case of Cyprus and Ireland), economic failures (in Spain), too much government borrowing in the past (in Japan and Italy) and too much social spending (in southern Europe, Argentina, and elsewhere).

All these reasons for borrowing have no effect on the market because the market only cares about risk and return. It does not care "why" you borrowed the money and why you are in the Debt Trap, it just wants you to pay it back. Until you do, it will charge you interest that reflects the risk it perceives in your ability to repay the loans. Individuals and businesses may borrow too much money and go bust: this happens every day. It is part of life, and the downside is the people and organizations involved are devastated. However, their failure does not drag down and defeat an entire nation. When a national government goes bust, it *does* drag down the entire nation with it. That nation is defeated and is brought down because of its government: it borrowed too much debt.

Why do governments get into the borrowing game anyhow? To anyone who has ever borrowed money to buy a car, a house, or a business, it is a relatively easy thing to do. Paying it back is the hard part. It takes up a lot of your cash that you would otherwise have available to spend. It also increases the risk of a financial failure for you and your family. If you never borrow money, you cannot fail, or at least not spectacularly. The same is true with government debt. It is hard to pay back. The government has to use money it would otherwise have for other services. The downside to government debt is a failure of the government and the entire economy. This is the problem with government debt that is not present with personal and business debt. The government is risking the entire economy and devastation of millions of lives if it fails, so why would it take that risk?

In the past, governments have borrowed to finance wars, which on its face seems to be a valid reason to borrow money even with the risk of financial devastation. Had the United States not borrowed money to enter World War II, the world would be a different place today. I believe almost all Americans supported borrowing money for that war even if there was a substantial risk of dragging the country into the Debt Trap. I don't believe there was that kind of support for any of the other wars in which the country has participated. Since World War II, governments have also borrowed money to support their banks during banking crises, but mainly governments have borrowed to support social programs. In the last 10 years, many governments that have defaulted on their national debt and are now in the grips of the Debt Trap have done so to provide social benefits to a group of recipients who were lucky enough to be recipients during the 2000–2010 period. Social program recipients before then did not get the benefit of all this borrowing, and recipients after 2010 will not get these benefits because these countries can no longer borrow and must live with a balanced budget.

The lucky recipients of cash from the government during the last decade will be the only recipients of government largesse from borrowed money. Until the last decade, the country operated on a pay-as-you-go basis, more or less, and over the last decade the government borrowed up to its borrowing capacity. (I believe it far exceeded safe borrowing capacity.) Americans will not have that borrowing capability in the future, and the people who were the cash recipients in the last decade were lucky to be there when they were. No one in the future will be that lucky. For the next 100 years, if we can survive the Debt Trap, taxpayers will be paying interest on debt incurred by the government to distribute to the lucky few who were in line to get cash over this short period of time. Is this a valid use of the country's borrowing capacity?

MORE BURDENS TO THE ECONOMY

The federal government burdens individuals and businesses in many ways. Taxes burden all of us. Without taxes, many of us would have twice the spending ability we have. As we have seen previously, government spending always equals taxation, and many governments have figured this out and have lowered spending and consequently taxation to relieve the burden on their citizens. The United States had this figured out until the last 20 years or so. We have also seen that the greater the percentage of GDP a government represents, the lower the growth in GDP for that country. This is simple economics of the burden of overhead. Since the United States already has a very large component of government spending in the economy (42 percent), the salvation to the debt crisis the country is in is not more taxation. More taxation will only further slow GDP growth, exacerbating the deficit. The most competitive countries with the higher rates of GDP growth are those with lower spending as a percentage of GDP. We saw this in Figure 3.2.

Businesses borrow money just as the federal government borrows money, and they actually compete in the marketplace for money. Over the last four years, the federal government has borrowed from the market around $6 trillion. This is money that would have been available to businesses in the future but was taken out of the market by government. This money would have been invested by businesses, which would have created jobs and a better economy. While demand today for business debt is very weak, when the economy rebounds debt will be harder for businesses to obtain. Had the government not borrowed $6 trillion, businesses would have far more access to capital to create jobs. Further, borrowing by the federal government has worsened the unemployment situation by restricting the amount of funds available to businesses.

John Taylor in his book *First Principles: Five Keys to Restoring America's Prosperity* aptly describes both as follows: "The higher level of government purchases as a share of GDP since 2000 has clearly not been associated with lower unemployment. Though correlation does not prove causation, it is hard to see what plausible third factor could reverse this correlation. To the extent that government spending crowds out job-creating private investment, it can actually worsen unemployment. Recent government efforts to stimulate the economy and reduce joblessness by spending more have failed to reduce joblessness."

In their quest to do everything possible to help the economy, the current Congress and administration did not even do so much as research the ramifications of their actions to stimulate the economy by deficit spending. They may have been well intentioned, but their actions have made the situation far worse. They have dramatically grown the national debt and at the same time burdened the economy so much that there has been no job creation and no economic growth. When the government spends a billion dollars, it must take it from people who would have spent it in the economy or invested it. The taking process (overhead) reduces GDP by a billion dollars. The spending process does not replace the GDP lost.

The Keynesian economists working for the current administration have a thin façade covering the underlying "liberal" mind. The current administration pushed government spending programs in an attempt to restart the economy. Trillions of dollars were spent despite the economic data we have and that the OECD has collected over the last 50 years that shows that government spending does not help GDP growth. To the general public it may appear that the equation is simple: if the government spends a billion dollars on new roads and bridges, this will create jobs. Unfortunately, this is very far from how the economy really works. All this spending has done nothing but hurt the economy and maneuvers the country right in between both jaws of the Debt Trap. The scary part is how politics can distort objective research and thinking for a better America.

REGULATIONS

Most government entities (89,000 in the United States) issue regulations. In 1949, the federal government had 19,000 pages of regulations, but by 2005 that had grown to 134,000. The pages on Obamacare alone could top 100,000 by the time all its regulations are adopted. Regulations to a business owner are identical to a tax: it costs you cash but there are no new sales, revenues, or profits from spending that cash. Regulations, like tax, take cash from businesses and individuals without creating a transaction that increases GDP. The cumulative effect of regulations in the United States is staggering.

According to Professors John J. Seater of North Carolina State University and John W. Dawson of Appalachian State University in their paper entitled *Federal Regulation and Aggregate Economic Growth, January 2013*, "Regulation's overall effect on output's growth rate is negative and substantial. Federal regulations added over the past fifty years have reduced real output growth by about two percentage points on average over the period 1949–2005. That reduction in the growth rate has led to an accumulated reduction in GDP of about $38.8 trillion as of the end of 2011. That is, GDP at the end of 2011 would have been $53.9 trillion instead of $15.1 trillion if regulation had remained at its 1949 level."

We tend to dismiss the concept of reducing regulation because it has become such an everyday part of our lives, but the aggregate impact on our economy is no doubt enormous. Even at a fraction of the numbers that Seater and Dawson have calculated, regulation is choking the economy. This, of course, means less tax revenue to the government, which leads to higher deficits.

WHY DIDN'T ANYONE SEE THIS COMING?

What caused the housing crash of 2007–2008? Why didn't anyone stop the madness before the crash? There have been at least 25 books written about the crash and the cause, along with thousands of articles and probably millions of blog posts. The primary issue that any politically oriented person is concerned with is whether or not the federal laws and regulations surrounding the

Community Reinvestment Act caused the housing bust. Under regulations issued, financial institutions (Fannie Mae and Freddie Mac) were required to loan in low-end neighborhoods. These were subprime loans. Conservatives point to this starting point as the cause of the crash. Liberals counter with the observation that only a small percentage of the subprime problem related to these loans. This, of course, is not true because Fannie Mae and Freddie Mac ended with $2 trillion of subprime loans, a large part of the market. Like everything in economics, all arguments have some validity, and although I think this may have had some signs of a starting point for the disaster, the cause was somewhere else. Many writers have blamed the buildup of mortgage-backed securities and credit default swaps as the cause. They also blame very lax credit requirements. Worldwide demand for mortgage-backed securities drove bankers to sell to investors things they wanted and sometimes things they didn't want. All this is true, and all this contributed to the crash.

Few people have looked at the actions of the Federal Reserve and the Securities and Exchange Commission. During the 2001–2007 period, the Federal Reserve kept a lot of liquidity in the market, making money easy and interest rates low. Had interest rates been higher, people buying houses could not have afforded to buy homes nearly as expensive. For instance, if a buyer is paying 3 percent interest, he can purchase a house that costs twice as much as he could buy if he were paying 6 percent. So had interest rates been higher, total housing debt would have been lower and the problem would have been significantly smaller, if not completely nonexistent. Under this simple analysis, the Federal Reserve actually played a role in the housing bust. The Federal Reserve regulates banks and therefore had the ability to stop questionable lending practices, particularly since they had many regulators on premises. They no doubt had the information necessary to make changes, but they just didn't do it. John Taylor, in his book *Getting Off Track*, explains how the Federal Reserve, the Securities and Exchange Commission, and other government organizations could have prevented the crash. Taylor, having worked as an economist for the Federal Reserve and the Treasury most of his professional life, believes in the power of the Federal Reserve to regulate the economy, as do I.

Add this cause to the myriad of other claims for the cause of the crash, and you probably can understand the complexity of the analysis of the cause. All the claimed causes are somehow interrelated, and the end result was a bubble that burst; the entire world suffered.

The "crash," however, is not the cause of the United States falling into the Debt Trap, since the economic downturn represented a revenue loss of only about $1.6 trillion to $2.2 trillion and increased "social expenses" of $200 billion. The massive deficits were the result of increased spending by Congress and the Obama administration in the false hope of stimulating the economy and escalation of various social programs.

The federal government debt problem did not happen overnight. It was not caused by some catastrophic event like a banking system meltdown, and no one stole all the money and ran off with it. The problem has been one of slow accumulation of more government regulation, spending, and commitment to do more things for people. The administrations and agencies referred to previously were not created in a single day. They were created one at a time over the last 80 years. The funding programs were also not created in a day. To normal citizens, the slow creep of more and more spending and regulation by the government has gone unnoticed. We each go about our everyday business and do not pay attention to the daily activities of Congress. This is simply human nature. Congressional actions are also human nature. U.S. citizens elected representatives to go to Washington and spend money ... and that the congressmen and senators have done. Most people in government want to do something "for the country" and "for the people," which inevitably leads to spending Other People's Money.

All these agencies and programs were conceived to help people and are the financial cause of the United States entering the Debt Trap. The major cause is spending on so-called social programs, clearly the single biggest financial cause. Why would Congress spend the country into the Debt Trap? I used to believe the answer, my friend, was blowing in the wind. It is not. The answer to this question exposes the real causes of the country entering the Debt Trap: the psychological causes of the Debt Trap.

PSYCHOLOGICAL CAUSES OF THE DEBT TRAP

Any man who thinks he can be happy and prosperous by letting the government take care of him better take a closer look at the American Indian.

—Henry Ford

While there are obvious financial mechanisms that have led the United States into the Debt Trap, as discussed in Chapter 4, these are still not *the* cause of the Debt Trap. Why would a group of congressmen and congresswomen knowingly lead the United States into the Debt Trap and push the country into a depression that can economically destroy us as it has economically destroyed Greece and probably Spain and possibly Italy in the next year or so? Why does a group of politicians dramatically overpay state employees, giving them pensions that are so outlandish that future generations of taxpayers will be saddled with an enormous overhead burden so that one small group of people can be enriched by government at the expense of the taxpaying public?

These behaviors have puzzled me ever since I started my professional career. Over the last 30 years, I have studied the human mind and how it works and pored over literature produced by both liberals and conservatives on the psychology of "the other." Interestingly, liberal psychologists love to denigrate the conservative mind, and vice versa. They do not seem to write about themselves, which would be more interesting to me. Nevertheless, the concepts underlying both are continuing to develop, and even genetics has entered the field.

The real cause of the United States entering the Debt Trap lies in the individual and mass psychology throughout the country that is reflected in its elected representatives, primarily those with a "liberal" mind but also those within the conservative groups. Liberals and conservatives have very different psychological characteristics and use different methods to abuse the U.S. system of government. The liberals use government as "Mommy" and "Daddy," or more frequently as the "nanny" state, in an attempt to equalize the life condition of everyone, as well as dramatically overpay union members; conservatives use it to milk business from the government to boost their sales and profits. These two groups are vastly different, but both have a parasitic effect on the government and are both to blame for the Debt Trap America is entering.

This abuse of the state by both types of people certainly explains why the country is entering the Debt Trap, but it is still not what "causes" these things to happen. The real causes are even deeper—they lie deep in the subconscious minds of millions of people in the United States and probably billions around the world. As any psychologist will testify, there are a myriad of psychological characteristics that make up any person. Additionally, there are many influences of nature and nurture that affect each of us. What I have done here is to review the top three culprits within the mind that are at the root cause of the U.S. financial crisis.

ETHICS OF GOVERNMENT DEBT

The principle of spending money to be paid by posterity, under the name of funding, is but swindling futurity on a large scale.

—Thomas Jefferson

I have to make a note here about the moral and ethical principles underlying government debt. When we as individuals borrow money, we know we have to repay it. An identity thief is someone who steals money by borrowing in someone else's name and consequently makes someone else repay the money borrowed. It is inescapable that making someone else repay money you borrow is stealing, whether you are a person or government. The U.S. government, for instance, cannot borrow money and make Japan or France repay it. That would be stealing from another country. So, when the government borrows money, just who is going to pay it back? The answer is that it never gets paid back but each successive year as new taxpayers are added to the tax rolls they have to pay the interest on that money borrowed. After every 50 years or so, the entire tax roll has changed and all the new taxpayers have to pay interest on the money borrowed, whether it was borrowed yesterday or 200 years ago. And, the interest expense every 12 years or so equals the amount originally borrowed. We are today still paying interest on the money we borrowed to fund World War II.

A current U.S. taxpayer is paying interest on money borrowed by some Congress 100 years ago. In the future, millions of people who have not even been born yet will have to pay back the money the government has borrowed that benefitted only people alive now. Why are we, and unborn people, getting stuck with the cost of someone else's folly? This is nothing but a fraud, an outright theft from people who can do nothing to stop it, on the next generations of taxpayers: but the fraud is legal because the government did it. I couldn't do this, and you couldn't do this. The fact that Congress and the president don't even consider the ethics of borrowing is scary. I could certainly understand if the Congress in power in 2020 said, "Some jerks in 2000–2016 borrowed all this money, but we are getting no benefit from it. We are going to default and repudiate it." Of course, this is precisely what Mexico did, as referenced in Chapter 1.

PSYCHOLOGY OF THE CORPORATE WELFARE GROUP

In the business world we say that companies that sell to the government or have the government give them tax credits or require others to purchase their products or services are "companies dependent on corporate welfare." Companies receiving this "corporate welfare" are many: the Cato Institute estimates that this "corporate welfare" system costs the government over $100 billion a year. The list is a long one (see Table 5.1), and it includes all businesses that are dependent on a government subsidy, tax credits, regulations, or any other strong-arm method of creating wealth for the owners of the business. It includes both liberals and conservatives and some of the highest-profile businesses and businesspeople. There is an entire industry of registered lobbyists whose full-time job is to get government-mandated benefits for their clients. I consider this to be abuse of the government to get easy money from it. Both liberal and conservative congressmen and congresswomen participate in handing out money and benefits as they get political contributions from the beneficiaries. And remember, congressmen and congresswomen are not handing out their own money; they are handing out "Other People's Money." It is very easy to hand out Other People's Money.

Table 5.1   Corporate Welfare Programs in the Federal Budget
(millions of dollars[1])

Program	2012 Outlays
Department of Agriculture	
Agricultural Marketing Service	1,289
Applied R&D	1,143
Farm Security and Rural Investment programs	3,175
Farm Service Agency	11,863
Foreign Agricultural Service	2,164
Risk Management Agency	3,829
Rural Business-Cooperative Service	372
Rural Utilities Service	1,330
Total, Department of Agriculture	25,165
Department of Commerce	
Applied R&D	785
Economic development Administration	531
International trade Administration	379
Minority business development Agency	24
National Institute of Standards and Technology	
Technology Innovation Program	8
Manufacturing Extension Partnership	131
National Oceanic and Atmospheric Administration	
Fisheries Finance Program	6
Fishery promotion and development subsidies	4
National Telecommunications and Information Administration	
Broadband technology opportunities program	2,227
Total, Department of Commerce	4,095
Department of Defense	
Applied R&D	4,737
Total, Department of Defense	4,737

Program	2012 Outlays
Department of Energy	
Energy supply and conservation	9,834
Fossil energy research and development	1,402
Advanced technology vehicles manufacturing loan program	4,834
Innovative technology loan guarantee program	1,260
Total, Department of Energy	17,330
Department of Housing and Urban Development	
Federal Housing Administration mortgage subsidies	15,739
Community development block grants (to businesses)	285
Community development loan guarantees	17
Total, Department of Housing and Urban Development	16,041
Department of the Interior	
Bureau of Reclamation	1,254
Bureau of Land Management	1,354
Total, Department of the Interior	2,608
Department of State	
Foreign Military Financing	5,201
Total, Department of State	5,201
Department of Transportation	
Federal Aviation Administration	
Commercial Space Transportation	16
Essential air service/payments to air carriers	203
Federal Railroad Administration	
High-speed rail	1,251
Railroad rehabilitation and improvement	17
Railroad research and development	33
Maritime Administration	
Assistance to small shipyards	37

Program	2012 Outlays
Title IX guaranteed loan program	99
Ocean freight differential subsidies	175
Maritime security program	193
Total, Department of Transportation	2,024
Other Programs and Independent Agencies	
Appalachian regional commission	53
Export-Import Bank	*
International Trade Commission	91
National Institutes of Health: Applied R&D	13,845
NASA: Applied R&D	2,799
National Science Foundation: Applied R&D	450
Overseas private investment corporation	*
Small Business Administration	3,157
Trade and Development Agency	46
Total, other programs and independent agencies	20,441
Grand Total	97,642

The group of corporate welfare programs in Table 5.1 does not include government contractors that provide a service that the government needs to operate. There are thousands of businesses that provide the U.S. government with products and services that it needs, such as networks, computers, automobiles, personnel, accounting services, military support, and electricity generation. These companies bid competitively and do not receive any special treatment by the federal government. The companies I am referring to as parasites are those receiving "earmarks" or another form of subsidy from Congress that they somehow justify as needed. Policymakers somehow justify treating some companies or industries differently as a kind of "adjustment" to the market that is needed. One example is Amtrak, which receives $1.5 billion a year in subsidies.[2] It turns out that total revenue of Amtrak in 2011 was around $2.7 billion, and it is proud that it lost only $1.3 billion in 2011. PBS receives $1 billion a year in subsidies. Satellite and cable television only have 550 television channels available, so what is so important about having the government support this one channel? The Discovery Channel, History Channel, Science Channel, and Nat Geo have Nova equivalents. Disney and Nickelodeon have a dozen children's channels. Old music concerts that are popular on PBS are also shown on MTV and VH1. I believe that there is little content on PBS that is not available on many other channels. I also believe that these support programs exist solely for some political gain for some group of congressmen and women and all at the expense of the taxpayer.

There is a game of "I'll scratch your back if you scratch mine" among congressmen and congresswomen that perpetuates this. If only 10 percent of Congress would support your "earmark," you'd get it passed by agreeing to vote for other members' earmarks. This is a practice called "log rolling" and is how individual congressmen get spending for their pet projects through Congress. It is easy to spend Other People's Money.

Pure outright "earmarks" are requirements by Congress to have some administration spend money on something the government does not need. This practice is perpetrated on the public by both Republicans and Democrats, but thanks to a weak economy and so much focus on federal deficits, "earmark" spending is down significantly from 2008. To give an example of how the system works, I used to own a network engineering company, and we had built a number of networks for federal government agencies. After 9/11 and the creation of the Department of Homeland Security, I considered my company in a unique position to build a highly secure, independent (that is, no public sharing of) high-bandwidth network to help the administration of Homeland Security. After meeting with a powerful registered lobbyist about the potential, he offered that he could get an "earmark" requiring Homeland Security to spend a lot of money to purchase a network from my company. His fee was $2 million. Just thinking about participating in that system made me feel dirty. As tempting as the offer was, my network engineering company decided to go with a straight sales approach, but Homeland Security did not build that network because at that time the organization was so early in its development it had bigger issues to deal with (such as securing airports). Many other companies have no scruples and would be happy to pay a fee to get a large contract.

In April 2013, Congress passed a spending bill that included $436 million for new Abrams tanks. The military said it did not want or need new tanks but Congress nonetheless required the administration to spend this money even though the tanks will never be used. The tank manufacturer is receiving enormous revenue for something no one needs or wants, all because it is good at the "special interest" game. The justification is always, "We are saving jobs." Like all earmarks, the flow of funds is a little from every taxpayer and a lot to a single company.

These "earmarks" have existed for thousands of years. It used to be that courtesans in the king's and queen's courts would hang out and ask for handouts, now termed "earmarks." In Gustave Le Bon's *Psychology of Socialism*, published in 1898, 115 years ago, he describes this phenomenon:

> State Socialism, or the centralisation of all the elements of a nation's life in the hands of the Government, is perhaps the most characteristic, the most fundamental, and the most obstinate of all conceptions of Latin societies ... Those over which it does not actually preside it is obliged to support lest they should be endangered. Without its subsidies most of them would promptly become insolvent. In this manner it pays to the railway companies enormous subsidies under the title of "guarantees of interest."
>
> The private enterprises—maritime, commercial, or agricultural—which it is forced to subsidise in various ways, are numerous; subsidies for the shipbuilders, subsidies for sugar-makers, subsidies for silk-spinners, for cultivators ... The most hostile political parties are perfectly at one on this point, and unhappily on this point alone...

This perpetual intervention is ending by entirely destroying in the breast of the citizen those sentiments of initiative and responsibility of which he already possessed so little. It obliges the State to direct, at great expense, owing to the complexity of its mechanism, such undertakings as private persons, with the motive power of personal interest, might successfully manage at far less expense, as they do in other countries."[3]

Sound familiar? These words are as true today as they were 115 years ago and very well describe what is going on. Le Bon, however, does not follow the money as I do, and if you follow the money it is easy to see the motivation of all the politicians and companies receiving earmarks. Companies receiving earmarks are making easy or free money or getting an investor (that is, the government), so it is no wonder why they do it. It is a scam on taxpayers. Politicians give earmarks away to get financial or vote support. The only people not at the table when all this is going on are the people paying for it: you and me. This, of course, is a form of socialism in that the government is in the business of taking money from a large group of people and distributing it to a small group of people. Once again, it is Other People's Money and very easy to give away, especially when you are rewarded for doing so. Unfortunately, this has been going on for a long time with hundreds of companies and millions of individuals, but it is nonetheless still a fraud on the taxpayer.

America has long since surpassed anything Le Bon could have conceived in 1898 and has reached a level of pure communism with a large portion of society. "Subsidies" come in all shapes and forms and now permeate the society. In addition to "earmark" scams, there are 18 federal government nutrition (which offer free food) programs, 47 employee programs for "training" (which make payments to for-profit schools for tuition), 22 housing "assistance" programs (which pay your rent or mortgage), 80 programs for free transportation, and 77 welfare programs (which distribute free money), but the real number of programs is unknown, even to the General Accountability Office. There is even a *Catalog of Federal Domestic Assistance*

(CFDA) listing over 2,200 programs to support states, local governments, special interest groups, individuals, and so on.

Figure 5.1 depicts the growth in the number of federal "subsidy" programs since 1970. This is a preposterous bunch of handouts made to voters and companies that went to the effort and expense of hiring lobbyists to get the handouts. The system that allows this is the core problem, as there have always been and will always be people with their hands out for easy money and the government is a great source of easy money. The politician who creates another handout program gets the votes of those with their hands out.

Most people are aware that federal spending is soaring, but the federal government is also increasing the *scope* of its activities, intervening in many areas that used to be left to state governments, businesses, charities, and individuals. To measure the widening scope, Figure 5.1 uses the program count from the current edition of *The Catalog of Federal Domestic Assistance.*

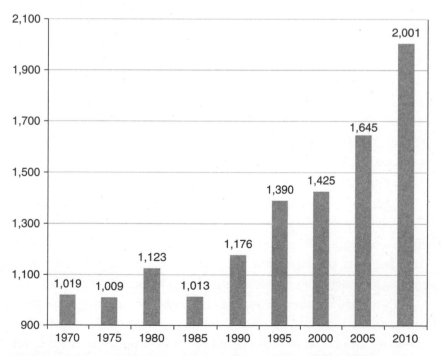

Figure 5.1 The number of federal subsidy programs, 1970–2010.[4]

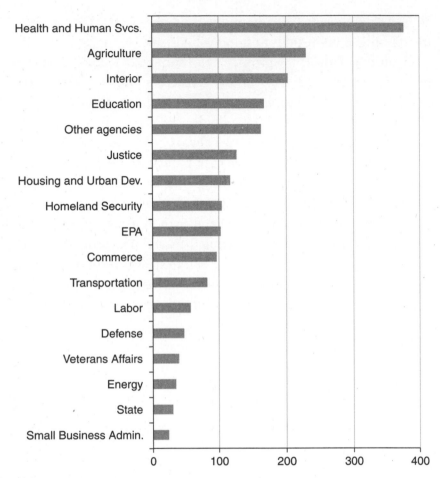

Figure 5.2 The number of federal subsidy programs by department or agency, 2010.[5]

Figure 5.2 shows the number of subsidy programs listed in the *CFDA* by federal department. It is a rough guide to the areas in society in which the government is most in violation of federalism (the constitutional principle that the federal government ought not to encroach on activities that are properly state, local, and private).

Grants are another area of government easy money. Instead of someone with a good idea for a product or service having to find investors and create a business, all he or she has to do is apply for a grant and the federal government money machine will take the money the taxpayers earned and hand it out to him or her. On the surface, all grants seem like noble wealth redistribution by the state, but the underlying problem is that the people distributing the money are not the ones who made it. They are using Other People's Money. The grant programs are administered by people who do not have any of their money in the game and, consequently, they can make large errors in judgment without any ramifications to them at all. In fact, the situation is just the opposite: they become the king or queen of a small kingdom with all the subjects begging for money for every imaginable project.

There are so many government subsidies I cannot begin to even categorize them. Some recently experienced handouts in Texas include restrictions on mailing wine directly to Texas residents. This is a particularly interesting issue to me, as I, a Texas resident, enjoy wines and have a couple of friends in the liquor and wine distribution business. I heard the inside track. For a year prior to the vote in the Texas legislature, distributors gave any member of the House or Senate free beer and wine during any fundraiser. When the vote finally came up, despite having no real reason to prevent direct shipments (the distributors argued that underaged kids could buy wine by mail), the legislators voted to restrict direct shipments, making it mandatory to purchase wine from retailers so that distributors and retailers could make their fees.

Government regulations benefit many industries. States have protected their businesses from out-of-state competition. In the early 1900s, there were the famous "milk wars," where a state would prohibit imports of milk from another state because of "health" reasons. Some states require that abstract and title companies compete for business by a bid process. Other states fix prices for these companies so that a title policy must be priced as a percent of the purchase price of a property. Title companies love this. (By the way, the Supreme Court of Iowa outlawed title insurance as "invidious to business." The state runs a service for $110 per transaction and makes money with it.)

The alcohol fuels program, which costs American taxpayers roughly $38 billion a year, benefits only corn farmers and a handful of wealthy investors. The steel industry has been the recipient of many beneficial regulations and other government actions since the 1960s in order to "protect" our industry here. There have been import quotas, minimum price limits, and antidumping and countervailing duty cases brought against many foreign producers. The federal government's "Market Access Program" that helps finance agricultural product promotion (advertising) is nothing more than a handout of free advertising. "Clean energy" companies receive outright cash infusions by the government. This list goes on into the thousands of things governments do to help a business or industry. All of this constitutes a nice, simple transfer of wealth, but this type of thing costs citizens hundreds of billions of dollars a year nationwide.

It seems the handouts and subsidies are never-ending, and if your business or industry is not receiving some, you may be in the minority. The point here is that governments, both federal and local, have forever protected and subsidized businesses that have asked for it. The common term in politics is "special interests." So, any time you hear that term, start looking for a subsidy. If you follow the money (and there is always money involved), you will find that the businesses are benefitting in ways that translate into money and the politicians are benefitting by receiving money or votes. The only one not at the table is the person paying for it ... and it adds up to a lot. Politics has always been an easy place to get money by selling out the citizens.

The list of federal and state-sponsored subsidies includes laws, regulations, tax benefits, outright investments, and other handouts. Each recipient of this largesse has a reason why they "need" a law or regulation. The recent investment by the Obama administration in a failed solar power company, Solyndra, wasted $500 million; that expense was justified by the administration as an effort to help develop alternative energy sources. Neither Obama nor anyone in his administration possesses special knowledge that enables him to invest capital more wisely or efficiently than investors in private enterprise. Government officials are not omnipotent and do not possess special powers about technology innovations, market movements, or, for that matter, anything to do with the business world. The only motivation for administration officials was to help develop the solar power industry. Notice they didn't round up everyone in the administration and have them use their personal funds. They used Other People's Money— your money. They would have never used their own; that would be too risky. This is why government does such a poor job at choosing which businesses to subsidize. In fact, money is always wasted when the government tries to steer the market in favor of some product such as solar energy. Trying to "create" a market for solar power, in the face of far cheaper energy alternatives, is very poor judgment. If there is not a market for a product or service, it is a risky business to try to establish one. This is the domain of venture capitalism, not government.

In his book *First Principles: Five Keys to Restoring America's Prosperity*, John Taylor, an economics professor at Stanford who spent most of his professional career with the Treasury Department and Federal Reserve, described the negative economics of "crony capitalism" as follows:

> This is textbook crony capitalism: the power of government and the rule of men—rather than the power of the market and the rule of law—to decide who will benefit and who will not. Economists have identified a specific version of crony capitalism that they call regulatory capture: the tendency for regulated firms and their government regulators to develop mutually beneficial relationships that harm the economy, public safety, and people's lives more generally. The benefits to the regulated firms may include lax supervision, protection from competition, or government bailouts. The benefits to the regulators may be lucrative post-government employment, political contributions, or favors to family and friends, which may be implicit or explicit.[6]

There is always a justification for having Congress give away something to some business. Each giveaway may be small, but the total adds up to very large numbers and a society dependent on the government. The horrible part is that federal, state, and local governments have become the major industry in the United States. Today, this aggregation of government exceeds 42 percent of the country's GDP. The society has become a dependent one, and the economy is highly dependent on government.

This whole handout industry is not the cause but the manifestation of the underlying psychological drive (by everyone involved) to survive and prosper. Nature still programs us to hunt for food and reproduce. Hunting for food today has been supplanted by making money, which can be traded for food. I am all in favor of unleashing the drive to make money, for this is the energy behind all progress. I am not in favor of obtaining success by fraud, which is precisely what these government handouts are. The taxpayer is always the dummy and the victim of this process. If you follow the money, it always comes from the taxpayer and goes into the pockets of some business or other group asking for easy or free money. That business or group of people directly or indirectly channels money and/or votes to the politicians who made it all possible.

Unfortunately for us taxpayers, the system and process is so endemic and there is such a large industry built on making it work that we have little chance of stopping it. In the counties surrounding Washington, D.C., are millions of people whose full-time jobs are getting favors from the government. Further, the system is a significant means of building political capital for congressmen and congresswomen to keep their jobs. Then, there is the large population who believes it is the role of government to tax and then dole out money to corporate welfare recipients in order to direct the economy. All of this is, of course, flat-out corruption because it is spending Other People's Money.

OPIUM

Opium is a terrible drug for illegal drug users: it is addicting and ruins the lives of almost everyone who uses it. This is not too different from the opiate being used in this situation: it is known in the finance circles as OPM or Other People's Money. It is very easy to give away, waste, and recklessly spend Other People's Money. The phenomenon is well known to everyone starting around adolescence. When Dad gives you the credit card to buy clothes, you spend way more than you would if it was your own money. When someone else is buying dinner you order a more expensive meal. In business, when it is the shareholder's money, managements buy jets, lavishly decorate their offices, have hunting camps, stay at the finest hotels, and so on. Everyone knows that the only person who takes good care of your stuff is you. This is because to everyone else, your stuff is Other People's Money.

This is the main reason Congress and state and local money machines frivolously spend money. It is not *their* money, it is *your* money, and these people are "paid" to take your money and redistribute it. That is what they are there for—if they did not spend money, there would be very little for them to do. They can legislate things like the Americans with Disabilities Act and No Child Left Behind, but these are means of making you, your business, or local governments spend money without the federal government acting as a collection agency. These types of laws are called "unfunded mandates" because the federal government mandates that you do something but does not pay you for doing it. They make someone else spend the money on a charity or special-interest group that wants a handout or some other special treatment. So when folks in Congress or another government entity sit around considering legislation, it is almost always going to cost someone something, and it is going to benefit some other person or group. Either way, it is really the same thing: Congress is spending Other People's Money, and the burden continues to grow on people who are earning money.

Who doesn't like to spend Other People's Money? Going on a company or government boondoggle is spending Other People's Money. Winning something is spending Other People's Money. Being invited to dinner at a friend's is spending Other People's Money. It changes everything when it is your money. Consider a company golf outing. The real cost of a weekend of golf with a bunch of company executives may be $3,000 each, after hotels, airfare (preferably private plane), dinners, drinks, green fees, caddies, and entertainment. It is very fun, no doubt because everyone knows Other People's Money—the shareholders' or the government's (taxpayers')—is paying for it. The lucky participants feel as if they are stealing the money from someone else. All this would change if each participant had to pay his or her own way. Unless they were millionaires, few people would pay that much money to go play golf with business colleagues.

Just recently, the press exposed a scandal involving General Services Administration managers on a boondoggle to Las Vegas. They spent $500,000 on a group meeting that included lots of champagne and outside activities. These people don't make enough to afford this kind of lavish partying if they were using their own money. They spent the money because they were using Other People's Money. There is also the story of the British parliament discussing whether to give disaster relief to a foreign country, and the debate was over whether to give 1 million, 2 million, or 5 million pounds sterling (£) for aid. When a member of the House of Commons suggested that as a gesture of good faith each member should give one day's pay (£290.00), he was soundly rebuked. Few members were willing to contribute even £290 of their own money, but they were happy to give millions in Other People's Money.

PSYCHOLOGY OF SOCIALISM

In my quest to determine what exactly causes the kind of deficit spending we have seen in the last 10 years in the United States and in Europe, it is obvious that the inability to balance a budget is due to the meteoric rise in the amount spent on so-called social programs and, to a lesser extent, subsidies. This is abundantly clear after reading Chapter 4. Almost all European countries have socialized to a significant degree over the last 40 years, particularly in healthcare, unions, and welfare. More and more of the population live on welfare, get "free" healthcare, are part of unions, retire earlier than employees in the private enterprise sector, work fewer hours than employees in the private enterprise sector, get pensions that are too high, and rely on the government to pay for all of it. This, in turn, means that governments have to tax more or borrow more, and this cycle will not end until countries are consumed in the Debt Trap. The behavior of the population receiving all these benefits is to always demand more free stuff, no matter how much they are receiving for free now.

The United States spent very little on healthcare in 1960. Today, the federal government spends $2.2 trillion on healthcare, welfare, and other social programs. This "socialization" of America and subsidy handouts are the primary cause of the U.S. economic crisis. Without these expenses, the country would have balanced budgets and no federal debt. Both these "causes" are directly related to a socialist psychology that admittedly exists in a large portion of the population. Let's say America's core psychology was for everyone to work and pay all living expenses, including healthcare and retirement, and each person was responsible for her or his own planning. The government would have never borrowed any money in the last 30 years, would have no debt, and we would have a balanced budget. It is this underlying psychology that we used to have here in the United States, and the recent changes to a different psychological base are the "cause" of our economic crisis. The result of this psychology is the problematic rise in government spending on healthcare and other "social" expenses.

The liberal mind is associated with some of our greatest creations in the arts, sciences, psychology, fashion, and many other areas of creative thought. I will grant that a large portion of our highly creative talents have a liberal mind. I acknowledge their contributions. The other side of the liberal mind is the part of the mind that creates financial problems. This aspect of the liberal mind is the primary cause of the Debt Trap.

Is there a difference between a "liberal" and a "socialist," "communist," or "progressive"? The answer is no. A "liberal," now termed a "progressive" (a term made up by the liberals to put a hue of "advanced thinking" on themselves), believes that the government can create an ideal life for people, that the government can create jobs, that the rich should pay a higher percentage rate in taxes, that union members should be paid more and work less than other workers, that the workers should unite into a strong political force, and that wealth should be distributed "more fairly" (that is, equally). This is the current "liberal" mind. Is it socialism or communism, or maybe the modern term *progressive?* Of course it is. These concepts are not "modern" at all. Here is a list of communist principles from *The Manifesto of Communist Party* by Karl Marx and Friedrich Engels written in 1848:

1. Abolition of property in land and application of all rents of land to public purposes.
2. A heavy progressive or graduated income tax.
3. Abolition of all rights of inheritance.
4. Confiscation of the property of all emigrants and rebels.
5. Centralization of credit in the banks of the state, by means of a national bank with state capital and an exclusive monopoly.
6. Centralization of the means of communication and transport in the hands of the state.
7. Extension of factories and instruments of production owned by the state; the bringing into cultivation of waste lands, and the improvement of the soil generally in accordance with a common plan.
8. Equal obligation of all to work. Establishment of industrial armies, especially for agriculture.
9. Combination of agriculture with manufacturing industries; gradual abolition of all the distinction between town and country by a more equable distribution of the populace over the country.
10. Free education for all children in public schools. Abolition of children's factory labor in its present form. Combination of education with industrial production, etc.[7]

Liberals consider their concepts and beliefs some sort of economic theory and often cite Karl Marx's *Manifesto* as the basis. I can assure you that the *Manifesto* has not one word of economic theory in its 30 pages. In fact, there is no "liberal" economic theory, there is only a "dream" that the government will somehow take care of everyone. Gustave Le Bon was the first psychologist I could find who studied socialism from a psychological perspective. He concluded that in France, the concepts of the "socialist" mind were simply "dreams" that socialists lived by. Le Bon concluded that their psychological makeup was a dream world—a place where everyone is "happy," no one has to work hard, everyone has plenty to live a rich, meaningful life, and above all, everyone is exactly equal. This is true today; there is a dream of how they would like the world to be but there is no plan of how they can actually get there.

PSYCHOLOGISTS ON LIBERALISM

I have read a myriad of papers from psychologists on the subject of politics and the liberal versus the conservative mind. In my research, I found that for every paper on the liberal mind there were five hundred on the conservative mind. In addition, not only was any paper that had as a subject matter something to do with the conservative mind negative but the authors also could not help but move quickly from a scientific discourse to emotional catharsis. Their passion of liberalism has made them violate real science—they are nothing but demagogues. For instance, a group of four psychologists (it turns out only two were members of psychology departments; the other two were from political science and business school departments) from Berkeley (two), Stanford, and Maryland compared Ronald Reagan to Hitler. They also determined conservatives were motivated by fear and aggression and were dogmatic and intolerant, simple minded, and fearful. Many make statements to the effect that "conservatives" just have a lower IQ. These "psychologists" are certainly not scientists because they cannot rise above their emotions to discuss the issue objectively. I file their "work" in the circular file; their work is not interesting because it is not science, it is boring demagoguery.

Why so much attention to bashing the conservative mind and so little to actually studying the liberal and conservative mind from a scientific perspective? The answer to that question came during a talk a psychologist by the name of John Haidt (from the University of Virginia, my alma mater) gave at a meeting of the Society for Personality and Social Psychology (one of the largest conferences for psychologists). Haidt asked the participants in the audience to raise their hands if they considered themselves to be liberals. Of the several hundred attendees, it appeared to me that over 90 percent of them raised their hands. Then he asked for all those who considered themselves conservatives to raise their hand; the total count was 8 to 10. This explains why there is a dearth of research on the subject but also sheds light on the entire profession of psychology. Why is most of the field made up of "liberal"-minded people? Why are media, entertainment, journalism, fashion, psychology, and education industries chock-full of "liberal" minds? They seem to attract each other and are drawn to these fields. Clearly the answer is that something about all these endeavors draws the same type of liberal mind and is a place where few conservative minds care to spend much time.

The liberal philosophy that has led to the massive social spending is nothing more than a psychological condition of the liberal mind shared by a large number of people. This is the primary cause of the United States entering the Debt Trap. But what exactly is this psychological condition?

THE HISTORY OF SOCIALISM: THE RESULTS OF LIBERAL MINDS TAKING OVER GOVERNMENTS

There is a large group of U.S. society that does not hesitate to further the effort to have socialism triumph over capitalism. And, as Le Bon pointed out in his works, the communists' first desire is to destroy the current system so that they can rebuild their "dream." That victory over capitalism necessarily means the destruction of capitalism and democracy so that they can reconstruct a new society based upon their dream of a utopia where the living conditions of every person are exactly the same, and all determined by an all-powerful state government. To the people who believe in it, the road to this great achievement is simple: destroy the current system and build the new utopia. They have no plan of how they are going to do this, but that doesn't matter. They are simply "dreamers."

I found it difficult to believe that a large portion of America's own citizenry would actually want to destroy the capital system Americans have built, but as depressing as it seems, that is exactly what the liberal mind wants. Pythagoras in 550 BC did just that in ancient Greece. Karl Marx in 1848 advocated it. The Bolsheviks in 1917 did just that in Russia. Hipólito Yrigoyen in Argentina did that in 1916. Fidel Castro did that in 1960 in Cuba. Mao Tse-Tung did that in China in 1949. The list goes on. It has been happening in the United States slowly over time: during the Great Depression, Franklin Roosevelt's administration was rife with communists. During the 1930s there were many articles and cartoons about the communist takeover of the United States, including many accusing Roosevelt's administration of "spend, spend, spend in the guise of recovery; break the country and blame capitalists." The press at that time was less liberal and even accused Harvard and Columbia of being communism progenitors.

Those with an overly liberal mind are all too aware of the desire to destroy America as it is today. Their plan is to overwhelm America with debt, welfare, and entitlements—in other words, to bankrupt it. This will cause the collapse of America, and the government could then turn to pure socialism. Their concept is that capitalism will collapse and the government will have to step in and take over all businesses, controlling everything. The government will of course treat everybody fairly and equally. Their scheme has been so well researched it has its own name: the Cloward-Piven strategy. Still shaken by this prospect, I decided to do my own unscientific survey of my liberal friends, and these are business and legal professionals. They concur with the destruction of the current capitalist system . . . scary.

Communists promise a utopia where equality trumps over human beings' natural differences despite the indisputable fact that nature has imbued unequal qualities in each of us that neither human nor government can change. Of the two main aspects of socialism, namely economics and social, economics is the easier to analyze. The issue is how wealth is best produced and divided. The capitalists believe in the laws of nature: you eat what you kill, and the "market" determines how the economy works. The communists believe everyone should share equally the earnings made, no matter who makes the money and how much. They don't even believe that the one making the money should be credited with doing so. Karl Marx popularized the saying "from each according to his ability, to each according to his needs." What a great slogan to garner support! Each person gets to have his needs met, which means everyone will be happy! This is utopia: "I can get everything I 'need.'" This sounds like a great plan. What could possibly go wrong? There are actually millions of people who believe this system will work.

In July 2012, Barack Obama, a man who displays some socialist tendencies, declared that individuals who built a business should not be credited with building it: it was really the government that was responsible for their success. We all know the story of the Little Red Hen: how she made the bread herself and the other animals hanging around who would not help her but wanted to eat the bread anyway. If they were Obama and his liberal Congress, they believe that even though the other animals played while the Little Red Hen worked and made the bread, that somehow the animals playing miraculously made the loaf of bread happen. I actually think they are deceiving themselves into believing that they are not doing anything wrong when they vote to take the bread away from the Little Red Hen because "the Little Red Hen didn't make it, we made it." This "dream world," where the liberal mind lives, was recognized as exactly that back in 1898 in France by Le Bon.

All forms of economic socialism have sprung up since antiquity, including those that exist today. As far back as we can go in recorded history, and most notably in ancient Greece (and contemporary Greece, for that matter), governments have tried socialism and died in doing so. Plato's *Republic* described the practice; Aristotle describes and denounces them. In his book *Landed Property Among the Greeks,* M. Guirand states, "All the contemporary doctrines are represented here, from Christian Socialism to the most advanced Collectivism." The concept of taking from the rich and distributing it among the poor was practiced during ancient Greece. The concept of renouncing your worldly possessions which would then be distributed by the state was the mantra of Parmenides and Pythagoras in 550 BC. The social and economic revolutions that took place in ancient Greece sometimes succeeded, but their success was fleeting. Pythagoras built a state where the most intelligent and educated people ran the government. To get into this "elite" group, you had to give them all your worldly possessions. The government then would tax the remainder of the people. Because the "elites" were so much smarter than the general public, they were the ones who would decide how to spend and invest all the money. This was socialism in 550 BC. The Pythagorean society failed spectacularly with a massive rebellion. The core problem then—and now—is that the goal of the socialists is to destroy first and then rebuild. After the destruction of a society, rebuilding the promised utopian society somehow never could be accomplished.

Socialism did not die with the Greeks. It appeared later during the Roman Empire as they experimented with it in agriculture—the socialism of the Gracchi. This was an attempt to limit the amount of each citizen's property and make equal distribution of agricultural products among the poor. Socialism also appeared among the Jews, including Jesus, who denounced riches and asserted the rights of the poor. After all, he did profess the Kingdom of God is reserved for the poor alone: "It is easier for a camel to go through the eye of a needle than for a rich man to enter the Kingdom of God." The Christian religion was socialism for the poor and was successful in creating a moral basis for taking care of the poor. The core tenets of socialism were established in at least 550 BC and have survived to this day. Many generations have attempted to explain their concepts as "new" (for example: the American liberal is not a "communist"; he is a "progressive"). These concepts are not new. They are thousands of years old, and they have not changed at all.

The concepts of Karl Marx were not new; they were only a rehash of the same communist doctrines published in 1755 by Morelly in *Code de la Nature*. Tocqueville comments on *Code de la Nature*:

> You will there find, together with all the doctrines asserting the omnipotence of the State and its unlimited rights, several of the political theories by which France has been most frightened of late, and whose birth we flatter ourselves to have witnessed: the community of goods, the right to work, absolute equality, uniformity in everything, mechanical regularity in all the movements of the individual, regulated tyranny, and the complete absorption of the personality of the citizen into the body of society:
>
> 'In this society nothing will belong to any person as his personal property,' says Article 1 of the Code. 'Every citizen will be fed, maintained, and occupied at the expense of the public,' says Article 2. 'All products will be amassed in the public magazines, thence to be distributed to all citizens and to supply their vital need. At five years of age every child will be taken from his family and educated in common, at the expense of the State, in a uniform manner,' etc.[8]

In the early twentieth century, Argentina rivaled the United States as the second largest economy in the world. It was a capitalist country with no social spending: no handouts. Everyone had to work. In 1916, Hipólito Yrigoyen, a member of the "Radicals" was elected president, and he promised change. That he did by implementing mandatory pensions, free healthcare, and subsidized housing for the poor: all this, of course, by levying taxes on the "wealthy." The government had in essence taken over a large portion of the economy. When Yrigoyen tried to pay for all this by taxing the "wealthy," he found out there was not as much money there as he had dreamed. He then turned to taxing the middle class heavily. Labor unions grew rapidly, and payouts of entitlements grew, especially under Juan Perón. All this spending with few left to tax led Argentina into deficit spending, which it did until markets refused to loan the country any more money. Then, as we shall see in Chapter 7, it tried every trick known to humankind to keep the judgment day from ever coming; that led in the late 1980s to printing lots of money, which resulted in hyperinflation ravaging the country. Inflation hit 3,000 percent in 1989.

The government at this point had lost control of the country, and its power to govern had evaporated, because it had no money. In 1994, Argentina raised payroll taxes to 25 percent, tacked on a value-added tax, taxed wealth, taxed sales of companies, and killed capitalism. By 2002, the country lived in a perpetual depression, worse than the one the United States faced in the 1930s. This terrible, tragic story is told over and over throughout history, yet the "dream" that everyone can be equal and happy if the government takes over wealth distribution is the dream that captures the everyday thoughts of the liberal mind. This dream runs on a continuous loop and is the underlying drive to the compulsive, financially destructive behavior we witness every day from the liberal mind.

Russia now produces one-third the amount of GDP per person that is produced in the United States, and Cuba currently produces less than one-fifth of the U.S. GDP per person. North Korea is one 25th of the U.S. GDP per person and China one-sixth.[9] Cuba has been a communist country since 1960; for 50 years its retired leader, Fidel Castro, told everyone that communism will work someday but first the country must pass through this *"periódico especiales,"* or special period, to get to utopia. Fifty-three years and counting and utopia has yet to be reached.

To feel how desperate the citizens of these countries are, close your eyes and think for a minute how you would feel if you, a U.S. citizen, were instantly transformed into a Cuban citizen and were now making one-fifth of what you are making today. China and Russia have both turned to capitalism to bring themselves up substantially from the depths of pure communism 20 years ago. None of the countries that have tried communism have done anything but impoverish their citizens. The poorest welfare recipients in the United States live a better life than most of the populations in any of these countries.

Communism has been nothing but a colossal disaster every time it has been tried from 550 BC in Greece to modern-day Cuba and North Korea. From an economic point of view, pure communism is nothing more than a state with 100 percent tax rate, where the central government controls all expenditures.

Over the last two thousand years times have changed, and so has socialism. The desires and needs of human beings two thousand years ago were minimal. The survival focus of most of society was simple enough: food to make it another day. There were no transportation needs; everyone walked or rode animals. There were no medical needs; the few medicines available from plants were scarcely available to anyone, rich or poor. There was no housing authority; everyone built his own very modest abode. Comparatively, men and women today have great desires that could not have been conceived back then, even by kings and queens. What we consider today to be basic essentials (housing, electricity, running water, plenty of food, unlimited healthcare, big-screen television, cell phone, unlimited education, and transportation) were grand luxuries only 50 years ago. Clearly, a lot of these are not needs at all—they are desires.

Somehow, these "needs" have become necessary for happiness (happiness being defined as what percentage of your "desires" is available to you) and certainly indispensable to equalize everyone. Those who work to produce their own way in the world can afford more of these items. No matter how small or large your desires are, your happiness is based on the ratio of "desires" to satisfaction of desires. When these two sides of the equation are equal, people achieve happiness. People who have not made a lot of money persist in the belief that making money will somehow, miraculously make them happy. This, of course, is not the case at all. The most important aspect of happiness is finding and maintaining love, connecting with people, having rich relationships with friends and family, and so on. Money cannot make you happy. Somehow, the socialists have completely missed this point; they view happiness as having equality in the amount of money each person has, and when everyone has the same amount, that is utopia.

Humans can either decrease desires or increase satisfaction in order to achieve happiness. Many people from the Far East achieved happiness long ago by decreasing desires. The Norwegians do the same thing now to achieve a happier society. In the United States, on the other hand, desires have increased exponentially, making it impossible for everyone to actually fulfill each one. That doesn't stop the socialists from trying to fulfill every last person's desires and dreams, always using Other People's Money. With the blatant marketing of finer and more exciting material things, the desire of even the poorest people in the United States is constantly increasing. Unhappiness exists throughout the citizenry because not everyone has attained his or her desires. The socialists have done everything possible to increase the government's redistribution of wealth from taxpayers to the poor so that everyone can live in equal conditions. Figure 5.3 shows the total federal government expenditures as a percentage of GDP since the formation of the country.

Prior to World War I, the U.S. government spent on average less than 3 percent of GDP per year. That government was not involved

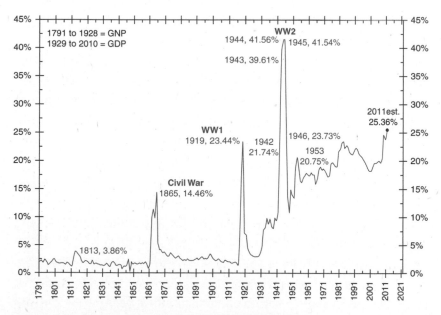

Figure 5.3 Total outlays (spending) to GNP/GDP.[10]

in the day-to-day lives of its citizens. The current federal government is not the only form of government spending on your behalf. Adding federal, state, and local government spending, total government expenditures in the United States were over 40 percent of GDP in 2010. The phenomenon that is driving this outrageous growth and leading to the creeping socialism we have today is the desire of Congress to meet more and more desires of the poor so they can live in the same conditions as wealthier citizens. The more congressmen and congresswomen hand out, the more votes they get. There is, of course, a never-ending growth in the desire to make everyone happy, and it seems that Congress is there to keep funneling Other People's Money into the mouths of those who want it. The socialists hope we can get this graph to 100 percent of GDP; then we would all be happy.

Why do so many people not work? I have always had the mindset to work and contribute to my development ever since I can remember. I mowed lawns, took paper routes, and worked in an ice cream parlor, a hamburger stand, a pizza joint, and a bakery. I did my own auto repair and bought and sold used cars. I started with zero. This is not the mindset or psychology you generally find today among the poor. I always wanted to work, but there is a large segment of our population that does not want to work. A contractor in East Texas told me he could not find even unskilled workers at $10 an hour because anyone can sit at home in front of their big-screen television and make that doing nothing. This is the reality of America today. The "dream" of helping the poor get through the day is in reality creating a psychological "jail" to them. It is making infants out of them. These people can work; they just do not want to. The argument by the socialist that we have to help the poor, handicapped person because he would have difficulty surviving otherwise is specious. For every one of those, there are 50 able-bodied workers who do not want to work.

The vast majority of people on welfare are trapped there for life because the government is encouraging them not to work. And this, of course, perpetuates itself to each succeeding generation. During a 10-day guided tour of Israel, the most interesting country I have visited outside the United States, our guide explained the genesis of communes in Israel. When modern Israel was first formed in 1948, there quickly formed 200 communes used for farming. There are now 3. The original concept was the same as the hippie movement in the 1960s in the United States: let's all live on a farm and work it together, and we will all share in the crops. In the second generation at the communes in Israel, there were many who wanted to be actors, singers, and artists. They wanted to stay inside and do their thing while the others toiled in the fields. The communes, however, didn't need or care for their work; they needed field hands. These communes quickly broke down and now exist as money-making commercial farming enterprises where workers are paid for their work and the artists are nowhere in sight. They are either working in the fields for pay or have gone elsewhere trying to sell their efforts to others. This is an example of local handling of the unemployment and poverty problems.

During the Clinton administration, a few simple changes were made to the welfare system. The central concept was to make welfare a temporary fix for the unemployed. The Clinton era law, Temporary Assistance to Needy Families, limits assistance for unemployment to 60 months of lifetime unemployment. During the first few years of the new law, unemployment fell from 12.2 million people to 4.2 million *and* average income for the hardest-hit group, single women, rose an average of 25 percent over the level of assistance they were receiving while on welfare.[11]

The federal government system of handing out welfare is centrally managed in Washington, D.C., and can only manage a few simple procedures to hand out free money. Did you apply for a job this week? If so, here is some more money until you get a job. This is the problem with centralized management. Centralized management can never get to the heart of each person's situation and figure out the best solution for him or her. They can only provide a simple one-size-fits-all approach, which of course means that no size will ever fit you. If the decision to hand out free money was made at the local level and taxed at the local level, there would be a lot more employment and very little poverty. The centralized system has enabled people who do not want to work to stay at home and do nothing. This is why management of large corporations has evolved to move decision making to the local level where employees have the most information and control and where they can hold people accountable for their actions. Accountability cannot happen in centrally managed organizations. To help alleviate the management nightmare of managing the welfare state in Washington, D.C., the federal government handed most management decisions to the states, as well they should. They also funded most of the cash needs by block grants.

Imagine a system of local control over the U.S. welfare system or even a smaller system of friends controlling the welfare of friends. Say one of your friends lost his job and the rest of you gave him money so he could make it to the next job. How long would it take for him to get a job? Not long. If the money was your money, you would make sure he did something quick and you would audit his actions ... or cut him off. If he had extenuating circumstances, like a medical problem that prevented his working, friends who were supporting him would best figure out what they should do. This is the benefit of local control and is completely lost in a centrally managed organization.

Le Bon concluded that over time, the major source of discontent among the masses is the unequal distribution of wealth. It is in this discontent that the socialists justify their attacks on the people who make money. The feeling of the discontents is jealousy, one of the seven deadly sins. In the hallowed halls of Congress, the liberals have been debating for the last four years just how much income constitutes wealth that should be taxed at a higher rate; after all, the wealthy should pay their "fair share." President Obama has had a difficult time determining this point and has used $200,000, $250,000, and $1 million as the defining amount that makes someone "wealthy" enough to be taxed more. Currently, he is using $1 million in annual income as the mark of wealth that should be taxed at a higher rate. His recent proposal to raise the marginal tax rate for people making over $1 million a year is not intended to actually increase any revenue but is used to play into the collective mindset to ignite the jealousy already residing in the minds of the socialists. The United States is facing what Obama estimates is a $9 trillion deficit over the next 10 years, which I think will be at least $12 trillion. The congressional Joint Committee on Taxation has concluded that the increased tax will raise only $3 billion a year. This tactic addresses nothing about the deficit, but it plays into the minds of the socialists. The ploy is used nevertheless to get votes and enrage the jealous and angry feelings of Obama's constituency.

But let us not delude ourselves: over 60 percent of Americans think the wealth distribution in the United States is "unfair." So the issue is, is it? The market method of determining wealth is reward by the marketplace to those who contribute to GDP and make a profit. The other method of distributing wealth is by someone in government deciding how it should be distributed. The dream is that everyone will be rich and we will all drive Mercedes and fly Gulfstreams, be good looking, and be happy.

DREAMLAND

All the ideas of utopia are in the dreams of socialists, and that is where they will always stay: in dreams. The dream of creating a perfect state seems to be the consistent theme of the various groups that make up the liberal society. It can be termed "Rainbow Coalition," "Occupy Wall Street," or any other name, but the thread that ties them all together and makes them a "team" is that they all believe that the government makes everybody happy. When socialism has succeeded in taking over a state, like Cuba, North Korea, China, and the Soviet Union, it has succeeded in destroying the government it replaced but it has never succeeded with the dream and promise of utopia and equality. Not only have the governments of these countries failed from a perspective of generating wealth because socialism destroys incentive to work and produce, but they have failed from simple management science.

Steven Pinker in his book *How the Mind Works* throws another bucket of cold water on the concept of communism and why it will never work. According to Pinker, whom I agree with, the human mind evolved over thousands of generations mostly in the savannahs of Africa and was reverse-engineered to support life needs thousands of years ago. Further, the end game of human reproduction is to keep the genome alive and replicating, and not for any other purpose. He gives some examples of the human communism experience and how it failed:

> The Woodstock Nation "was the first utopian dream [in the United States] to be shattered. The free-love communes of the nineteenth-century America collapsed from sexual jealousy and resentment of both sexes over the leaders' habit of accumulating young mistresses. The socialist utopias of the twentieth century became repressive empires led by men who collected Cadillacs and concubines."[12]

The point of Pinker's research is that despite the fantasy of anyone who has a dream of how things should work (that is, socialists), the way the mind and humans in general actually work is quite different. A significant portion of our behavior is programmed into our DNA, and dreaming that socialism can ever work is against human nature. The fantasy of a utopia is merely that: a fantasy. The liberal mind has forever believed that, with government leading the way, we can change human nature and somehow make everyone equal. Moving from dream to reality is the hard part.

There are a few clever techniques to demonstrate a real social experience to people. The first and easiest is to get a group of kids, adults, or both to sit at a table. Give each one $20 in $1 bills. The rules of the game are to have each person put in an envelope in the center of the table any amount he wants and then the pot will be distributed equally. Track the amount of the pot during each round, and you will find the pot diminishes as everyone figures out he can keep more money by not contributing to the pot. This is exactly what happens in a socialist society. Another is to tell a child or liberal who wants to take care of the poor that she can work for you pulling weeds for an hour and you will pay her $10. Then you will take that worker to a beggar, and she can give the panhandler the money she earned. She will question on the first try, "Why am *I* working? Why not that guy?" Another method is to have a class in school share grades so that everyone gets the same grade. By the end of the semester, everyone will flunk because there is no reward for personal achievement. Unfortunately for all of us, communism has never worked and never will.

Another primary reason that socialism will never work is that no management team can possibly centrally manage a large, diverse organization. The business schools in the United States study large-company management techniques, and large corporations spend a lot of time and money in studying and educating management in making a large organization more efficient. The simple answer to managing a large organization is that you must decentralize decision making. There are so many decisions that have to be made in any organization that centralization makes management of a large organization collapse.

General Electric is a good example of decentralized management. I worked for a subsidiary of General Electric and spent some time with Jack Welch, chairman of GE, and went through several of their management training courses. As was taught in business school at the University of Virginia and practiced at GE, decisions need to be made as close as possible to the source of the business issue. This is what I did with my companies. One company I owned had 4,000 employees in over 100 locations, and we made sure that decisions were made at those locations. Jack Welch flattened his management structure so that there were no more than three layers of management between him and any employee.

As is the plan with Obamacare, having most decisions made in Washington, D.C., by some bureaucrats will amount to a monumental disaster. They have to decentralize most operations today. There is no way a centralized system can possibly handle the millions of decisions that have to be made every day. Unlike unemployment, where there are but a few questions to be answered before a check is written, healthcare decisions are wildly complex and need to be made minute by minute. The decision process is made with a local group of people, including doctors, nurses, claims personnel, pharmacists, and so on. If everyone is put on hold while some bureaucrat in Washington is asked to review the file and approve the next test or procedure, the system will fail due to its own weight. Centralized healthcare I believe is another death march of socialism. Great Britain's experiment with national healthcare has brought that country back to a decentralized system of decision management and competition. The central government should never have taken on the responsibility.

The dream of the socialist is to have a central government organize and manage every aspect of life, when the real-world experience is that it has never happened and cannot happen. Socialists have never actually been able to produce a working model. When Hugo Chavez took over food distribution in Venezuela, he had destroyed almost $1 billion of fresh produce within two weeks because his government knew nothing about food distribution. He and the people in his government were just a bunch of dreamers put in charge of a distribution machine that they had no idea how to operate.

Under Obamacare, the system will be managed in Washington D.C. To date, there are 29,000 pages of regulations, 14,000 exemptions, and a deficit of $2.6 trillion associated with the legislation. Centralized management of a massive industry like this is impossible. It is unbelievable to me that with the advanced business management knowledge and skills we have today they were all bypassed by a liberal Congress to enact Obamacare despite a long history of failure of centralized management. That is because the "dream" of the liberal mind is to have everyone taken care of by the state even though there is no "plan" on exactly how the government can possibly accomplish this. My prediction is that Obamacare will be a disaster because it can never be managed.

The socialists promise utopia with extreme simplicity without any idea or plan of how to manage such a complicated organization. They wave a magic wand over it and proclaim that it will just happen and not to worry. Their new society will, of course, be perfect and will be accomplished by some train of miracles that will astonish even the most educated and experienced managers of organizations. Their dream is that all the wealth in the country will be piled in a big heap, everyone can have as much as she or he wants, and the money supply will somehow magically replenish itself every year. In England, socialists are called "dreamers" and conservatives "pragmatists." I think that is a valid assessment. Looking back on all the management work, headaches, and hours I put into companies, I can see no way that the socialists can ever manage such a dream. That is what socialism is and will always be: just a dream.

How can the vast differences between a conservative and a socialist on almost every issue facing Americans be explained? Has it always been this way? Thomas Jefferson thought so when he penned, "The same political parties which now agitate the U.S. have existed thro' all time. And in fact the terms of Whig and Tory belong to natural as well as to civil history. They denote the temper and constitution and mind of different individuals."

Judging from the readings of history, my conclusion is that it has always been this way. The issue to me is why do the socialists continue on the path that has failed every single time it has been tried? What is causing this phenomenon? Why is this thought process and psychology so prevalent in so many levels of our society? That is the issue to me, and ultimately I see it as the cause of the United States and several European countries becoming Nations in the Red.

Lyle H. Rossiter, Jr., published his book *The Liberal Mind: The Psychological Causes of Political Madness* in 2006. It is undoubtedly an accurate portrayal of the manifestations of the socialist mind:

> What the liberal mind is passionate about is a world filled with pity, sorrow, neediness, misfortune, poverty, suspicion, mistrust,

anger, exploitation, discrimination, victimization, alienation and injustice. Those who occupy this world are "workers," "minorities," "the little guy," "women," and the "unemployed." They are poor, weak, sick, wronged, cheated, oppressed, disenfranchised, exploited and victimized. They bear no responsibility for their problems. None of their agonies are attributable to faults or failings of their own: not to poor choices, bad habits, faulty judgment, wishful thinking, lack of ambition, low frustration tolerance, mental illness or defects in character. None of the victims' plights is caused by failure to plan for the future or learn from experience. Instead, the "root causes" of all this pain lie in the faulty social conditions: poverty, disease, war, ignorance, unemployment, racial prejudice, ethnic and gender discrimination, modern technology, capitalism, globalization and imperialism. In the radical liberal mind, this suffering is inflicted on the innocent by various predators and persecutors: "Big Business," "Big Corporations," "greedy capitalists," "U.S. Imperialists," "the oppressors," "the rich," "the wealthy," "the powerful," and "the selfish."[13]

Rossiter concludes that the liberal mind "cure" to all this tragedy is to have the government take over every aspect of life and caretaking. The government will rescue everyone from their troubled lives.

I believe all this analysis is accurate and clearly shows a vast difference in the thinking process of a liberal mind and a conservative mind. The "enabler" to this mass of liberal minds are the liberal "intelligentsia" and the liberal politicians. They are "heroes" to the liberal masses. This thinking process clearly leads to the financial problems the country is dealing with today and is the primary cause. Nevertheless, I have always been mesmerized by how things work, and we have still not answered the question of why the liberal mind works like this. Is there a central subconscious feeling that ties all the liberals together or perhaps a difference in brain formation? Maybe so.

HOW THE MIND WORKS

In 1997, Steven Pinker published *How the Mind Works*. This effort had nothing to do with politics but instead was a scientific analysis of the mind, and the findings were important because they altered a lot of theories on how the mind works. Using modern tools, Pinker was able to shed light on some of the oldest mind concepts. First, he defined the mind as "a system of organs of computation, designed by natural selection to solve the kinds of problems our ancestors faced in their foraging way of life, in particular, understanding and outmaneuvering objects, animals, plants, and other people." He goes on to show that people do not behave for the long-term good of society but for the short-term reward for themselves ... how do I get the most for me now, even if it costs someone else much more later? The concept that humans really feel and do what is best for all mankind (the "group") is not how the mind works. Reciprocal altruism is a technique of preparing your mind to believe that you will be taken care of ... [and is] a major self-deception. ... I think it unwise to confuse how the mind works with how it would be nice for the mind to work."[14]

The supposed emotions of the liberals for all their diatribes are "sham emotions" and not what they really feel. What they really feel is "how can I get the most for me with the least amount of work even if it hurts someone else?" If I play like I support everyone who is outcast, then they all will support me and we will have a large group of self-supporters: everyone will be so happy ... what a wonderful dream I am having!

The first, and rather obvious, group psychology that defines socialism is free handouts from the government. This group is enormous and by some measures represents almost 20 to 30 percent of America. Before the concept of social security, the poor and truly needy, such as people with severe physical or mental disabilities, were handled on a local basis. This was due to the great human trait of altruism; the human characteristic that drives humans to take care of others. This system worked well for a very long time, although it wasn't "perfect" in many eyes. In the early 1900s, there was no national system of caring for the poor and needy. There were no social security, no food stamps, and no unemployment payments. Today, there are thousands of federal social programs, but the big three are social security, Medicare, and Medicaid. There is no doubt that this is the number-one contributor to the Nation in the Red, but it is still not the "cause." Why would politicians let this happen as they have around the world, and why can't they stop spending before the Debt Trap closes on all of us and a financial collapse ruins the entire country? This psychology, particularly what is going on in the subconscious minds of leaders, is the "cause" of the Debt Trap.

Dr. Rossiter outlines the underlying messages that liberals either blatantly espouse or tacitly allow:

> The government will take care of you.
> You cannot make it by yourself in the world.
> You do not have to take care of yourself; the government will.
> Free speech is OK unless it is not in line with our belief system.
> It is OK to take money earned by the "rich" to be spread among the poor.
> The free market is rigged to oppress us and take our rightful money.
> Unions are good; businesses are bad.

DEEPER CAUSES

The next level of cause brings us into the realm of psychological analysis. There have been thousands of papers written about the liberal and conservative mind, and many, if not a majority, are designed to denigrate a liberal or conservative mind. This, to me, is not science or helpful because the focus is not how the mind works but an emotional release of the author. The truth is found in objective testing and analysis, and this is plentiful today. A history of the psychological studies of the liberal and conservative mind may be helpful.

In ancient Greece, Plato and Aristotle both remarked about socialism, but the first real studies in the psychology of socialism were in the late 1800s, in particular Gustave Le Bon's *Psychology of Socialism*. These liberals were viewed as a menace to society. Even by this time, psychologists knew that the Marxist ideas that liberals were liberal because of their economic "class" were false. The liberal mind is nothing more than a psychological trait.

Current psychological theories are focused on open-mindedness as the defining liberal psychological characteristic and conscientiousness as the defining conservative one. Several studies have shown that liberal and conservative characteristics are present in children as young as nursery school age. This points to genetic determination of this personality trait, which I believe is the case. So, we have the age-old B. F. Skinner behaviorists and the geneticists to help us: is it nature or nurture?

The very short summary of a number of studies on testing, analyzing, and reporting on what is the psychological basis of the liberal mind is that liberals tend to be open to experiences and conservatives tend to be more conscientious. These two character traits correlate closely with liberalism and conservatism but certainly are not definitive determining factors in my mind. Much psychological work goes on in detail about liberals and conservatives and many other character traits that define them. On the face of many of these conclusions, however, there are exceptions to the behavior and psychological traits of liberals and conservatives everywhere, and there is not a strong correlation to me between destroying capitalism and "open to experiences." Furthermore, these are character traits and not the cause of character traits, which is what I am pursuing.

Jonathan Haidt (now at New York University) has studied liberal and conservative minds extensively and has published many works on the subject. He analyzes five sets of morals and clearly delineates a fracture between liberals and conservatives. He studied morals and values over many cultures in many eras and concluded these best define the two minds. The five sets of morals are: (1) harm/care (preventing harm and taking care of everyone), (2) fairness/reciprocity (making sure that everything is fair and everyone treats everyone else the same way), (3) ingroup/loyalty (affirming the importance of group participation and valuing the group), (4) authority/respect (having an authority and respect for authority) and (5) purity/sanctity (being physically and mentally immaculate). He studied thousands of subjects using scientific methodology and concluded that liberals, in making moral decisions, believe that harm/care and fairness/reciprocity are slightly more relevant than conservatives believe they are. On the remaining three, however, liberals do not view ingroup/loyalty, authority/respect, and purity/sanctity as very relevant in their moral decision making, while conservatives rank them almost as important as harm/care and fairness/reciprocity.

Rossiter and Haidt have done amazing work defining the core characteristics and moral basis of the liberal mind, shedding much light on the issue. I find their research is helpful in understanding the liberal mind, but I have not found research concluding what causes the liberal mind. For instance, no one has concluded that a physically abusive maternal figure immediately after birth causes these character traits. The closest approximation I have heard from researchers is that the common underlying emotion of liberals is the feeling that they are "outcasts" in society. This "outcast" group includes minorities, Jews, Muslims, religions other than Christianity, artists, journalists, environmentalists, and so on. They feel unaccepted in society. Outcasts come in many variations and special interest groups. As Le Bon discovered in the 1890s, these disparate groups have only one thing in common and that is to destroy the current system of capitalism and replace it with a system that accepts and values them. They will no longer be "outcasts." During the Democratic National Convention in September 2012, one speaker said, "Government is the one thing we all belong to." While I am not really sure to what he was referring, I believe it is the concept that a government that accepts and values them is their "club" in which they are not outcasts. Underlying all this somewhere is the ultimate "cause" of the liberal mind that has put many nations in the red. Is there a "silver bullet" that can define why the liberal mind is like this? Maybe so!

> A man's admiration for absolute government is proportionate to the contempt he feels for those around him.
> —Alexis de Tocqueville

BEHAVIORAL GENETICS

"Behavioral genetics" is the study of the role of genetics in defining behavior and is of particular interest to me in understanding the liberal and conservative minds. Genetics was my favorite subject in college, and I even wrote my senior thesis on genetic control of the behavior of fruit flies and mice. In animals at the fruit-fly level, all behavior is determined by genetics. There is no "learning" or behavioral development. My experiment was to genetically separate flies that would fly toward light from flies that would fly away from light and breed a clone that would always behave this way. This was easy enough to do, and once I made a generation that would fly away from light, I could mark them with some type of genetic marker. I chose eye color and made flies that would fly to light with black eyes and those that would fly away from light with red eyes. These flies would always produce offspring that would behave in the same manner generation after generation. All aspects of their behavior were controlled by a gene in their genetic code.

Mice, on the other hand, could alter their God-given behavior significantly and learn quite a bit. They can learn their way through a maze and change their behavior to earn food. My conclusion was that while genetically programmed behavior existed at the lower levels of animal development, the higher up the phylogenetic tree you progress, the more behavioral modification a species can undergo. This I believed was true, and there was no real study of this issue back in my college days in the mid-1970s. Things have changed since then, and the subject, as well as the research and developments in genetics, have progressed at a rapid pace. There is now a defined discipline called "behavioral genetics," and I believe this subject may hold one of the keys to the true "cause" of liberal and conservative minds.

Humans are more complex than other animals and have a broad mix of genetics and environmental psychological issues that affect them. They also learn more than any other animal. This, however, doesn't stop the search in genetics for a gene that controls a basic personality trait like liberalism or conservatism. Research has discovered four potential genes that they believe are "liberal genes," but one in particular is very promising: it is the gene DRD4. In a paper entitled "A Genome-Wide Analysis of Liberal and Conservative Political Attitudes" a group of geneticists and psychologists led by Peter Hatemi (University of Sydney) and Nathan Gillespie (Virginia Institute for Psychiatric and Behavioral Genetics) (14 contributors in all), studied the entire human genome (all 23 pairs of chromosomes) and found four genes that are statistically significant markers of liberal behavior. The focus, however, is on DRD4. James Fowler, both a professor of medical genetics and political science at the University of California, San Diego, termed DRD the "liberal gene," publishing his report in the *Journal of Politics* in 2010. The gene, it turns out, has been the subject of many psychological studies, including attention deficit hyperactivity disorder (ADHD), Parkinson's disease, and schizophrenia. Whether this gene is determining who is liberal and who is not is yet to be determined, but this would give me some comfort that the ultimate "cause" of our financial crisis is a genetic trait.

The DRD4 gene regulates dopamine receptors in the brain. The 7R allele is associated with the "novelty-seeking" behavior found in liberals. An allele is an alternate form of a genetic trait: blue eyes and brown eyes are different alleles. While there is still plenty of work to be done on DRD4, it could be that this one gene is the "cause" of the liberal mind and hence "the" cause of the Debt Trap we are all facing. Dopamine regulates the brain's reward and pleasure centers. It enables us to recognize rewards and take action to get them.

Dopamine also regulates emotional reactions. Could it be that this one gene causes liberals to swim in dopamine at the "dream" of a government regulating all happiness where everyone is equal and happy? Is this why they are so emotionally extroverted? Maybe so.

In their paper "Friendships Moderate an Association between a Dopamine Gene Variant and Political Ideology," Jaime Settle, Christopher Dawes, Nicholas Christakis, and James Fowler researched twins and concluded that if a twin had the 7R allele and during childhood had lots of friends, he or she would develop a liberal mind. They concluded that at least one-third of liberals are genetically determined and at least one-half are environmentally determined. They also reiterated that "novelty seeking" is the personality trait most commonly linked to liberals. Further, peer pressure, especially from classmates, strongly correlates with political orientation. If children hang out with liberal children, they have a tendency to become liberals; if they hang out with conservatives, they have a tendency to become conservative.

IS DOPAMINE THE CULPRIT?

Dopamine is a neurotransmitter that helps control the brain's pleasure and reward centers. Drugs such as cocaine and methamphetamine work by dramatically increasing the effects of dopamine in the brain. The feelings that are generated from dopamine are so strong that some observers have described dopamine as the most evil chemical in the world. Robert Sapolsky, a neurologist at Stanford University, has been studying dopamine and its effects on behavior. The interesting part of his studies with monkeys is that, like Pavlov's dog, when the monkey gets a signal that a reward (food) will be coming soon, dopamine levels increase. The monkey stays high during a work period when he knows he will be rewarded at the end of his work. When the reward finally does come, the dopamine level drops during the feeding. The obvious conclusion is that the reward is not why the monkey is motivated to work; it is the dopamine produced in anticipation of the reward.

More interestingly is that when the reward is produced only part of the time, say 30 percent, for the work the monkey is doing, dopamine levels rise dramatically over the levels seen when the reward is given 100 percent of the time. Sapolsky points out to a room of psychologists and neurologists that they have all done just what the monkey has done: they have worked very hard through high school, college, and medical school to get their reward of a stable career and money. The audience quickly grasped the conclusion.

With such great differences between the liberal and conservative mind, can it really come down to a simple chemical difference causing the chasm between the two?

CHAPTER 6

THE EUROPEAN ECONOMIC AND CURRENCY CRISES

The euro will not survive the first major European recession.

—Milton Friedman, 1999

Anyone who pays even a modicum of attention to the news is well aware of the financial and currency crisis spreading throughout Europe. This crisis, described by many as a contagion, is brought on by government spending more than it takes in as tax revenue and borrowing the difference—sovereign debt. That practice is well-accepted by many European nations and unfortunately the United States as well. Sovereign debt is debt issued by a government in another currency, but for purposes of this book, it is the same as any government debt. Most European debt is issued in euros, although no one country controls this currency.

The European crisis is relevant to the United States in several ways. First, the European countries facing the largest national debts, led by Greece, and followed by Cyprus, Spain, Portugal, Ireland, Italy, and France, are giving America a preview of what it is facing in the next few years. Second, the market reaction in European debt securities (the debt the foreign governments are issuing) shows what will happen to the United States when the market perceives the risk in U.S. debt reaches the levels of risk it sees in Greek, Spanish, and Italian debt. Third, we can study what the financial and psychological causes the overspending of the indebted European nations were. Fourth, we can study the economic problems each country caught in the Debt Trap has undergone and what actions have alleviated the suffering and what actions have exacerbated it. Hopefully, the United States can learn from the mistakes of others and not get caught itself. Lastly, if the nation cannot wrest itself from the Debt Trap before it gets caught, people should take action to protect themselves and their families from the devastating horror the Debt Trap can bring.

DEBT LEVELS

Although too much government debt and government default on debt have existed since ancient times, there is no need to study early defaults since current defaults are happening before our very eyes, in a modern global economic environment, with international finance and trade, the global issuance and trading of credit default swaps, knowledgeable investors with sophisticated trading strategies and tools, and global markets to trade and hedge currencies. The parallels between the situation in the United States and the European countries mentioned previously are too much national debt, large government deficits, government efforts to stop the bleeding by cutting spending and raising taxes (which, by the way, has only occurred in state and local budgets in the United States), slowing economies as a result of the global recession and, particularly in the United States, the housing bust. Let's take a look.

The place to start is the "official" debt-to-GDP ratios reported to the European Union (EU) and European Central Bank (ECB). The average European country debt to GDP has risen to 90 percent. Table 6.1 lists each member country, its "official" debt, and its ratio of debt to GDP. Pay particular interest to the ratios of Greece, Spain, Italy, and France. We will study them in more detail.

Table 6.1 Debt-to-GDP Ratios (%) in European Countries, 2012[1]

Austria	74
Belgium	102
Bulgaria	17
Cyprus	75
Czech Republic	44
Denmark	45
Estonia	7
Finland	49
France	89
Germany	82
Greece	132
Hungary	79
Ireland	109
Italy	123
Luxembourg	21
Netherlands	67
Poland	56
Portugal	112
Spain	72
Sweden	38
United Kingdom	87

It's a toss-up as to which European country has the worst debt problem to date, but the most studied economy is Greece's. The GDP of Greece is around US$300 billion, roughly the size of the economy of Dallas, Texas. While it is only 2 percent of the U.S. GDP, the same economic rules apply. The Greek debt crisis was triggered by investors around the world. Greek sovereign debt grew to approximately 165 percent of Greek GDP by the end of 2011. In 2009 savvy investors started worrying about that country's ability to repay the debt, when Greece first admitted to lying about its finances: it had much higher debt and deficit than reported. This is lesson one: you cannot trust the government to be open about its finances, as governments lie about their financial situation and the financial condition of their banks. Financial analysts can look into each country's finances and bring out more clearly what the real financial condition looks like. As you may recall, we did this exercise with France and the United States in Chapter 2. Members of Congress are calling for more transparency into the U.S. Federal Reserve Bank balance sheet.

Many commentators think the "official" debt-to-GDP ratios submitted have become a joke because each country "masks" its true level of debt and inflates its GDP numbers to give the appearance that it has control of its finances and should keep its high debt ratings. The exercise we did in Chapter 2 for France led us to the conclusion that the true debt-to-GDP ratio of France is around 121 percent. Let's do that exercise for Spain (see Table 6.2).

Spain has a real debt-to-GDP ratio of 141 percent. As you should remember, this same analysis we did for the United States in Chapter 2 gave us a real debt to GDP of 121 percent, and that was without adding the $20 trillion in underfunding of social security and $24.5 trillion underfunding in healthcare. Italy has lived with "official" debt to GDP of over 90 percent for more than 20 years; it is currently 120 percent. In the 1980s, the government went on a borrowing binge, and the country has been unable to grow out of it or pay it down since.

Table 6.3 is a list of countries currently in the news that are in financial trouble, with their reported debt to GDP and current deficits.

As you can see from Table 6.3, the United States is in the thick of it, along with all the troubled countries of Europe. Its debt-to-GDP ratio puts America on par with Italy by 2015.

Italy is the only country actually reducing its deficit below the benchmark limit of 3 percent of GDP set forth in the Maastricht

Table 6.2 Spain's Financial Commitments[2]

Spain's reported GDP	$ 1,295 billion
Admitted "official" debt	$ 1,090 billion
Contigent Liabilities:	
Liabilities to ECB	$ 332 billion
Cost of EU budget	$ 20 billion
Liabilities for stabilization fund	$ 125 billion
Liabilities for Macro-Financial Assistance Fund	$ 99 billion
Total European debt	$ 576 billion
Total national and European debt	$ 1,666 billion
Spain's estimated GDP	$ 1,178 billion
Spain's "official" debt-to-GDP ratio	68.5%
Spain's actual debt-to-GDP ratio	141%
Guaranteed bank bailout debt and European Investment Bank debt:	
Guaranty of EIB debt	$ 67 billion
Guaranty of bailout of banks	$ 125 billion

Table 6.3 Countries in Financial Trouble[3]

	Debt-to-GDP Ratio (%)	Deficit as a Percentage of GDP
Cyprus	75	–5%
France	89	–5.2%
Greece	132	–9%
Ireland	109	–12%
Italy	123	–2%
Portugal	112	–3%
Spain	72	–8%
United States	100	–7%

criteria. (The treaty that created the European Union and ultimately the common currency [euro] is called the Maastricht Treaty, and the criteria for member countries regarding total debt and deficits are called the Maastricht criteria.) Italy is making substantial progress. Spain and France are reducing their deficits as a percentage of GDP but are still far above the 3 percent target. The trick for these governments is to reduce expenses and increase taxes to get the deficit below 3 percent of GDP without pushing the economy into a recession. The United States, on the other hand, is not making progress. America's deficits have run almost 9 percent of GDP for three years (although the projected deficit for 2013 is 5.7 percent), making it a "violator" of the Maastricht criteria for a stable economy. The nation violates both the debt-to-GDP ratio (maximum 60 percent) and the deficit ratio (no more than 3 percent of GDP deficit). After looking at the most troubled European countries (other than Greece and Cyprus, both of which are toast), we can easily tell that the financial condition of the United States is as bad as that of Spain, France, or Italy, if not worse. What these countries have done is to wait until the markets have forced them to quit deficit spending rather than control it themselves. The question is, does the U.S. government have the willpower to actually cut spending to the point of balancing its budget?

HOW THE MARKETS AFFECT EVERYTHING

When Greek finances became more transparent in 2009 (meaning that Greece finally disclosed its true deficit and debt numbers), the interest rate on its national debt started to rise. By April 26, 2011, the Greek debt market had pushed the interest rate on Greek 10-year bonds to 17 percent. In December 2011, the yield hit 37 percent. In contrast, 10-year bonds in the United States and Germany yielded less than 2 percent. This is how the market reacts to a country that has a high debt-to-GDP ratio and a large deficit: investors lose confidence and require higher interest rates on the country's debt to account for the risk that they may not get paid back. After all, as we saw in Chapter 1, governments default regularly, and no investor wants to lose money on a default.

The recent economic history of Greece is a tragic one; the country was so overborrowed that it failed in dramatic fashion. Spain is not in as bad shape; nevertheless, it's not doing well. Its economy is not diverse and had been substantially dependent on the construction industry, which has essentially shut down. Spain's real debt-to-GDP ratio is similar to that of the United States at around 146 percent. It is also running deficits of about 5 percent of GDP. So how does the market price Spain's, France's, Germany's, and Italy's 10-year bonds? Figure 6.1 shows the answer.

The U.S. 10-year bond yields (that is, the interest rate) are under 2 percent, and Spain and Italy were suffering with 6 to 7 percent. As you can tell from Figure 6.1, the market is telling everyone that it has lost confidence in Spain and Italy. The market knows that Spain's economy is not diversified and its major industry sector (construction) is dead. The market also knows that Italy's economy is teetering on recession and has a very large

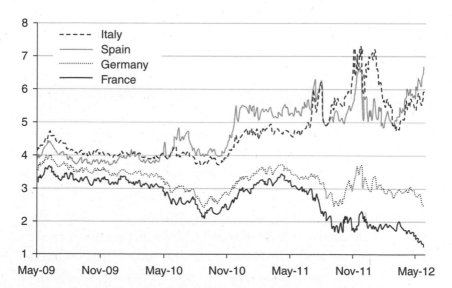

Figure 6.1 Ten-Year Bond Yields in Four European Countries, 2009–2012[4]

debt-to-GDP ratio. The market, on the other hand, still has confidence in Germany, France, and the United States. Since June 2012, the yield on Spanish and Italian debt has fallen 2 percent in response to a statement by the European Central Bank that it would become a direct lender to Spain if current interest rates remained this high. The market took that as a form of guaranty on Spanish debt, which lowered the perceived risk and consequently the interest rate.

If the United States keeps deficit spending, this is how the market will treat federal debt soon. In Chapter 2, we calculated the impact of higher interest rates on the national budget. Today, the cost of interest on the U.S. national debt is about 2 percent of the national GDP—around $360 billion a year.[5] If interest rates for U.S. debt rise to the levels that Spain and Italy were paying on their debt, that cost would increase U.S. interest expense over time to nearly 6 percent of GDP. That would mean the nation would be paying around $720 billion a year in interest expense instead of using that money to help people.

"The market is the market is the market" is a common phrase used throughout the finance industry to mean that what the market says is always the answer. If you own a share of Exxon and the current market is $80 per share, even if you think in your heart of hearts that it is worth $100 a share, try to sell it for that; you can't do it. The market "tells" you what something is worth no matter what you try to argue. The "market" is cold, devoid of human emotions, only interested in facts and profits, and far bigger than the U.S. government or the entire U.S. economy; it does not care why a country got into financial trouble, even if it was to save Grandma from having her house taken away. So, when the market turns on a country, as it has with Greece, Spain, Ireland, and Italy, it is ruthless. Even actions by the Troika to lower interest rates on these countries' debt are temporary at best. The lesson to be learned is that the market soon will turn on the United States, and the country will see dramatically higher interest rates.

When market confidence in a country's debt gets bad enough, as it has in the case of Greece, Iceland, Portugal, and Cyprus, the market simply stops loaning any money. When a country's finances get this bad, investors do not believe they will be paid back. This, of course, forces a country to balance its budget because it has no other source of cash to pay its bills. Further, with no additional loans from the market available, the country has to default on its debt as it becomes due, triggering a chain of defaults throughout its entire debt structure. In the case of Greece, when the market stopped loaning the government any more money, it could not make its next interest and principal payments because it could not borrow any money to make those payments. Further, in the case of the European Union, the members all agreed to adopt the euro as the currency for all member countries. Consequently, in the event a country gets into trouble it cannot manipulate the currency. Greece, had it kept its currency (the drachma) instead of joining the European Union, could have printed money to get its economy going. This is why Milton Friedman stated that the euro could not survive the first major European recession: the countries in recession would want stimulus but couldn't get it because someone else controls their currency.

The market will ultimately cut off the United States just as it has these European countries. The Obama administration budget for 2014 which projects budget deficits for the next 10 years is overly optimistic in its assumptions. Chapter 2 reviewed this period and concluded that the aggregate budget deficit will be much higher than the Obama budget plans. By 2018, the debt-to-GDP ratio will exceed 118 percent, and the market will not let the United States borrow any more money; it will be forced to one form of default, as explained in Chapter 7. At this point, the market will stop lending to the United States just as it has to Greece and probably will to Spain, forcing the nation to stop deficit spending and most likely default. Faced with this eventuality, the government will take one or more of the five options out of the Debt Trap.

GETTING BEHIND THE POWER CURVE

The laws of economics are like the laws of physics: they are scientific and cannot be changed by government action. Interest rates are the product of the laws of the market and are affected by a number of factors, including perceived risk, deferred consumption, liquidity preference, inflation expectations, taxes, and investment alternatives. Even though a central bank such as the Federal Reserve can artificially keep short-term interest rates down, it can't do so forever.

There is a long history of adjusting interest rates based on risk. As far back as 175 BC in Mesopotamia, Babylon had adopted the Code of Hammurabi, which limited interest rates to 33.3 percent. Between 600 and 100 BC, Greek city-states held down interest rates.[6] The manipulation of interest rates for control of the economy is a relatively new economic science; it started with the creation of the Federal Reserve in 1915. We now know that money supply and interest-rate changes control the economy and economic growth.

In the investment community, there are a number of companies that analyze and rate debt (credit risk) issued by companies, countries, counties, cities, and even municipal utility districts. The most well known of these are Standard & Poor's, Moody's Investors Service, and Fitch Ratings. When a country (or corporation or another issuer of debt) wants to sell debt to investors, the rating agencies will analyze the issuer, determine its creditworthiness, and assign a rating. Investors use this rating to price the debt. The higher the rating, the lower the interest rate on the debt. The AAA rating is the highest rating and reflects the safest investment. Once a rating agency determines that an issuer (a country, county, city, or corporation) is no longer risk free, it downgrades the issuer's debt, and the interest rate rises. This is what is happening in many of the European countries, such as Spain, France, Italy, and Greece. This group is now known as "Club Med." It is also happening in the United States for many cities and states. California and Illinois are the lowest-rated states, although California recently revised its pension obligations to help solve its ratings problems. When a country or state loses its higher credit rating, the interest rate it pays on its debt rises and investors who own the debt become concerned that the issuing country or state may default on its obligations to pay interest and principal on its bonds, just as we have seen above with respect to Greece, Spain, and Italy. The United States had carried an AAA rating since ratings began, but in 2011 Standard & Poor's downgraded the United States to AA+, one grade lower, and forecasted a negative outlook. This means the country is starting its fall.

When a country like Italy or the United States has such a high level of debt and spends 5 to 10 percent of its national budget on interest payments, it is "behind the power curve." Currently, Italy is running a "primary" surplus of almost 1 percent of GDP. A "primary" surplus (or deficit) is the measure of a government's cash flow before its interest expense. So Italy is actually generating positive cash flow from taxes to run the government. The problem with the Italian government is not today's government; it was the government back in the 1980s that borrowed all the money. Since the mid-1980s Italy has suffered under debt-to-GDP ratios of over 90 percent, the worst of the large economies in Europe. In 2012, Italy is expected to have an interest expense of over 4 percent of GDP. That compares with 2.3 percent (1.6 percent on debt to the public) of U.S. GDP and 10 percent (6.4 percent) of total U.S. receipts being paid. When the United States returns to normal interest rates (6 percent), the government will be paying 6.9 percent of GDP and 30 percent of total receipts on interest expense.

There is no benefit today to Italians from the overspending 30 years ago, just as there is no benefit to Americans for the overspending of the previous Congresses and administrations (and, for that matter, of this administration). There is only "expense," a dead "overhead" item that is so big that it represents a national "sales tax" of 4 percent in Italy and 2.3 percent in the United States. And, by the way, the only reason the number is not higher in the United States is that the interest rates on U.S. government debt are low because the market perceives the risk of a default by the United States as low. When the market turns, this will be a different story. Today, the market is still operating under the assumption that the United States can actually fix its debt problem.

CAUSES OF THE EUROPEAN DEBT CRISIS

The obvious cause of the debt crisis in the United States and around Europe is too much borrowing by governments or some form of banking crisis that was supported by the government. In the case of the United States, this has all happened since 1980, primarily since 2008. In the case of many of the European countries it has happened at different times.

Ireland

During the 1990s, Ireland experienced a building boom, and money was readily available. From 1993 to 2000, the economy grew almost 10 percent per year based on the building bubble. The Irish banks ended up going bust when real estate values plummeted in 2006–2007, and the banking crisis was converted into a sovereign debt crisis because the government guaranteed the banks' debt. The banking bailout cost over 50 percent of 2009 GDP.

Ireland's debt is already rated at below investment grade, and interest rates on its debt are over 8 percent. Although Ireland has actually cut government expenses in a major government austerity program and is slowly recovering, its only source of debt is from the Troika. Moody's in its report says it "sees a possibility that the end of the current support program at year-end 2013 will not only prompt a need for further rounds of official financing … but that *private sector creditor participation is also to be required as a precondition for such additional official support.*" (emphasis mine) This, of course, would be disastrous for Ireland, because the private sector will not be there to loan the country any more money, and it will need additional debt financing. Ireland should be the first to receive it from the Troika, since it has actually complied with austerity requirements.

Ireland's problems are a result of too much government debt.

Greece

Greece is a well-known subject, and the causes of its debt problems are systematic. It dramatically overpaid public union employees, the government became the major component of the Greek economy, and there was no effective tax-collecting mechanism. Greece has been known for its liberal economic policies, where the government provides most of the jobs and the social programs are extremely generous. Unionized government workers retire at 50 and live on lavish pensions for the rest of their lives. There was little work and lots of play. The country became essentially socialist. To support this lifestyle, it had to borrow money. When it disclosed that it had borrowed 160 percent of GDP, the market stopped loaning the country money.

Greece is on permanent life support from the Troika. It has no access to the debt markets and no other source of cash. It is dead-flat broke. It has not implemented any significant austerity that the Troika required, and its population would rather riot than comply. The actual reform in Greece is to convert from a socialist country to a capitalist country where people actually work for pay. This seems to be the hard part, and there has been no real movement in this direction. The government keeps asking for more borrowings so it can continue giving away money to the people, but there have been no real reforms to date. The public seems oblivious to the economic reality that the government has no money to give them. They demand more money, and the entire socialist country is failing in a spectacular fashion. Greece is in an economic depression as a result of its government borrowing too much money.

Greece's problems are a result of too much government debt.

Spain

Spain, like Ireland, suffered a building bust. The country's economy was substantially built on the construction industry, and when it stopped in 2008–2010, unemployment skyrocketed to almost 25 percent. That was the percentage reported; the real number could be much higher. Spain has a large component of social costs and strong unions. Since 2008, Spanish debt has almost doubled due to heavy unemployment and having to borrow almost $125 billion to shore up the banking system. Spanish citizens and international companies have been getting their money out of Spain at a rapid pace. Over the last year, outflows of money are almost one-half of Spanish GDP. The market is closely watching what happens to the Spanish economy. I believe that Spain's economy will continue to decline and it will need a bailout or it will default on its debt.

Spain, along with Italy, is a very large economy, and it is Europe's second-largest risk. It has already received a $125 billion bailout of its banks and will surely be asking for more bailout money to help finance its regional governments. Moody's has downgraded the country's debt to just above junk bond status, and if there is further deterioration of its economy Spain will be downgraded below investment grade (that is, junk), meaning it will have very limited access to debt from the market. Most financial institutions are not allowed to invest in junk bonds and would sell any bonds that fell below investment grade.

Spain's problems are a result of too much government debt.

Italy

As we discussed earlier, Italy's debt problems were inherited from a prior government in the 1980s that was a loose spender. This debt, which has persisted above 90 percent of GDP since then, is now around 120 percent "officially," and 146 percent "really." Italy's debt is $2 trillion, and it is therefore too big to fail. If the Italian economy failed as Greece's did, it could bring down most other European economies. That, of course, would be a disaster and would be prevented by every country stable enough to help Italy cure itself. The country's debt is barely above junk-bond status debt.

To get an understanding of how the market thinks about government debt, here is an excerpt from Moody's Investors Service when it downgraded Italy:

> A key factor underlying Moody's two-notch downgrade was the assessment that the risk of a further sharp increase in Italy's funding costs or the loss of market access has increased due to fragile market confidence, contagion risk emanating from Greece and Spain and signs of an eroding non-domestic investor base.... In this environment, Italy's high debt levels and significant annual funding needs of EUR 415 billion (25% of GDP) in 2012–13, as well as its diminished overseas investor base, generate an increasing liquidity risk.[7]

As you can see, the countries that are in trouble got there by different means, but the common problem is that they borrowed too much money. They are now in deep financial trouble, as is the United States. Looking back at the charts of yields on the bonds issued by these countries (see Figure 6.1), we can easily see what the market does to them when it perceives risk. It runs up the interest rate on the bonds, making it more expensive to borrow money and using more of a country's resources just to pay interest. That is why understanding the European crisis is so important to Americans. The United States is now operating in the same desperate mode as these European countries.

Italy's problems are a result of too much government debt.

GREEK DEBT TRAP

The United States is in a position like that of the countries just mentioned, although the U.S. government has a few more games it can play, since it controls its own currency. It also has one fewer option: no one can bail the country out as the rest of Europe has bailed out Greece. The United States is too big, and its debt is too great. The lessons of the European debt crisis are going to help America, as the nation is just a small step behind them. The first lesson for Americans is to recognize and admit to ourselves that the country has a serious problem and we must take action now. Deficit spending is like a drug addiction: it is an easy thing to get into, and most of the time it ends in a bad crash with devastating consequences.

The market for sovereign debt, both the willingness to buy and the interest rate on the debt, is determined on the basis of supply and demand for that debt—the simplest market mechanism. In the case of Greek debt, buyers became wary of the likelihood of Greece defaulting on its promise to repay, and thus the demand for its debt dried up. Investors in Spanish and Italian debt also perceive a significant risk and are demanding more return. While all this market turmoil hurt individual Greek bondholders (they lost about 70 percent of their investment), the problems of the country of Greece had just begun.

When the market finally said no to Greek debt and would not purchase any more, the European Central Bank, European Union, and International Monetary Fund (Troika) stepped in to lend Greece money to give it a little operating cash. As a condition to receiving these loans, the Greek government was forced to cut spending and tax dramatically more in a move to balance its budget. This is also the case with Spain, Italy, and France. They are all cutting government spending, and the cuts are painful to the people. The cuts are to pensions, current salaries to all state employees, many government grants, and so on. These cuts in spending have also pushed these economies to the brink of recession and, in the case of Greece, into a depression. The Troika is forcing Greece to lay off thousands of workers and reduce social benefits to the poor.

What triggered the dramatic interest-rate rise for Greece and the other economically distressed countries was loss of confidence by the market that the countries could stop spending. The cause of the decline was a fear, and a likelihood, that if you bought the countries' bonds today you could not resell them in the market in three or six months, or at any time in the future, for what you paid for them.

Furthermore, purchasers feared that if they held the bonds to maturity, these countries would be unable to pay back in euros, as they were supposed to. No investor expected that these countries could actually generate the cash internally in order to pay principal and interest on the bonds. What investors had to decide was whether the market would still be there for these countries when they decided to sell their bonds. These countries would have to go to the market to issue new bonds to get the money to pay back the bonds that were maturing. Investors also had to assess whether or not these countries would still have the desire to pay principal and interest. After all, if paying interest and principal on bonds means that citizens will go hungry, politicians will stop paying interest and principal on the bonds. With all this risk, the market demanded more interest rate, as you see from Figure 6.1.

MUSICAL CHAIRS

For the investors who purchase the bonds issued by financially troubled countries, the game they are playing is musical chairs. Everyone in the market has known the music would eventually stop and whoever owned Greek bonds at that time would lose all or most of his or her investment. As Greece piled on more and more debt and investors started demanding more interest to compensate for the risk, no investor ever thought that Greece could actually pay off the bonds as they matured. That was impossible, because the Greek government was deficit spending and it had no cash to pay off the bonds. The only cash it had was what it got from issuing new bonds. Investors were only interested in ensuring that they could sell their bonds, and so long as other investors would buy them on the market, many investors stayed in the game—and they got burned. For example, MF Global, a large fund based in the United States, played the game too long and went bankrupt because it was still holding Greek bonds when the music stopped.

This game is precisely the one being played in the United States with federal government debt. By deficit spending, as all the aforementioned countries have done, the government is putting its economic future in the hands of the market. Currently, investors from around the world are buying U.S. Treasuries because those investments are viewed as some of the safest ones in the world, with enormous market liquidity. Unfortunately for the government, this very low interest rate environment makes the cost of borrowing money today very cheap, so why not keep borrowing? Well, when the economy recovers or investors become afraid of the risk of default, interest rates will return to normal ... and normal is not good in the case of the United States.

During better economic times, the average interest rate of Treasury securities (U.S. debt) is around 6 percent. If the federal debt to the public is $12 trillion, interest on that debt at normal interest rates would be $720 billion. This money could have been used to fund Medicare, Medicaid, or social security. This massive federal government expense, which must be paid annually, is not the only burden: the government still has to pay back the $12 trillion somehow. In lieu of having to ever pay back the debt, the country will be paying an average of $720 billion a year in interest forever. This debt and the annual interest expense is a massive burden on all members of U.S. society, not only for today but for the next 100 years. After all, the country still has not paid back the debt it borrowed for World War II.

Growth in economies around Europe, as well as the United States, is controlled by managing money supply—specifically, a measure of money supply called M2. The M2 supply is calculated by adding up all paper currency plus the check demand deposits plus savings deposits plus time deposits. M2 growth in Europe has been around 3 percent in the last year, with the exception of Greece and Spain. M2 declined 17 percent in Greece and 7 percent in Spain, which is due to smart people getting their cash out of these countries. This is a typical "run on the bank," and, of course, causes the economies to implode. And imploding they are! In 2012, the Greek stock market declined 60 percent and Spanish market 30 percent. In March 2013, Cyprus had a run on its banks and had to close them, leaving wealthier depositors with losses that could approach 60 percent.

For those living thousands of miles away, it is hard to imagine the effect these changes have had on the people living in Greece, Cyprus, and Spain. From 2009 through 2012, the Greek economy declined more than 12 percent, and this is a definite indication of a depression. The lesson to be learned from these countries is that too much debt *will* lead to large portions of the economy being dedicated to payment of interest on the debt, which will result in large declines in the economy itself. Another lesson is that the people who got out first saved their investments while those who stayed in lost a significant part of theirs.

MOVE TO SAFETY

With the fear of a Greek-type default hanging over the heads of Spain, France, and Italy, which have economies of approximately one-sixth, one-seventh, and one-eleventh the size of that of the United States, panicky investors are trying to get their money out of these countries and into safer investments. This has had an impact on the United States. Hundreds of billions of euros have been converted to dollars and used to purchase U.S. federal debt and buy into U.S. capital markets, which has the effect of strengthening the U.S. dollar over the euro as well as pushing interest rates in the United States lower. When the market turns on America, the opposite will happen. Investors will take their money out of the United States and find safer places to put it. This will leave the country in a freefall in both the debt and equity markets, and investors will get out at a fierce pace.

A dramatic fall in the market for federal debt will affect almost everyone in the world. The fall will start when interest rates either return to a normal 6 percent range due to a return of normal economic activity or a default risk perceived by the market.

Another significant unknown is the effect of the Federal Reserve selling back into the market over $3 trillion in government debt it owns. This is 25 percent of the total outstanding federal government debt and were this debt to be sold in the market, the market would crater. Since there has never been a central bank operation of this magnitude, we are in an experimental state of affairs regarding our national debt and economy. The pundits have speculated about everything from forgiveness to holding the bonds to maturity; but since no central bank has faced this scenario, no one is sure exactly what will happen. I cannot imagine any scenario that would be positive.

OTHER COUNTRIES IN TROUBLE

The Europeans and the United States are not the only countries in trouble. Japan, Zimbabwe, Lebanon, Jamaica, Belgium, Iraq, United Kingdom, Hungary, Canada, and Germany all have debt-to-GDP ratios greater than 80 percent. Many Latin American countries, such as Venezuela and Argentina, have systematic financial problems even though their debt-to-GDP ratio is less than 50 percent. The governments in many countries do not have market access, so rather than borrow money, they just print it. Easy enough. Printing money brings on another problem: inflation. I encourage the reader to go now to TradingEconomics.com and toggle the "Debt/GDP" column so that it shows the debt-to-GDP ratio from highest to lowest. It is a sad sight indeed to see that the United States has the ninth-worst ratio of 183 countries listed.

CRASH IN REAL TIME

I will never forget a recording we were required to listen to during driver's education class. It was clever and had a lasting impact on my driving, and I've been driving for 40 years. At the beginning of the recording you were asked to lean back in your chair and close your eyes so you could better visualize what you were about to hear. A man started by saying the driver had been distracted and let the car slip off the side of the road, hitting some gravel at 60 miles per hour. After one-tenth of a second, the car was completely out of control and 30 feet from a culvert. During the next three-tenths of a second, terror had struck the driver as she realized there was nothing she could do to avoid a catastrophic collision and almost certain death. During that three-tenths of a second, she thought about her family and children and what would happen to them without her in their lives. Without her livelihood and the presence of a mother in their lives, her young children were going to suffer tremendously.

As that three-tenths of a second came to an end, the first contact between the culvert and the front right quarter panel occurred. The metal crumpled lifelessly against the concrete and steel barrier, setting off the airbags in one-hundredth of a second. As the airbags deployed, the car crushed through the right front quarter panel with the impact rippling through the entire frame and the momentum of the driver just starting a forward movement. Metal continued to crush the engine through the firewall and into the back of the instrument panel. The short-circuiting of the broken electric motors, switches, and wires set off the fuses, which shut the entire electrical system down … a safety mechanism to try to avoid a postcrash gasoline fire.

As the engine was crushed against the firewall, the fuel line ruptured under the unimaginable stress from the cracked engine block and pumping pistons. The torque of the running engine twisted against the now-crumbling cylinder walls as fuel started spraying a fine mist into the engine compartment. The fireball was now only one-tenth of a second away. During that one-tenth of a second, the mass of the shattering engine crushed through the cabin, splintering the windshield and side windows. The engine was headed straight for the driver and would crush her against the driver's seat during the next one-twentieth of a second. The first fragments of broken glass started penetrating the driver's face and neck, starting the cascade of blood that would spray the dashboard and drain the precious oxygen from her brain just as the steering wheel hit her chest and started the crushing of ribs that would end her life in the next one-twentieth of a second…

The end of this tale is a little too gruesome to write, but no one could project a good outcome because there is not one. This car crash was predictable and avoidable. It never had to happen. Had the driver simply paid attention and not become distracted there never would have been a crash. The consequences of the crash are also predictable: the husband will lose his wife, and the young children will lose their mother. Anyone can predict that the children will suffer greatly all their lives. The mom, being a wage earner, may be putting the family in financial jeopardy. The business she worked for may be losing a key employee, which can cost others their jobs and support for their families. We can all visualize and predict what will happen during the crash and the later consequences because crashes happen enough to inform us of all the events that unfold from the experience. The concept is very simple.

The economic crash that is happening now in Europe, particularly the one that has already happened to Greece and Cyprus and is currently happening to Spain, is identical to a car-crash scene. Every car and every crash are different, but the general theme is the same. The Greek tragedy started 30 or 40 years ago when the government became the "nanny" of the citizens. The handouts and freebees started, unions rose to power, workers worked less, workers retired early (at 50 years old), the few people and businesses that paid taxes did not pay much, and the government spent more than it took in and borrowed the deficit. Because the government borrowed so much and put it into the economy by giving it to citizens, its debt mushroomed over the years, and interest expense ate away a substantial amount of the cash that was borrowed. But this story, like the car-crash story, does not have a good ending. It never does.

Like the car crash in our slow-motion visualization, this Greek tragedy has played out in front of our eyes. After years of deficit spending and borrowing by the Greek government, the debt markets finally stopped lending to Greece. As debt became due, the government tried to borrow money to repay the debt, but no one would loan it the money to do so. Finally, the Troika rode in on its white horse and arranged a massive loan to Greece. When the dust cleared, Greek debt had been reduced and the bondholders, mostly banks around Europe and foreign governments (in particular, Germany), picked up the bill. Remember, many of the investors were pension funds that needed the cash invested to pay retired workers: these workers are getting far less in pensions today.

The conditions of the bailout, required by the Troika, were dramatic reductions on Greek government spending and an increase in taxes. These are dramatic changes for the Greeks, since they have operated as essentially a socialist country for the last several decades. The government was everything. It was the source of 50 percent of the jobs. One could retire at 50 and receive lifetime pensions that were very rich. The country did not really have a tax collection mechanism, and few people paid taxes. Healthcare was paid for by the government. In short, no one really worked, and the few businesses that were successful paid little in taxes. It was a modern-day socialist country that thumbed its nose at its obligations to pay back the money it borrowed just as it has five times in the last 200 years.

The problems of Greece's debt default have started a chain reaction in the country that is as predictable as the slow-motion automobile accident described above. With no government cash, it passed a law that the people and businesses that owed taxes must pay them or have their electricity cut off. The lawsuit that followed went to the Greek Supreme Court. The court ruled that the country could not cut off electricity for failure to pay. So what happened next? Everyone quit paying the electric company, and it is shutting down electricity production, creating massive blackouts. The government has also not paid for a year's worth of drugs delivered to Greece by drug manufacturers. These manufacturers have now cut off any further deliveries until they are paid for past sales. This billion-dollar problem is yet to be resolved, but pharmacies are now bare. They have no drugs. Desperate citizens are ordering from out of state and paying with their own money (now, *that's* a novel idea!).

Many people in Greece have already run out of food, and neighbors have taken up feeding those without. Even institutions dependent on the government for food have been getting none. Here is an excerpt from an article on prison food:

> The financing for many prisons has decreased to a minimum for some months now, resulting in hundreds of detainees being malnourished and surviving on the charity of local communities.
>
> In Corinth, citizens took it upon themselves to support the prisoners as food warehouses ran dry and the government could not round up food for soldiers or prisoners.[8]

Electric power has been reduced in Greece due to nonpayment:

> Power traders in at least four countries have reduced or halted electricity exports to Greece due to non-payments, helping to force market prices sharply higher in a potential blow to struggling industries and raising the risk of blackouts during the tourist season.
>
> With Greece deep in crisis, power grid operator LAGHE owes foreign and domestic suppliers 327 million euros ($410 million), a court document obtained by Reuters showed, as its revenue falls due to the recession and a refusal by many Greeks to pay their bills.[9]

Rioting and looting have become commonplace in Greece. Crime has increased. Banks have reduced credit on credit cards or cancelled the cards completely. The bad part is that the situation has only begun and will get much worse. Nationwide strikes are planned, and by the time this book is printed they will have occurred.

The primary lesson from this research is that the government of Greece is missing in action. It is not there to take care of things, because it is powerless at this point. The country does not have any money to buy more food, drugs, or electricity. Consequently, a system of bartering has taken hold … and no taxes are collected on barter transactions.

The official unemployment in Greece is 23 percent, but that is certainly understated. The economy has shrunk by over 12 percent in the last two years, according to official statistics. The IMF predicts further declines of at least 3 percent this year. This is a depression. Food lines are long; farmers are giving away food without a source of capital to grow next year's crops. All the banks would be technically bust except that they have been given capital by the ECB to keep their doors open. The Greek stock market has plummeted 60 percent from 2010 to 2012, and real estate has fallen around 50 percent. People are not paying their rents, and borrowers are not paying their mortgages. There have been riots by unions and students protesting lower wages and pensions as well as increasing fees for education. The students chant: "education should be free" and "we should be guaranteed jobs." The austerity measures Greece has promised are necessary, and they are also causing a depression. The amazing thing is that no cuts have actually been made yet. As I write this book, Greece is asking the Troika to loan it money without having to make the cuts because they are hurting the people. This is the effect of the Debt Trap. Greece became used to deficit spending, and the economy was dependent on it. Once that is taken away, the economy crashes because the deficit spending is what kept it propped up. Do you see any parallels with the United States?

Spain and Italy are on the front end of the Debt Trap closing around them. The recent bailout of Spain's banks by the ECB is meant to help shore up the economy, but the economy has grown dependent on the government's largesse and deficit spending. Currently, the unemployment rate is hovering around 25 percent in Spain and above 10 percent in Italy. The governments made recent announcements of improvements, but I doubt their veracity. First, the economy in Spain was almost 50 percent construction industry.

The real estate boom of the 2000s is now a bust, with construction at a standstill, meaning that the millions of workers who made livings with construction are now unemployed. That means fewer people are going to restaurants or buying cars and other consumer items. The Spanish stock market (IBEX 35 Index) has fallen around 45 percent from 2010 to 2013, meaning that a lot of wealth has been lost. Consequently, there are fewer people who have capital to build businesses, buy houses, and so on. M2 money supply fell 7 percent in 2012 alone as people have transferred their savings out of the country. In Seville and Cadiz, Spain, crowds broke into grocery stores and stole food to give to local food banks.

Italy has a more diversified economy, but the downturn in the economies throughout Europe will drag down the Italian economy with it. Moody's just downgraded Italian debt to just above junk. Spain and Italy are caught in the Debt Trap, and I suspect that things are worse than what is reported by the governments. We may be looking at another Greece, except substantially larger. The Greek economy was about 2 percent of the size of the U.S. economy, but Italy and Spain together are 25 percent of the size.

RELEVANCE OF THE EUROPEAN ECONOMIC CRISIS

It is not difficult to understand the links that Europe has to the United States. Europe sells $380 billion of goods to the States, and the States sell $270 billion of goods to Europe.[10] An economic decline in Europe will reduce the amount of imports from America, hurting the U.S. economy, jobs, and so on. The greatest reason for studying the European crisis is that the United States' financial condition is very close behind Spain, Italy, and Greece in terms of debt to GDP and deficits. The country is falling headlong into the Debt Trap, and the past and current Congresses and presidents, and maybe the way the political system was set up in the Constitution, is to blame. If the sequence of events leading up to where America finds itself now had happened in an hour instead of over the last

80 years, citizens would violently rebel against an instant conversion from a purely capitalist country into a socialist country. The fact that the conversion happened slowly over the last 80 years has made the transformation palatable in the minds of the public and everyday working person. The fate of Argentina was similar: it was the second-largest economy and second highest GDP per capita in the world in 1916 when its new leader, Hipólito Yirigoyen, implemented mandatory healthcare and mandatory pensions. It took almost 70 years of slow conversion to communism to wind up in a default on its national debt. The country is now a smoldering carcass of its once great past. In all these cases, the slow conversion to communism and willingness to borrow money to pass it around to the masses ends up in the train wreck we are witnessing in slow motion in the United States.

In Chapter 7, I explain the five ways countries deal with the Debt Trap. The European situation brings up all these methods with the exception of printing currency. Since the countries that have adopted the euro as their currency cannot directly print any money, they are left with all options of dealing with the Debt Trap except for printing money. The exceptional amount of time and energy spent by all these European countries in dealing with the Debt Trap has confirmed that there are no magic potions and no pixie dust: there is no easy way out.

WHAT WOULD A U.S. FEDERAL GOVERNMENT DEFAULT FEEL LIKE?

Every country has a different story and a different economy. All countries have different debt structures, different psychological makeups, and different economic behaviors under the same pressure. Therefore, it is difficult to predict what the behavior of the United States will be once it is caught in the Debt Trap other than to say it will be depressing. Here's what pundits have to say about the precarious financial situations of various countries. It looks as if it's always a case of "it can't happen here." We'll see.

Italy is not Spain.

> —Ed Parker, *Fitch*, June 2012

Ireland is not in "Greek Territory."

> —Brian Lenihan (Ireland Finance Minister),
> November 2010

Neither Spain nor Portugal is Ireland.

> —Angel Gurría, Secretary-General OECD,
> November 2010

Spain is not Greece.

> —Elena Salgado, Spanish Finance Minister,
> February 2010

Portugal is not Greece.

> —*The Economist*, April 2010

Greece is not Ireland.

> —George Papaconstantinou, Greek Finance Minister,
> November 2010

Spain is not Uganda.

> —Mariano Rajoy, Spanish Prime Minister,
> June 2012

Uganda does not want to be Spain.

> —Uganda Foreign Minister, June 2012

A default by the U.S. federal government would not feel like the Greek default because Greece actually had someone to come bail it out. The government was loaned over $125 billion to keep things going, and that is after defaulting on its bonds and leaving investors with a loss of 70+ percent on their bonds. I believe the United States will be more like Argentina or even Japan, where economic activity has come to a standstill over the last 20+ years.

If the federal government does not start behaving responsibly and cannot reduce expenditures, many bad things will happen. I believe the first thing that would happen in the United States is that government with the aid of the Federal Reserve would start printing money to make short-term relief possible. This is what Argentina, Germany during the Weimar Republic, and many other countries have done. That effort of course would never fix the problem because it would do nothing but start an inflation cycle. The currency is not the problem; federal and state spending *is*. All that printing money would do would be to postpone the crash a year, and then the country would have both a depression and a currency crisis, which is much worse than just a depression. At that time, the Federal Reserve would become the only buyer of Treasuries. As the economy slowed down and started spiraling in on itself from the sudden cutoff of government spending, the people who are directly dependent on the government would feel the depression first. They would be laid off or have salaries cut significantly. Government contractors, grant recipients, university and state recipients, and thousands of other recipients would not receive any cash or would have dramatically reduced amounts of cash. This would be very painful to these people. When "social" transfer payments were cut, such as food stamps, welfare, student loans and healthcare benefits, there would be riots in the streets. More and more people would become idle, with nothing to do all day, because there would be no jobs.

Fewer people would be buying cars, boats, and motorcycles, and fewer people would be traveling. Businesses would likewise cut back on salaries, travel, building new facilities, and hiring. All this reduces the amount of currency circulating and the speed of circulation. The economic crash would now be at full speed. Local groups would set up soup kitchens to feed the millions of unemployed. Real salaries around the country would decline dramatically, and a wave of home foreclosures would sweep the country. Banks would then start to fail, and the Federal Reserve and U.S. Treasury would start taking them over. People in the United States, as in Greece and Spain, would want to get any savings they have out of the country, and money would flow out of the country in trillions of dollars, making the economic cycle worse. America would now be in a full depression.

The solitary cause of this depression would be that our irresponsible federal government borrowed too much money. That is the only cause. The devastation to this country would overwhelm most people and businesses. Our economy would fall, and the countries such as China, India, and Russia that have not borrowed money would control the world economy. The United States would become a smaller player in the world economy, and more of the population would have a much lower standard of living. That is how government debt works. The country would become just another victim of the Debt Trap.

Moody's has written that if the deficits continue, the U.S. debt rating will be downgraded. This language is essentially the same language used by Moody's at the start of the debt debacles in Greece, Spain, and Italy.

The problems of the United States are simply the result of too much government debt.

THE 5 WAYS OUT OF THE DEBT TRAP

We all know what to do, we just don't know how to get re-elected after we have done it.

—Jean-Claude Juncker, prime minister of Luxembourg and president of the Euro Group

Governments over time have tried hundreds of ways to avoid the pain of the Debt Trap. I think the most creative (and least successful) country at doing everything it could imagine to get out has been Argentina. None of its tricks have worked, and the Argentine government has done nothing but bring further pain and heartache to that country. The five ways out of the Debt Trap are (1) let the economy grow the country out of the trap, (2) default and repudiate the debt, (3) print money to pay for it, (4) raise taxes and/or reduce expenses to create a surplus, and (5) bail out. Let's examine each of these methods and understand the implications. But first, I think we should review the "gimmicks" that have been tried by many governments to attempt to avoid or escape the Debt Trap.

THE GIMMICKS FIASCOS

When a government gets caught in the Debt Trap, unfortunately for its citizens, investors, trading partners, and really everyone, there are a lot of people sitting around thinking up clever ways to avoid the pain associated with the real methods of getting out of the trap. In many countries, especially those run by a dictator who can legislate by edict, almost every "gimmick" or "trick" to keep from entering the Debt Trap has been tried. In light of readily available economic data and other information, it seems implausible to me that governments are so naïve as to believe these actions could actually help. But desperate people do desperate things.

A common gimmick used by many countries is exchange control. This restricts people and businesses from exchanging, say, Argentine pesos for American dollars. The idea is that citizens want to get their money out of a particular country so they can keep and protect their wealth. They would like to put their money in American stocks, real estate, and other investments. But if the government lets them exchange their pesos for dollars, that money leaves the economy and the economy suffers. In the United States, it is hard to conceive of this type of restriction because the country has never had it. The U.S. investment environment has always been one of the most stable in the world. In many other countries, however, particularly Latin American ones where there are revolutions frequently, there is not a stable investment environment and people want to keep what they have earned. Any smart person can get an exemption or a business can get consent for international transactions and figure out a way to get money offshore. The only ones who cannot protect themselves are the common people who are caught in the squeeze and always go down with the ship. In the 1980s Argentina's currency was the austral, and conversion to dollars was restricted. When that proved to be ineffective, the government allowed conversion in the 1990s. Countries such as Greece and Spain have seen massive savings transfers out of their countries because they have no exchange controls or money movement controls.

Many countries have forced conversion of other currencies and gold into the local currency. Argentina actually had banks go into safety deposit boxes and remove dollars and gold and replace them with pesos. Smart people and businesses were ahead of the game and had already removed their dollars and gold, but the general public was not. Even though the state ordered people to exchange their dollars and gold for pesos, who would be so dumb as to do that?

Ordering a fixed exchange rate is always popular with politicians of countries in the Debt Trap. Argentina tried it, ordering the exchange rate of the peso to the dollar at 1 to 1. Now that the exchange rate was fixed, they could print lots of their pesos, and their economy would grow without inflation. What a beautiful solution. Wrong! While the government thought it was so smart, international exchange dried up, hurting exports and throwing the economy into a worsening recession/depression. In addition, the black market went on with market-based exchange rates, and the peso traded down on the dollar. In the case of Argentina, inflation in the late 1980s ran 10 to 20 percent a month and hit a high of 200 percent in one month and over 2,000 percent in a single year. The devastation to the economy was enormous. When the fixed rate was at last formally released, the exchange rate to the dollar went from 1 to 1 to 4 to 1 in one day.

Another mechanism is to freeze bank accounts so that people cannot get their cash out and flee, commonly known as a run on the bank. Argentina tried this and, of course, it had a devastating effect on the economy. Obviously, if everyone's cash is trapped in the bank, no one can spend it and economic activity ceases. The repercussions of a freeze are so bad and so imminent that it is hard to believe politicians could actually do it. But they do.

Cyprus just added a new tool to the ever-increasing number of gimmicks a country will use to try to get out of the Debt Trap. When its banks failed from overexposure to Greek debt, it confiscated the deposits of anyone who had more than 100,000 euros on deposit. Billions of euros were confiscated. On the face of it, it seems as though uninsured depositors should take the risk of failure. After all, they are uninsured. The problem with this approach, however, is that there is no way anyone can know the solvency of a bank. The Cyprus banks had passed ECB tests within the last few months. There was never any disclosure in advance to warn depositors of a risky bank. Quite the opposite, countries reassure depositors that banks are solvent to prevent runs on banks. They continually do this until the day the bank fails. So, there is no way to actually analyze banks for safety. In addition, in Europe the banks are allowed to carry all sovereign debt, such as debt in government bonds of Spain and Greece, without any reserve and without discounting to market (until there is a default). This all came crashing down in a few days in March 2013 when the effects of this lax regulation became apparent to the world.

The Cyprus banks reported that they had billions of euros of Greek debt, but on their books they showed the value to be the price they had paid for the bonds. In reality, the banks were broke because the Greek debt was now worth only 30 percent of the value that the banks reported on their books. When the banks failed and depositors tried to get their money out of the banks, neither the Cyprus government nor the European Central Bank came to rescue the banks and the depositors ended up losing their deposits.

This new approach to paying for a bank collapse is dismaying to investors here in the United States. This method essentially forces depositors to become investors in the banks, so they now need to do a financial analysis of the banks in which they make a deposit and continually monitor the financial health of those banks. But as we have seen in the Cyprus story and in every bank failure here in the United States, no one can really monitor the financial health of a bank except for those inside the bank. Almost every bank failure is a surprise to depositors, and were we to allow depositors to lose their deposits when a bank fails here in the United States, every time there was a rumor of a bank having problems there would be an instant run on that bank and it would fail immediately.

Creating a new currency is always a great gimmick. Once a country has ruined its currency by inflation or other contrivances, it can simply print a new currency with an entirely new name and replace the old one. Of course, it does this at a new exchange rate determined by the politicians in the blind hope, by some set of unknown miracles, that it will be accepted by the people. As money (currency) is nothing more than a belief system that someone will take your currency in exchange for a good or service, these politicians hope that people will buy into the new concept because "this time things will be different." Germany did this in the Weimar Republic during the 1920s and the new currency (Rentenmark) was exchanged for the old Mark at a rate of 1 to 1 trillion.[1]

Price control is another gimmick that has been tried, and it was actually applied in the United States by Richard Nixon in 1971. Nixon is also the president who took America off the gold standard for good. None of these gimmicks have ever worked, and none ever will. The market is bigger and stronger than any government, including that of the United States. The one sure thing that works for gimmicks is that they send a signal to investors that it is time to get their money out. So, when you see the federal government start trying these gimmicks, it is time to run for the door, convert your currency to a stable one, and get your wealth out of the United States.

Another gimmick is to have the central bank buy your debt. Whether or not the market has reacted by raising the interest rates because of the risk in a country's bonds or a government knows that this is getting ready to happen, a country can simply have its own central bank buy its bonds. It's a great trick and is nothing but a shill in a bidding contest. When the central bank buys a lot of government bonds, that means there are fewer bonds for investors to purchase, which drives interest rates down and the value of the bonds on the market up. This, of course, is a fake market and, like all fake market ploys, fails in the end and causes damage to future generations. This gimmick has already been seen in the United States. In the last few years, the Federal Reserve has purchased almost $3 trillion of Treasuries. The Fed had better get prepared to buy a lot more when the market turns on it.

A particularly pathetic gimmick is lying to the public about economic statistics. Greece recently revealed its lie, and the market ended up shutting down that government. Argentina has taken to criminalizing opinions by the press and economists that conflict with "official" economic statistics. The Argentine government is particularly fond of fabricating numbers, but let's not forget that the U.S. government has also done this for quite some time. For instance, each administration, and sometimes several times during an administration, the definition of *unemployed* is modified to make the unemployment numbers look better than they are. It is inconceivable to me that modern-day governments actually attempt these contrivances, but they do.

LET THE ECONOMY GROW THE COUNTRY OUT OF THE DEBT TRAP

The slow, painful way out of the Debt Trap is by letting the economy grow to such a level that the debt-to-GDP ratio shrinks back down to a manageable level. My idea of the best level for government debt is zero, but if government debt were 25 percent of GDP, that would stabilize government finances and make government workable for a more healthy economy. In order to escape the Debt Trap, the economy must grow faster than the deficit is growing as a percentage of GDP. This can be accomplished, of course, by increased economic activity and lower deficits. Economic growth is a complex problem, as we discussed in Chapter 2. Liberals believe government can somehow magically increase economic activity by spending money ... in spite of the fact that no country has ever accomplished this. In order for GDP growth to exceed the government spending deficit as a percentage of GDP, the GDP would need to grow at around 10 percent per year, a feat never accomplished for more than one or two years.

To understand how growth effectively reduces debt, look at American history. During World War II the country borrowed a little over $200 billion. At that time, the entire GDP of the United States was around $175 billion, and the debt represented 120 percent of GDP. The country has never paid that debt back, but the economy has grown to nearly $16 trillion at an average rate of 3.2 percent per year. So that $200 billion, instead of being 120 percent of GDP, is now just 1.25 percent of GDP. This is how GDP growth can shrink national debt even without it being paid off. This is the hope for the United States with respect to the current debt. The hope is to grow GDP fast enough to effectively shrink the debt.

Lest we forget, the government did pay interest on the $200 billion in debt since 1945. Let's say the average interest rate since then was 6 percent: that means that the federal government actually paid $804 billion in interest expense on that money through 2012 (67 years). Further, it will pay $12 billion a year on average for that debt forever. Your great-great-grandchildren will be paying this. This continuing cost is also an example of the power of long-term interest expense. On the debt the government owes today ($12 trillion), it will pay on average $720 billion a year forever. Let's look 67 years into the future, and we can calculate that the United States will have paid over $48 trillion—yes, *trillion*—in interest expense on the $12 trillion borrowed ... and our grandchildren will be paying $720 billion a year forever. Was the party worth the pain?

Unfortunately for the United States, growing GDP is not what it used to be. The country is facing a number of factors that will slow GDP growth for at least the next decade. The real GDP growth rate will probably be somewhere between 1 to 2%. The factors leading to this slow growth are outlined in Chapter 2. They include the overhead associated with the national debt and overblown government spending, demographic changes, and slow international GDP growth. Consequently, growing the way out of the Debt Trap is going to be very slow and painful. During the last 10 recessions, the economy grew briskly starting the year after the recession. Not so with the recession of 2008.

Japan has been in the Debt Trap since 1990 and is trying to grow out of it. This strategy is not working well for that country. During the 1980s, Japan was the juggernaut in the world economy. The country was buying assets all over the world, and its real estate and stock market were skyrocketing. I was working in New York then, and I remember when a Japanese company bought Rockefeller Center in New York City. The collateral the company used for the debt financing was a parking garage it owned in downtown Tokyo. All this growth and money making, of course, was based on debt, and in particular government and bank debt. Japan now has debt equal to more than 200 percent of GDP. Unlike in the United States, in Japan the government has ownership in many banks, banks have cross-ownerships with one another, businesses have cross-ownerships with banks and government, and in the end there is an undecipherable web of equity and debt that no supercomputer could figure out. Japan has not required banks to mark down their loans as banks in the United States have to do, and the Japanese government is trying to grow the economy out of the problem. Its economy has stagnated for two decades.

The goal is to grow the economy and create equity, or "wealth." If the economy grows, this will create some value above a person's, company's, or bank's debt and will create equity. If the entire equity in Japan grows to a large number, the debt will shrink as a percentage and become manageable. However, this will create another problem for the government: interest rates on government debt would rise, wiping out most of the increased tax revenue received by the government, meaning that other government programs will suffer. So the government has to keep interest rates very low, holding the economy at very low growth and the creation of "wealth" at a very low growth rate. Japan has seen 20 years of low and restricted growth and will see another 20 years at least. This is the damage the Japanese government of the 1980s did to that country. In exchange for a decade of fast growth, Japan will have to suffer three or more decades of no growth. What the politicians did there was sacrifice the future of their children and grandchildren so that the generation in power in the 1980s could live well.

The goal of this method to get out of the Debt Trap is to grow the economy at a faster rate than the growth in the national debt and interest on the national debt. This is the Paul Ryan plan. He is actually not planning to balance the budget. In order to get the national debt back to 50 percent of GDP, Ryan is proposing that some minor changes be made to Medicare. Over time Medicare would cease to exist, and a voucher program to help pay for health insurance would replace it. Likewise, changes will need to be made to social security and Medicaid. The current projected date that the national debt would decrease to 50 percent of GDP under the Ryan plan is 2040. That is 27 years. Let's think what could possibly go wrong during 27 years: I'm trying to decide whether to list the ways in alphabetical order or in order of economic devastation.

The assumptions used to come up with Ryan's numbers are terribly optimistic: tax receipts averaging 19 percent of GDP over the period, the growth rate of GDP at 4.5 percent without recessions, reduction of all other government programs from 12.5 percent of GDP today to 3.75 percent by 2040, and so on. That may be a political ploy to make some sort of move in the right direction, but I don't believe the U.S. economy can come anywhere close to his numbers. I strongly support Ryan's plan because it starts moving the country in the right direction. The issue is the same with the Obama budget: the numbers are just wrong—and badly wrong. In addition to the bad numbers, there is no chance that Congress, at the first opportunity by the liberals, would not modify all programs (with the exception of defense spending) and spend a lot more money, pushing the country farther into the Debt Trap. My only conclusion about the

Ryan plan is that he is trying to balance a political backlash with spending reductions. The plan is certainly better than any other politician's, but it definitely cannot ever work using his numbers. The country needs far more draconian measures.

Ryan's concept is to grow the economy faster than debt growth, which has actually worked three times in history. The first example is Great Britain. In 1815 that country reduced expenses and raised taxes, and the full recovery was accomplished by 1914, a mere 99 years. The second example is the United States. During World War II (1945), national debt hit 120 percent debt to GDP. With essentially balanced budgets, the national debt fell to approximately 50 percent by 1962 and 35 percent by 1980. The third time was again Great Britain. Also during World War II, that country's debt to GDP hit 250 percent, and it got the ratio back to 50 percent in 1972: a mere 27 years. This was accomplished by GDP growth and very slow or no growth in outstanding debt. These are very rare exceptions, as you can tell by the list of countries that have defaulted on their debt as outlined in Chapter 1.

Although this method of dealing with the U.S. national debt is the most responsible one, I doubt that politicians would ever let it work. First, the time period for all this to happen would be, I believe, 40 to 50 years or more, and during that time big spenders will gain control of Congress and do more damage. Second, during that long period, the country is certain to see wars, recessions, natural disasters, and many other unforeseen mega-expenses that politicians would determine to be worth borrowing money to resolve. Lastly, even minor impositions on the public, such as the plan Paul Ryan has proposed, have created a political backlash. Around 60 percent of the public do not want to cut back Medicare or other programs. This reminds me of the story of the Little Red Hen. Nobody wants to suffer any pain, but everyone wants to keep his or her benefits.

The method of growing the way out of the Debt Trap appears from all perspectives to have limited potential. I would not put much faith in this method of getting out.

DEFAULT AND REPUDIATE DEBT

Default is the number-one way that countries deal with too much debt. They simply don't pay it. There is not really anything anyone can do to them other than declare war. They may not get any more loans for a while, and they may suffer some economic consequences from other countries, but they can shed the heavy burden of debt with the stroke of a pen. Chapter 1 lists hundreds of countries that have done just this. The IMF has been stiffed many times and so have sophisticated investors who have been in the market for a while. The market has just experienced a number of defaults, and the investors who have absorbed the losses were well aware of the risks. Greece just stiffed investors to the tune of about 70 percent. Investors in Portugal, Ireland, Iceland, and Cyprus have likewise lost most of their investments. Spain is in the initial throes of its Debt Trap and would end up as a member of the default bunch were it not for the efforts of the ECB to shore up the market for Spanish debt. When the default happens, people get hurt.

When looking at the default option, countries are not thinking about how to protect investors from the harm of their actions. They are thinking about the burden the debt is putting on their citizens and how they can get rid of the problem they created. Imagine a debt-free United States today. The country is spending about $360 billion a year on interest expense on the national debt. If it had no debt, that $360 billion could be used to reduce the deficit. That $360 billion is the fourth-largest expense on the national budget, behind defense, healthcare, and pensions. The burden is only going to get much worse as interest rates rise, either due to a recovery or market perceived risk. Very shortly, the government could easily be paying $1 trillion a year in interest expense. To put this in perspective, it is only receiving around $2.7 trillion in taxes today. That would mean that government would be spending almost half of its tax receipts on interest expense, and for what? I think every American should be mad as hell at past Congresses and presidents for borrowing this money. Citizens are getting zero benefit from the government officials' profligate spending and have a massive burden that will cause harm for the next several generations. This money was squandered.

At some point people start saying that the debt was borrowed by some prior generation and so it is not their responsibility to have to repay it: "We got no benefit from it, why should we be responsible for repaying it?" This is a common refrain heard in any society in this position. And the people saying it are right. What benefit does the young generation receive? Their attitude and my attitude is that each generation should pay its own way. I certainly agree with that, but now what to do about it? So everyone looks at their options and just like millions of Americans who have declared bankruptcy, repudiation becomes a serious option. The study goes on and the obvious conclusion is that most countries in this condition repudiate. They may lose face, some international business, the ire of other nations and peoples, but they have shed the pain and burden of repaying their debts.

Repudiation does not mean that every investor gets hurt. The United States could pick out those investors who are weak or can otherwise not do much about it. For instance, if the U.S. government said all bonds held by China are hereby repudiated, what would be the result? I can assure you that this has been studied carefully. First, China could seize U.S. government funds and all United States-based companies' funds and other assets held or located in China. The United States could re-retaliate by seizing China's assets in the United States ... and so on. Since the United States probably has over $1 trillion of assets in China, especially private investments there, I doubt that such a repudiation would work. But this is the thought process. We can find some investors who are weaker and repudiate their debt. This is basically what happened in Greece, where investors were not treated equally. Another form of default is to unilaterally restructure debt payments and/or reduce the interest rate paid on debt. This operates the same as repudiation but somehow sounds better.

The real downside for repudiation by the U.S. federal government would be the enormous damage that such repudiation would do to the world economy. The U.S. financial system would collapse because its banks would have to reflect the losses in their portfolios, and these losses would wipe out the equity in most banks. Pension funds, hedge funds, corporate and individual investors hold trillions of dollars of Treasuries. If the debt was repudiated, most investments would collapse and pensioners would not receive their pensions, investors would lose their investments, and the entire economy would crash into a mighty depression far deeper than the Great Depression. The stock market, real estate market, commodities market, and virtually every market would collapse. This scene is too dismal to consider any further but would be worse than the collapse currently going on in Greece because there is no country standing ready to help the United States out. It has no safety net.

The federal government could simply extend bond due dates and lower interest rates to a manageable level. This, of course, is nothing but a thinly disguised default scenario; it is also exactly what the U.S. government did in 1790. The market for Treasuries would collapse, and the value of these bonds would drop significantly. In the event the government unilaterally reduced the interest it is paying on its debt, this would have an immediate impact on all outstanding debt. Say, for instance, you are a pension fund and you have $1 billion in 10-year Treasury bonds currently paying 3 percent. If the government unilaterally determined to pay no interest on the bonds, those would immediately fall significantly in value. You would instantly lose a large portion of your investment. The pension fund would have to reduce payments to pensioners, hurting millions of individuals.

Any banks holding that bond would likewise suffer a loss in value. Banks have to maintain minimum equity values, and this massive loss could wipe out any equity held in a bank. Nevertheless, this is an option.

PRINT MONEY TO PAY FOR IT

Printing money is also a favorite method used by countries caught in the Debt Trap. Why not just create a lot of new cash and pay off the bonds with that? How simple and easy can it get? So this scenario gets a lot of attention in countries that have their own currency and have issued bonds payable in their own currency. Had Greece not adopted the euro, it could have printed its own currency to pay off the debt if the debt was denominated in drachmas, the old Greek currency. The only downside to this method is that countries that do this create a currency crisis that in turn creates an economic crisis.

The United States through the Federal Reserve carefully controls the amount of money that is created. This careful control is used to regulate economic activity. When the Federal Reserve wants to slow down economic activity, usually when GDP growth exceeds 5 percent, it sells Treasury securities it owns to banks. This has the effect of reducing the cash banks have to loan to businesses and correspondingly slows down borrowing by businesses. This in turn slows down the GDP growth. When GDP growth is slow, as it currently is, the Federal Reserve does just the opposite: it buys Treasuries from banks, which puts more cash in the system so that those institutions will have to loan it to businesses, which in turn grows the economy. Through this mechanism, the Federal Reserve has been able to regulate the amount of money in circulation and has kept inflation at a very moderate rate for decades. It is necessary to have some inflation, as the economy is not perfectly efficient. For instance, to grow GDP at 4 percent, money supply must increase at 6 percent, meaning there will be an inflation rate of 2 percent. This is just how it works and what is needed to grow GDP.

The U.S. government is now $17 trillion in debt, and net of its debt to social security and several other government agencies ($5 trillion), it owes about $12 trillion to third parties that have loaned it money. So why not have the Federal Reserve simply make $12 trillion in new currency and loan the money to the government so it can pay off all outstanding debt? That sounds simple: with the wave of a hand the country would have no debt. The problem with this solution is that it would immediately cause hyperinflation. Today, there is approximately $10 trillion in M2 money supply. M2 is the primary means of calculating money supply in circulation and includes paper and coin currency, demand deposits such as checking and savings accounts, and money market funds. So if the Federal Reserve created $12 trillion of new money to pay off the national debt, which it could do by buying and forgiving it or paying it off as it matures, the "monetary base" would immediately increase.

The monetary base is the amount of actual cash and coins in circulation plus the amount of "reserves" that banks have deposited with the Federal Reserve. In 2013, the monetary base was around $3.2 trillion. All this extra cash in the system would quickly multiply into a high growth rate of M2 as banks loaned out all this extra money on their balance sheets and the impact on the prices would be extraordinary. As the banks loaned out this extra money, the M2 growth could easily reach 100 to 300 percent in the short term, meaning we could see inflation of 100 to 300 percent. This would instantly increase the cost of most commodities, energy, and interest rates by some horrific amount. The U.S. currency exchange rate would decline against all major currencies by a commensurate amount. The bondholders would receive the entire amount of their bonds in cash, but the cash would be worth only cents on the dollar. It is the exact equivalent of simply paying bondholders, say, 45 cents per dollar of debt and defaulting on the rest. Then, because of this massive amount of currency injected into the market, inflation would run rampant. It would convert the U.S. debt problem into the currency and economic crisis experienced by the Weimar Republic in Germany in the 1920s, by Argentina from the 1980s until today, and by Yugoslavia in the 1990s.

During periods of hyperinflation a number of bad things happen. People hoard things that are hyperinflating, such as commodities and food, creating immediate shortages, which, of course, make the values increase faster. Today, prices relative to products around markets have stabilized, so a gallon of milk is $4, gasoline is $4, a television is $500, and a basketball is $20. During hyperinflation, a gallon of gas can climb to $25, milk to $8, a television to $700, and a basketball to $24. These increases are not proportional, and the unequal rise in prices will put some companies out of business. Because of all the uncertainties, people do not spend their cash but get it out of the inflating currency and into a more stable one. This slows the economy. Some people and companies make extraordinary amounts of money while other go broke, creating a massive redistribution of wealth. People living on fixed incomes because they are pensioners or have a bond portfolio get crushed as the monthly cash they receive stays level while the cost of living skyrockets. A life insurance policy all of a sudden becomes worthless. There is the story of a German man who bought life insurance and paid the premium religiously his entire life. When he died in Germany in 1923, the policy paid off, so the family took the money and immediately spent it all on a loaf of bread. The currency becomes worthless, and those who can take advantage of it do well, while those who cannot suffer. Hyperinflation causes an enormous redistribution of wealth, mostly from the poor to the financially clever.

Hyperinflation is more common than you might realize and the list of countries that have hyperinflated their currency is rather long and notable; it includes Austria, Bolivia, Brazil, Chile, China, Greece, Hungary, Israel, Japan, Poland, Yugoslavia, Germany, Zimbabwe, Argentina, and Bosnia-Herzegovina, and even the United States Confederacy (1861–1865), when the Confederate dollar decreased to one-ninetieth of its starting value and fell to zero at the end of the war.

Yugoslavia went through it from 1917 to 1919, Germany (1920–1923) saw inflation of 466 billion percent, Zimbabwe (2003–2012) has lived through inflation of 6 quadrillion times the starting price, the former Soviet Union (1993–2002) saw inflation of 14 times the starting price, and Argentina (1975–1983) saw 1,000 percent inflation. At the height of inflation, Germany issued a 100 billion Mark note, which was equivalent to US$25. In 1923, Germany created a new currency, the Rentenmark, pegging it to the dollar at the exact exchange rate the Mark was to the dollar in 1920. The exchange rate for old Marks to Rentenmarks was 1 trillion to 1. The printing of money was done to pay the debts of Germany under its obligations. Of course, the payment method meant that the bondholders received a very small fraction of the value of the money owed. Table 7.1 shows the increase in the cost of a loaf of bread in Germany from 1918 to 1923.

Table 7.2 shows the price increases of a few other German items during this time period.

The final result of hyperinflation is a massive dislocation of the economy where some industries do very well and others go broke. The worst effect is that the middle class and the poor are crushed by dramatic price increases of almost every expense in their lives

Table 7.1 The Cost of a Loaf of Bread in Germany, 1918–1923 (in German Marks)

December 1918	0.5
December 1921	4
December 1922	163
January 1923	250
March 1923	463
June 1923	1,465
July 1923	3,465
August 1923	69,000
September 1923	1,512,000
October 1923	1,743,000,000
November 1923	201,000,000,000

Table 7.2 Price Increases of German Items, 1913–1923 (in German Marks)[2]

Item	1913	Summer 1923	November 1923
1 egg	0.08	5,000	80,000,000,000
1 kg. butter	2.70	26,000	6,000,000,000,000
1 kg. beef	1.75	18,800	5,600,000,000,000
Pair of shoes	12.00	1,000,000	32,000,000,000,000

without a means of improving their income. Relatively speaking, they lose everything.

RAISE TAXES AND REDUCE EXPENSES

In order to reduce the deficit, all of the United States is going to experience pain. Government expenditures must be cut and/or taxes must be raised. But, as discussed in Chapter 2, spending cuts have far less of an impact on the economy than raising taxes. Complicating matters, projecting government expenses is a notoriously risky business and is always wrong on the downside. The cuts need to be deeper than anyone can imagine. As discussed in Chapter 3, having to cut expenses when the deficit as a percentage of GDP is greater than the growth rate of GDP puts the country immediately into a recession. Furthermore, we know from watching the proposed cuts in Greek government spending that the general public that relies on all this free money riots at even the thought of cutting back anything they are currently receiving. They are completely unaware of the government's cash predicament and do not care. All they want is their money that they have been promised by the politicians.

Tax increases would only hurt the economy, as discussed in Chapter 3. Let's say the government taxed individuals and companies an additional $500 billion a year; this would take $500 billion out of the economy (about 3 percent of GDP) and instantly put the country into a recession. Additionally, taxing does not help the problem because the United States is already a high-tax country and can no longer compete on the world stage due to excessive regulation, high labor rates, higher material costs, high tax rates, and higher fixed-cost structure. Americans are taxed at over 40 percent by federal, state, and local governments, and the people making the money are really taxed much more. Increasing tax rates would be a welcome relief to many competitive nations who would view this as great news in terms of the outsourcing of U.S. jobs. Tax increases would make the United States even less competitive and hurt its economy in both the short and long term. The way to grow out of it would be to create more wealth. The nation needs more people making more money. Both spending cuts and tax increases would cause damage to the economy in that they would both take cash out of the economy. America would be caught in the Debt Trap, which Americans would carry around like a ball and chain for generations. As we all know, the sins of the fathers last three or four generations.

Can the United States actually cut over $1 trillion in expenses? This would be tough—not from the perspective of actually doing it, but cutting this much cash that goes into the economy will, in the short term, lower the GDP substantially and reduce benefits to millions of Americans that are principally received through Medicare, Medicaid, social security, and other so-called social programs. The Federal Reserve should pump a lot of currency into the system to offset the reduction, but there will still be casualties. While many Americans understand that the country is broke and cannot keep up these payments, a large percentage of them do not comprehend that, do not care about the nation's financial condition, and do not care about the damage to future generations; they only want their cash this week and this month, even if it means the entire country fails in a year and the current generation ruins the lives of many later generations. As appalling as that sounds, you have to look no further than the current situation in Greece and Spain, where millions who rely on government handouts and are threatened with cuts in their benefits are rioting in the streets, burning cars and buildings.

Spending cuts and tax increases do the same thing to the economy: they both reduce the amount of currency in the system. The significant difference in the two is that cutting expenses reduces government size and scope and does not have a dollar-for-dollar negative impact. As discussed in Chapter 3, the economic concept that the government can create jobs is a myth. Attempts at job creation actually do the opposite. If the government could really create jobs, the Soviet Union would have been a great success, Cuba would be the strongest economy in the world, and North Korea would be the juggernaut of Asia. Increasing taxes takes a dollar out of the economy for every dollar taxed. Furthermore, the multiplier effect for the economy is lost.

The process known as "austerity" is this process of decreasing spending and increasing taxes. It is a painful process, and as several European countries experiencing it can attest, it hurts a country's economy. The debt-stressed European economies have declined, of course, because of austerity, and several are suffering through recessions and even depressions. All the politicians and citizens are complaining about the pain. No one wants his or her benefits cut, and no one wants to pay more taxes; there are riots in the streets. People want to keep things the way they were. They are now electing politicians who are promising to return to the old days. France has elected a communist by the name of François Hollande (no relation to me, fortunately), who promises to keep the spending going by taxing the rich at 75 percent. This move has chased away many wealthy businesses and people, who have fled to surrounding countries. His new tact is to "grow GDP," which in turn will increase tax receipts and decrease the deficit. This has not worked because France does not control money supply and cannot stimulate the economy with M2 growth. The ECB controls money supply, and it is keeping money supply growth limited to prevent inflation. It seems as though France is caught in a trap, which it is: the Debt Trap.

BAILOUT

Due to the size of the U.S. debt, around $17 trillion gross and $12 trillion in debt to the public, there is no country in the world that could come close to helping America. Obtaining assistance is not an option for the United States.

OTHER OPTIONS

There are no other options.

Hundreds of countries have been in the Debt Trap, and the ways mentioned in this chapter are the only ways they can get out. Europe has a number of countries currently caught in the trap, and they are dealing with each country's debt in the manner that suits

the circumstances of that country. In Greece, the Troika has negotiated a default and then a bailout, combining two methods of getting
out of the Debt Trap. The Troika is bailing out Spanish banks now
and more than likely will be bailing out the country soon. The Europeans are very shrewd financial managers, and they have found no
other ways out of the Debt Trap. They are using every method of
getting out with the exception of printing money. This, of course,
is why the European Union may ultimately fail: the individual
European countries cannot print their own money to manage their
own economies.

When the United States gets helplessly snared in the Debt Trap,
it will be able to use all of the methods described above with the
exception of a bailout.

CAN THE U.S. GOVERNMENT ESCAPE THE DEBT TRAP?

> We all know what to do, we just don't know how to get re-elected after we have done it.
>
> —Jean-Claude Juncker, Prime Minister of Luxembourg and President of the Euro Group

Will the government go bust? This is the question that everyone would like answered. In Chapter 7 we reviewed the ways that countries deal with the Debt Trap. I think the United States already is in that trap, and so in dealing with it the country has five options. America is in very bad financial shape, maybe the worst it has ever experienced. Even after World War II, when the U.S. debt-to-GDP ratio was about 120 percent, the government was able to reduce its deficit to essentially zero without a massive depression, but it took 35 years to get that ratio down to a respectable 35 percent. Today, the federal government has borrowed from the public (and the Federal Reserve) almost $12 trillion, the economy has a GDP of about $16 trillion, and there is a public debt-to-GDP ratio of 74 percent. This, of course, disregards the debt to social security and other funds of $5 trillion, unfunded federal pensions of $7.5 trillion, and the $60 trillion or so in commitments to social programs with no way of paying for them.

The United States is already caught in the first jaw of the Debt Trap because the economy is dependent on the deficit spending of the federal government. The U.S. economy (that is, the GDP) grew at less than 3 percent for 2012 and around 2.5 percent for 2013. Federal government 2012 deficit spending was 7 percent of GDP and estimated to be 4 percent in 2013. If the federal government instantly balanced the budget by either spending reductions or higher taxes, it would instantly reduce GDP by 4 percent, and this would put the United States in a severe recession. This is the situation analysis. We need some financial heroes to lead the country into safe financial territory.

The next jaw of the Debt Trap has not yet closed in. That jaw is the market risk adjusting U.S. national debt and running interest rates substantially higher and then cutting the country off from the debt market entirely. We have seen a Standard & Poor's downgrade of U.S. creditworthiness, and Moody's has just released its intentions to downgrade the country's ratings. Egan-Jones, a smaller ratings agency, downgraded U.S. debt for a second time on September 13, 2012. When interest rates start to escalate, which they will as the debt continues to accumulate, the interest expense on the national debt will take up more and more of the budget, leaving less and less for other operating items such as military, medical care, and social security. Interest expense will become the largest budget item in the federal budget.

There is a chorus of officials from countries around the world warning the United States to fix its financial problems. In an article, the official Xinhua news agency of China said that America had a "runaway debt addiction ... [that could] jeopardize the well-being of hundreds of millions of families within and beyond the US borders."[1] In June 2010, when Treasury Secretary Timothy Geithner met with the finance ministers of the world's 20 largest developed and emerging-market economies, the G20, they rejected his pleas for more deficits, increasing Keynesian stimulus and recommended exactly the opposite: credible budget deficit reduction. Before a meeting of the G20, Treasury Secretary Geithner sent a letter to all his colleagues and called for all the others to join him in dramatically increasing government spending to try to stimulate all these economies and increase "aggregate demand." His economic plan was resoundingly rejected.

The official communiqué of the G20 did not mention stimulating aggregate demand with higher government spending, commonly referred to as "fiscal policy." The group specifically referenced countries that had been reducing their deficits in order to strengthen their financial institutions. The rest of the world knows that the U.S. government has borrowed too much money, causing the financial problems the country now faces. The smart financial managers of the most sophisticated countries know from their own experiences, especially those in Europe, that additional spending by governments does not benefit their economies. In the case of Greece, with its essentially communist economy, no amount of money supply funneled to the government has helped or will help. The country needs to turn to capitalism to get the economy started. Citizens there need to go to work 40 hours a week and receive a market rate of pay—probably far less than they are receiving from the government. Their government "overhead" burden of 50+ percent needs to be reduced to 20 percent. In the case of Ireland, on the other hand, spending cuts did work and it is on its way to recovery. Ireland reduced the size of its government, reduced tax rates, and let the private sector take over. The ultimate insult to Geithner may have been from the German finance minister Wolfgang Schäuble when he said Geithner's bailout concepts were "stupid."[2]

The sad thing about the handling of the housing bust and resulting "Great Recession" has been the incredible amount of money that has been wasted by the federal government. It started with George W. Bush and then went to another level under Barack Obama. The Troubled Asset Relief Program, or TARP (involving almost $800 billion), was needed to stabilize the U.S. currency and prevent the country from immediate financial collapse. Essentially all this money has been paid back. The United States could have handled the entire recession through the efforts of the Federal Reserve and avoided having government officials waste trillions of dollars because of their desire to have government save the day. The government could have $4 to $5 trillion less federal debt if it had pursued a Federal Reserve long-term strategy of quantitative easing (increasing money supply) to target economic growth of, say, 3 percent. Instead, the government borrowed almost $6 trillion, taking that money availability from businesses and individuals, further exacerbating a significant downturn. If deficit spending had been a proven remedy to recessions, I would feel differently. It has shown through 50 years of OECD data as well as experiences in America and Japan's experience over the last 20 years to not produce any economic benefits. Borrowing over $6 trillion in the last four years has taken that money away from the real economy and hurt the ability of the real economy to recover. The citizens of the United States will be paying an average of around $360 billion a year forever (federal debt averages 6 percent per year) because of the deficit borrowing in the last five years. Further, if the government had not borrowed that money, the investors who made these loans to the government would be looking for a place to put the money, and it ultimately would have been invested in the real economy. Due to a lack of confidence, the real economy (that is, the private sector) has stagnated.

On September 13, 2012, the Federal Reserve announced a new plan. It would buy $85 billion a month of government and other financial debt until unemployment recovered. This is probably a good move by Ben Bernanke and the Federal Reserve. All other federal government and Federal Reserve moves have been one-shot deals that are not policy. For instance, TARP was a one-time program over a short period, and no one knew what was going to happen after that. What was the policy? Would it change? The answer is that there was no policy, only one-off attempts to shock the economy back to life. The uncertainty of what would happen next was killing investment and spending. If investors and businesspeople were not confident of the future, why would they make long-term investments? The answer is that they would not.

Even tax policy is wildly fluctuating. The Bush era tax cuts were supposed to expire at the end of 2010 but were extended until January 2013. A vote in Congress did not happen until January 2013 to extend some cuts and change others. This vote was to avoid a "fiscal cliff," meaning that if the tax increases had gone into effect, the economy would decline into a recession. This method of congressional behavior has unfortunately become the standard method and consequently there is no confidence by businesspeople that the government can ever fix its self-generated demise. This has made more or less permanent a slow economic growth that will persist, along with a shrinking investment by business.

In his book *Five Keys to Restoring America's Prosperity,* John Taylor, who worked at the Treasury and Federal Reserve most of his professional career, asserts that consistent government policy is essential for economic progress. Taylor, by the way, concurs that the government wasted trillions of dollars that did nothing to help the economy recover. "At its most basic level," he says, "economic freedom means that families, individuals, and entrepreneurs are free to decide what to produce, what to consume, what to buy and sell, and how to help others. The American vision was that those decisions would be made within a predictable government policy framework based on the rule of law with strong incentives derived from the market system and with a clearly limited role for government." This is where we were in the 1980s and 1990s with over 20 years of economic expansion and progress. His five principles are:

1. Compel politicians to find a way to pay for each legislative act.
2. Limit the scope of government.
3. Provide incentives for politicians to spend taxpayer money wisely.
4. Rely more on the private sector.
5. Provide a predictable policy framework.

Can the United States actually implement "structural changes" at home? Economically, everyone knows that the economy would be much better off if more people worked and paid their own way. Could the nation actually ever go back to a government that would support this type of policy platform?

FIVE WAYS OUT

In Chapter 7 we reviewed the only ways there are to deal with the current financial position. The first and most popular method used by countries is to default and repudiate the debt, basically telling creditors they are not getting paid back. While the federal government is certainly capable of doing so, the global effect of such a default would surely cause a collapse of the world's financial system, including our own banking system. It is inconceivable to me that this method of dealing with the financial crisis would ever be implemented. Another method of dealing with the crisis is a bailout. This method is not available to the United States because there is no country or even group of countries that can or would "give" the country trillions of dollars to rescue the economy. Printing money is also by itself not a viable method for the United States to undertake to deal with the financial crisis. Many countries have tried this, and the resulting economic devastation from the hyperinflation it creates is as bad, if not worse than, a default. Consequently, while these three methods have been used by many countries, the resulting economic destruction is too grim to seriously consider for the United States.

TWO WAYS OUT

As we discussed earlier about investors and confidence that a country will repay its debts, investors are highly confident that the United States will repay its debts. The crisis is that the government has already incurred such massive debt that the interest expense will eat too much of tax receipts and leave too little for social programs. Unfortunately for U.S. citizens, there are only two ways left to get out of the debt crisis the country is currently facing: reduce the deficit and grow the economy. Both of these things are difficult to do, particularly since Americans have gotten used to living the high life off borrowed money. The blame for putting Americans in this position falls on Congress and several administrations who borrowed money when they should have balanced their budgets.

Nevertheless, this is the situation and the country must deal with it. The two available options can and should be implemented together. The variables are how fast the federal government can grow the economy without overheating it and causing another dot-com bust or subprime mortgage bust. The first and easiest method is economic growth. I believe this is where to start. Today in the United States, economic growth is handicapped by a number of items discussed in this book. First, demographics are against it as the baby boomers are retiring and women are leaving the workforce. Both of these will slow economic activity. Second, there is so much government regulation that, as we saw in Chapter 3, it dramatically slows the economy. And third, the federal government debt and the corresponding "overhead" burden and capital usurpation out of the markets hurt the ability of businesses to grow. And we all want growth of businesses: that is how the economy grows.

As a result of all these factors, real GDP growth will be limited. I believe that 2 percent real GDP growth will be the norm.

While this method of recovery is relatively painless, Congress can do little to stimulate growth. The entity that has the primary control over the economy is the Federal Reserve. In the past, it has been able to stimulate the economy by the methods described earlier, but the primary method is increasing the money supply. The Fed's efforts over the last five years have not worked to increase money supply, although there are signs of hope that the economy may see some growth in late 2013. The things Congress can do to help growth is reduce regulations, lower taxes, and stop borrowing from the markets.

While I expect some but not much GDP growth over the next two decades, which will help with the debt crisis, the remaining method of dealing with the crisis is deficit reduction. This is entirely controllable and absolutely will result in a solution without an economic collapse. Here is where the country needs to focus its attention.

THE SOLUTION

Without much support from GDP growth, the only remaining viable method of dealing with the debt crisis is to lower the deficit. There are only two ways this can be done: reduce expenses and/or increase taxes. Both of these moves are troublesome and involve long-term pain. As we calculated earlier, if the U.S. government reduced its deficit to zero and grew GDP at 3 percent a year, the country would return to 36 percent debt to GDP in 26 years. This was the level of the debt-to-GDP ratio at the start of 2008, not that long ago.

Increasing Taxes

It seems like a very simple thing to do, to increase the taxes, especially if just the "rich" are taxed. There is only one problem with taxation: it decreases GDP by at least the amount of taxation. So let's say we want to increase taxes by 4 percent of GDP so we can balance the budget. What will happen? The answer is that we will go immediately into a severe recession by taking that much money out of the economy. So if we want to stimulate the economy, we should reduce taxes: but this will cause the deficit to soar. This is the first quandary of taxation. The second quandary is the "overhead" burden of taxation discussed earlier. While everyone knows we need to have government overhead, when we get past the point of "necessary" government, the further taxation decreases the GDP. This is what we have seen earlier in the book, particularly in the graph of government growth over the last 100 years. All this growth is not free. It costs the economy dearly. So, the problem with taxation is that it brings in more cash to the government but lowers economic growth ... which in the long run hurts government tax receipts.

Decreasing Expenses

Just cutting spending seems like a simple thing to do. Most of the European governments are undertaking "austerity" measures, meaning cutting expenses, and having to make "structural" changes. Those types of changes mean governments cannot pay as well as they have been, they cannot give as much welfare, they cannot provide as many services, and so on. The U.S. Congress certainly *can* cut spending: it can simply pass a law doing so. So let's say the government wants to cut spending 4 percent to balance the budget. What will happen? There are two types of "expenditures" to cut. First are what Congress terms "discretionary" expenses, which are the government's operating expenses. A cut here hurts GDP almost dollar for dollar. "Mandatory" programs are simply transfer of payments from a taxpayer to another person under a social program. Economically, the GDP will fall but not as much as a tax increase or cut in "discretionary" programs.

THE ANSWER

The answer is that the United States has to cut government and grow the economy. As we saw earlier, over the last 80 years government spending has climbed from under 10 percent of GDP to over

40 percent. Almost all this growth has been for social programs and some has been for "corporate welfare." Both these types of programs amount to nothing more than a redistribution of wealth: taking money from the people who made it and handing it to people who did not. The United States has the same "structural" problems that many European countries have: the government is too large a part of the economy. The structural problem of too much government hurts the economy because the government takes money without producing anything and does not create economic growth: it hurts economic growth. The answer for the United States is to cut expenses 1 percent per year for four years to balance the budget and then keep it there for 25 to 30 years. If the country can get economic growth higher, the debt will reduce itself as a percentage of GDP, and the burden to society will be reduced.

HOW THE EUROPEANS ARE DEALING WITH THE DEBT TRAP

The European countries, particularly southern European ones, have found themselves in the Debt Trap. They have the same political factions as the United States has and have become trapped with too much debt, although their debt levels are not much higher than those in the States. So what has happened, and how are those countries getting out of debt? Europe has a lot of very smart, educated people working on the problem, and suffice it to say that the economic crisis those countries are in today is not worth the last 10 years of deficit spending that led them to this point. Since Europe has a central bank that controls the currency, the countries in serious crisis—Greece, Portugal, Spain, Italy, Cyprus, and France—cannot print money to get out of the Debt Trap, although there is still the possibility that one or more countries could withdraw from the European Union and restart their own currency. Their existing debt, however, is designated to be repaid in euros, so they would create a default if they tried to repay with their new currency. Portugal and Greece are the two countries most likely to do this. That is one option down ... probably.

European countries in trouble still can default and repudiate, but the impact on all other countries would be so severe economically that the debris field would include all of Europe. Greece is the only country that has actually defaulted, but the interest expense burden of Portugal's debt makes it another candidate to default. There is another option down, at least with regard to the larger countries such as Spain, France, and Italy. The smaller countries like Greece have received some bailout money. The group that loans this money, the Troika (ECB, EU, and IMF), requires "austerity" measures in order to receive bailout money, much like the markets will do to the United States. The bailout option, however, is about dead because the larger countries are too big to bail out. This is the third option down. So, the European countries in trouble are down to two options: grow the economy and balance the budget. The Europeans are enforcing "austerity," meaning reducing the deficit by increasing taxes and/or cutting spending ("structural change"), but they are having trouble growing their economies; the same two options left to the United States. Government spending has nothing to do with growing the economy, as we now know from 50 years of OECD data: only the central bank increasing money supply and lowering interest rates can improve the economy. So the European solution is the same as my solution: it is a logical conclusion from analysis of the options.

Unlike the U.S. central bank, the ECB has chosen to take a more conservative role and not increase money supply quickly or lower interest rates significantly. The bank's mandate has been purely to protect the value of the currency, which it has done well, but that is not how to get the economy growing. The ECB needs to dramatically increase money supply and lower interest rates to help the European economies, particularly those in southern Europe, rebound. This will help reduce the deficits by increasing tax receipts and reduce the debt as a percentage of GDP, helping solve the larger problem.

DEALING WITH THE PROBLEM

When you are a business owner or an individual and you have to cut expenses, you do it or you go bust. Almost all businesses go through growth-and-decline cycles and have to cut expenses. It happens every day, thousands of times a day, all over the country. This is not a novel problem. I have cut business expenses many times in business, and it is not fun. No one wants to do it.

The process that businesses undertake to cut expenses is the process needed by the federal government. The first step is to prioritize which government expenses are the most necessary. Let's say healthcare is determined to be the number-one priority. We need to make sure Medicare and Medicaid services are maintained. We need to implement all cost reductions that do not affect the medical outcome for patients. We then need to reduce expenditures by the federal government on other programs that are not priorities. For instance, giving billions of dollars a year to foreign countries may help the country in terms of its relationships, but the handouts do nothing for the U.S. economy and do not help feed our poor. These are not "necessary" expenses. All the "crony capitalism" expenses can be cut to zero without making an impact on the economy. There, in two sentences, I have cut almost 1 percent of GDP from the budget without hurting the economy at all. As a matter of fact, I believe making the cuts will help the economy because the federal government will be borrowing $100+ billion less, and things that are a burden on the economy, such as the alcohol fuel program, will have been eliminated.

Step two of the process is to run the government more efficiently, using modern business management techniques. There are hundreds, if not thousands, of ideas of ways to cut medical expenses. For instance, a Dartmouth study showed that some medical procedures varied in price by 800 percent in different parts of the country. Some procedures are ineffective; many are unnecessary. Doctors do too many tests to cover themselves from malpractice. There is rampant fraud throughout the system. And the list goes on. If Medicare were a business I owned, I would be working these points vigorously with smart businesspeople and medical personnel. There is no doubt that I could cut 25 percent of cost without affecting services one bit.

In business, we undertake time and motion studies to bring technology solutions to help people become more efficient with their time. We "outsource" functions that can be performed better by someone else. We "budget" everything—something Congress seems to be incapable of doing. We have processes and procedures for constant business quality improvement. All these things are lacking in a government operation. There is a severe lack of objective, business process, but this is how we can solve the debt crisis.

POLITICS

The conflicting political agendas, which stems from a difference in the psychology of two types of people, and our leadership will determine whether the United States can move to a path of fiscal responsibility and economic progress. This psychological conflict between two types of people has been around since human beings first walked the Earth ... and always will be.

> Men have differed in opinion, and been divided into parties by these opinions, from the first origin of societies ... the same political parties which now agitate the U.S. have existed through all time.
>
> —Thomas Jefferson

If I believed there was a way to restrain liberals from continuing to spend in the face of sure economic collapse I would be more optimistic. This nation belongs to those living here from time to time. One generation has no more right to borrow money to be paid back by the next generation than the country has a right to make another nation pay back its debts.

In order to keep from being destroyed by the Debt Trap, the United States needs to turn to GDP growth by re-creating a system that supports business rather than punishes it. The slower the growth in GDP and the higher the country's deficits, the longer it will take to grow out of the problem. For instance, if the nation can maintain an average GDP growth rate of 3 percent and a balanced budget for 26 years, it can get the debt-to-GDP ratio back to 35 percent. If there is 3 percent GDP growth and 1 percent deficits, it will take 39 years. To achieve this in the U.S. political system will be quite some feat, particularly in light of the avowed goal of some liberals to destroy the capitalist system through debt.

The only way to escape the Debt Trap before the country is completely consumed is to grow the economy and reduce the "overhead" cost to every citizen. The higher the "overhead" cost, the less the nation gets for its work efforts. Total federal, state, and local governments cost 42 percent of the national GDP, in aggregate (sales tax, income tax, property tax, license fees, and so on). For every dollar a U.S. citizen makes at work, he or she pays 40 cents of earnings to have government services and entitlement programs. Of that 40 cents, 16 cents are social programs of the federal government (there is no telling how much state and local governments spend on social programs). That is really nothing more than taking 16 cents of every dollar earned from a wage-earning American and giving it to another American or illegal alien who is not working. While many aspects of government are necessary, such as roads, military, and education, there are many that are not. The existence of government burdens every person and every aspect of the country's economy, like a ball and chain. As governments grow and increase this burden, many simply quit working and take the easy path of doing nothing and getting a free ride off of the government.

OBAMACARE

With respect to healthcare reform, the subject is so complex that many books could be written on it ... which happens to be my point. Just as large businesses can never be managed centrally, something as large and complex as healthcare has no chance of being managed by the federal government. If the federal government tries to manage this fast-moving, fast-changing environment, it will make a disaster out of it. Medical care and decision making is completely different in New York City than it is in McAllen, Texas, yet a centrally managed system can only have one set of processes and procedures for all. Obamacare already has over 29,000 pages of regulations, and 14,000 companies have been exempted from it. This is a disaster brewing. Healthcare needs to be managed by the states, and if the states have any sense they will transfer management to the cities and counties who should transfer it to the hospitals and other medical entities in the counties. Healthcare should be designed on a local basis: managed there and taxed there.

In Iowa, the state is working on a campaign to get all Iowans "healthy" and has recruited lots of community organizations to participate. Healthy citizens save a lot in healthcare costs. Now, can you imagine a program like that getting managed out of Washington, D.C.? At the local level, millions of ideas are put into practice to save millions and billions of dollars while achieving the same medical outcomes. If decisions are made at the local level, an idea generated in Fresno, California, can quickly be implemented in Atlanta, Georgia, with a simple meeting of the board of directors or administrator of a hospital. If each idea needs to go through a group of bureaucrats in Washington, D.C., and be reviewed and regulated there, it will take years to get a regulation passed. It's not that these people are idiots; the problem is that no management can work on a large scale with a centrally managed organization. If healthcare can be transferred to the states to manage, they will figure out the best ways to manage it and pass the best practices on to other states. If the federal government centrally manages it, the system is doomed.

HOW TO GET OUT

The federal government has put the entire country at risk of financial collapse; such is the predicament in which Americans find themselves. The country can get out of the Debt Trap before it crushes the economy. Americans will have to implement "structural changes" and make more people pay their own way. This is what most European countries have to do right now. They are forced to do it by the market, and soon the United States will be compelled to do it. The U.S. government has to stop spending, and the deficit needs to be reduced to zero or at most 1 percent of GDP. If government officials tax to get to a balanced budget, they will put the country into a deep recession or depression. The United States has to do what the European countries are doing, or it will be crushed by the Debt Trap.

Of the five hundred plus agencies and administrations, there are many that do nothing for the economy and others that are redundant. The first is the Department of Education. The Department of Education is a perfect example of too much management that does nothing but get in the way of progress. Education is perfectly manageable at the state and local level. Having the federal government provide a whole new level of management, oversight, and regulation does not add anything to education at the state level. It hurts education. The liberal fantasy that a centrally managed government is somehow good fails every single time. The list of other agencies that are burdens on the U.S. economy is a long one and should quickly be expanded to include any agency that does not benefit the economy and have a "necessary" purpose.

The concept of federal spending to "prime the pump" has never worked. As we experienced in the Great Depression, 10 years of large deficit spending did nothing to help the economy. Japan has run enormous deficits for 20 years, yet has seen its economy decline over that entire period. From 2009 through 2013, the U.S. government has spent $6 trillion dollars with no significant growth. This is not that difficult: deficit spending does not help grow the economy. The only method of restarting the economy is action by the Federal Reserve with a long-term strategic policy that is simple and understandable combined with no borrowing by government. Businesspeople can then plan long-term investments and know what the rules are going to be. The plan announced by Ben Bernanke in September 2012 I believe is the right plan. It is too bad he didn't do this when the problems of the housing bubble first started. Americans should support economic progress at the federal level with a tax policy that everyone understands and knows will be in place over a long period of time. The same goes with regulation strategy. This will get the economy back into growth mode.

There have been hundreds of ideas about getting the budget back in balance. One is to cut Congress's pay until the budget is balanced. As silly as this sounds, it may be very efficacious. Remember the discussion of OPM—Other People's Money—in Chapter 5. The case of the British Parliament not wanting to spend even one day's worth of the pay of its members is exactly the point. It is very easy to spend trillions of Other People's Money, but when it comes to spending a few thousand dollars of one's own money, people will go to extraordinary lengths to avoid that. With this congressional pay-for-performance plan in place, the United States might have a balanced budget in a month!

Liberals are concerned that if government spending is cut, unemployment will increase. Not so. As John Taylor recounts:

> Lower government spending as a share of GDP is not associated with higher unemployment. For example, when government purchases of goods and services came down as a share of GDP in the 1990s, unemployment didn't rise. In fact it fell. And the higher level of government purchases as a share of GDP since 2000 has clearly not been associated with lower unemployment. Though correlation does not prove causation, it is hard to see what plausible third factor could reverse this correlation. To the extent that government spending crowds out job-creating private investment, it can actually worsen unemployment. Recent government efforts to stimulate the economy and reduce joblessness by spending more have failed to reduce joblessness.

If America can get the economy to grow at 3 percent and reduce deficits to 1 percent over the next two- to three-year period, the country can actually get out of the clutches of the Debt Trap in 39 years.

If the government could actually balance the budget, the country could escape the Debt Trap sooner. It cannot cut expenses $642 billion (the amount of the deficit for 2013) immediately, because that would put the nation into a severe recession or depression. Therefore, it will have to cut expenses over a three- or four-year period to let the economy grow so that it can absorb these expense cuts. This is clearly the answer to getting the United States out before it is crushed. This doesn't mean the government would actually pay back one dime of principal, which I think it should do so future generations are not burdened with paying interest on money the current one borrowed for no reason. This country would still owe trillions of dollars in debt and still be paying around $1 trillion a year in interest forever. I believe this generation of politicians, and in particular the presidents who were in charge during the last 20 years, will be and should be blamed for heaping debt on the generations coming up. Had no debt ever been borrowed, the country would be almost $700 billion a year ahead of where it is now. Multiply this by the 40 years it will take to get out of this mess and America will have wasted another $28 trillion on interest. The political leaders who did this to the nation should be ashamed.

STRUCTURAL CHANGE

Throughout Europe, there is a cry for "structural change," particularly in the countries that have recently been bailed out: Cyprus, Greece, Ireland, Portugal, and Spain. As a requirement of receiving IMF and EU bailout money, these countries have had to undertake so-called structural changes. Even countries that have not been bailed out, such as France and Italy, are voluntarily undertaking structural change. "Structural change" is a euphemism for reducing dependence by citizens on government programs: in short, go get a job. This is what is meant by structural change, and it is exactly what is required in the United States to solve this financial crisis. Without a dramatic shift in the basic psychology of the liberal mind or at least in the number of people who want Other People's Money without working for it, the country will be doomed to be caught in the Debt Trap. At that point in time, the country will be forced to balance the budget and forced to make structural changes—much to the chagrin of those who have to go back to work.

CAN IT BE DONE?

The problem is not the economic understanding of how to do it; the problem is having a political environment for 30+ years that will support the plan. This, unfortunately, is a completely subjective opinion of future behavior of politicians and in particular Congress and the president. One thing I have learned in basic human behavior is that the best prognosticator of behavior in the future is to look at how someone behaves today, and I believe this is true in politics. The liberal mind will always behave like this. Liberal congressmen and congresswomen not only have no interest in solving the financial crisis, they are the ones who have led us directly into it in the first place. Taking a look at the Senate run under Harry Reid, an unabashed liberal, it has no plan to cut the deficit and did not even so much as prepare a budget for four years as required by the Constitution. Further, you can see their future plans by looking at the Obama 2014 budget for the next 10 years that will lead the United States directly into the Debt Trap and probably outright bankruptcy. The Obama 2012 budget was in reality a sham budget and was defeated in the Senate 97–0. Even liberals thought it was a joke. So with respect to a Congress and president who can lead the country out of the Debt Trap, a liberal group is not the solution: it is the problem. The basic dilemma is that liberals do not care about solving the financial crisis. They are not the solution to the problem; they are the cause of it. If a responsible president and Congress have the political will, we may be able to set a path out of the Debt Trap.

The American people need to make their voice heard. Any actual progress to fix the country's structural problems may work for a while, but if a liberal Congress is elected in the future, it will violate the slow plan of progress to get the nation out of the Debt

Trap, because the congressmen and congresswomen will just go back to spending. The American way out of the Debt Trap is not to cut and run, meaning to default and repudiate the national debt. It is also not to print money and stiff the creditors by paying them back with worthless dollars. It is not the American way to undertake gimmicks such as imposing exchange restrictions, prohibiting citizens from owning gold or other currencies, and manipulating the Federal Reserve System and the U.S. currency. The American way out of the Debt Trap is a long and painful one. The country will have to take its medicine and gut it up for a long 30-year period to get the nation back to where it was as recently as 2008. Americans can get it done, but the country must have leaders who have the understanding and fortitude to do it. The other methods of getting out are devastating, as every country that has tried them can attest. They are not the American way.

WHAT DOES ALL THIS MEAN TO YOU, AND HOW CAN YOU HELP?

I predict future happiness for Americans if they can prevent the government from wasting the labors of the people under the pretense of taking care of them.

—Thomas Jefferson

The events outlined in Chapter 6 will happen in the United States unless the federal government can make very large and significant "structural changes" (that is, spending cuts) during 2013–2015. While almost any business managed by rational women and men would make the spending cuts today, Congress, unfortunately, does not behave rationally; neither have all the countries caught in the Debt Trap throughout history. I believe no politician wants to actually make deep spending cuts because the masses will rise up in protest and vote the party out of office. Clearly, liberals want to continue the buildup of government and will never cut spending despite the full knowledge that the country is entering the Debt Trap. Their course is to keep spending the United States into the Debt Trap. It is my hope that more responsible politicians have the willpower to make dramatic cuts, but I still find it almost inconceivable they will actually do so.

In the event Congress actually cuts the deficit to 1 to 2 percent of GDP, it can stave off the Debt Trap until liberals return to office and start spending again. If for any reason the deficit is not cut to 1 to 2 percent of GDP in the next 12 to 24 months, I believe the nation will be caught in the Debt Trap by then, and the events that have already happened in Europe will start happening in America. There is very little good that comes out of all this except that the federal government finally will be forced to stop deficit spending. The downside is that more and more of the national budget will go to pay interest instead of helping the poor and the sick. U.S. citizens will be burdened with this debt and interest expense forever, since the principal will never be repaid. As we saw in Chapter 5, some liberals want to purposely bankrupt the country. In Chapter 5 we also saw that for the liberal mind to achieve its utopian "dream," liberalism first has to destroy the current system because it stands in the way of the liberal dream. To fulfill their dream, liberals want the government to take over everything—they continuously increase government functions and spending without any thought about the effect this has on the economy. All the liberal mind cares about is fulfilling the utopian dream. The United States is already caught in one jaw of the Debt Trap, and when the markets run up interest rates on the national debt the nation will be caught in the other jaw. Once caught in both jaws of the Debt Trap, the United States as we know it today will look like it did during the Great Depression. When this happens, all the aftermath that has happened to Ireland, Iceland, Cyprus, Greece, Spain, Portugal, and Italy will start happening in America.

On the national level, if the markets price U.S. debt as they have priced Spain's and Italy's, the federal government will see an enormous increase in the interest expense it pays for debt, especially on long-term debt. Once the markets run interest rates in the United States up to, say, 6 percent for 10-year bonds, it will take two and a half years to see the cost of that to our government. This is because it will take that long for existing debt to mature (become due) and be replaced by new debt at a higher interest rate. By that time, the federal government will be paying around $690 billion a year in interest expense and the markets will be forcing it to balance its budget or interest rates will increase further. Interest at that time would be around 25 percent of total federal tax receipts of around $2.7 trillion. Healthcare and social services would be around $2.5 trillion, and that would leave nothing for the military and all other federal government operations. Seeing how the current U.S. military budget is around $700 billion, grants to states around $600 billion, and other government operations are around $350 billion, the entire federal government would break. If Congress did not balance the budget at that time, the markets would completely block access to more debt, and the country would see interest rates escalate dramatically, just as was seen in Greece. If interest rates were to hit 20 percent, interest expense would consume essentially all the federal government budget. The government would then be faced with default, and the only option would be to default and repudiate the national debt or have the Federal Reserve buy all the debt by printing money. This is the option I expect the federal government will take. It is in reality nothing but another form of default and will put the nation into a hyperinflation period (see Chapter 7). In the event the government decided not to default and cut all government programs to almost nothing, this would put an enormous burden on the people. If the government decided to inflate its way out, the bondholders would be the losers by de facto receiving 50 cents or so on the dollar, and the economy and most people in the United States would be devastated by the hyperinflation that the printing of money creates. In Europe, to avoid this situation, which the Germans learned well during the 1919–1923 period of the Weimar Republic, the European Central Bank is keeping tight control on currency supply so as not to trigger another round of hyperinflation.

In a few years, if the United States has not cut the deficit to 1 to 2 percent of GDP, it will be faced with the choice of these two options. In the event we decide to inflate our way out, whatever bondholders are left owning bonds will be paid in inflated dollars that make their return negative. This is nothing but another form of default. As the market loses confidence that the United States can really pay all that interest without terrible hardship to its citizens, it will want out. In today's world, trading U.S. debt is so commoditized that trading programs run trading of bonds, not real live human beings. It is more than likely that yields will increase slowly over several months or a couple of years, as we saw in the case of Greece, as fewer investors would be willing to take the risk of owning federal government bonds. If things happen faster due to automated trading, this could make the exit by bondholders much like October 29, 1929, because when the avalanche of sellers decides to sell their debt, it will trigger a massive sell-off by the market, and the automated programs can make the fall happen within minutes. Whether it happens over a couple of years or a couple of minutes, the massacre will seem quick. There is also the Federal Reserve that will step in and start buying bonds to try to quell the sell-off, but at this point I believe the market will just want out. When this day happens, the reverberations will be felt worldwide.

So I believe the two options the government will consider are whether to make the citizens pay for the debt by cutting government expenses or make the bondholders pay by inflationary default. In the event the government chooses the latter, most citizens will be negatively affected anyhow. Most pensions and many mutual funds own government debt. Most banks own a lot of government debt.

This means that in real dollars pensioners will receive a fraction of their expected benefits. There was the story in the German Weimar Republic about the man who paid his life insurance premiums religiously for his entire life and when he died, his family got the insurance check, which by that time was enough to buy a loaf of bread. This is what will happen in America if the government decides to inflate its way out. Recall from Chapter 7 the descriptions of hyperinflation and the negative effects it has on the general public.

If interest rates increase and the government responds by cutting $650 billion to meet the market mandate, this will cause the GDP to fall about 6 percent, if the deficit spending is still at 6 percent then. This will start an economic depression, where GDP will fall over 10 percent (and probably much more). As millions of jobs are lost, this will start a cascading effect of business closures and more job losses. This is exactly what we are witnessing today in Greece and Spain and what we saw in the United States in the Great Depression. As millions of previously employed people hit the streets, riots will ensue and become violent. In Greece, crime has become so rampant that police are useless and a right-wing neo-Nazi party has taken up guarding people from marauders. Farm production in that country is down, survivalists are growing their own crops, few people even bother to pay taxes, and the entire life of the Greeks, as well as their economy, is broken.

As we have seen in Europe, stock markets can fall 70 percent, and real estate prices can drop over 50 percent. Since 2008 many markets across the United States have experienced a 50 percent drop in real estate prices. If you were a real estate owner in one of those markets, you would know what it feels like to lose 50 percent of the value of your property. This effect will happen nationwide, even during hyperinflation, because there will be no mortgage money available to purchase real estate.

The United States is not exempt from this mayhem; the country is under the same laws of economics as everyone else, and those laws affect its citizens just as they are affecting the Greeks and the Spanish. The United States is close on the heels of Greece, and after being burned by so many nations, the market will not let the country get to the point of Greece before it reacts with demands for higher interest rates. If the market actually stops the United States from borrowing, the Debt Trap will have closed and the entire economy will collapse due to a default or hyperinflation. The government will try printing money by having the Federal Reserve buy its debt, but this does nothing but change the default into a currency crisis, doing the same thing to the economy and jobs that we have seen happen in Germany, Argentina, Yugoslavia, and many other countries, while making the U.S. currency worthless. If the government does this, which I suspect it will, the depression will still hit and affect everybody, but hyperinflation will make the changes different.

EFFECTS OF AN ECONOMIC DEPRESSION

A depression is a terrible thing for a country and its citizens and does not affect everyone in the same way. Wealthy people who have protected themselves by transferring money to other countries, investing in gold, shorting the market, and staying liquid may not be impacted much at all. Others lose most, if not all, of their assets. That was the case during the Great Depression when unemployment hit 25 percent and real wages for those lucky enough to hold a job fell by up to 80 percent (that means living on 20 percent of your prior level of wages). For most people and the country as a whole, the Great Depression was an unmitigated disaster.

Today, the United States has a reported unemployment rate of around 8 percent. During the Great Depression, the unemployment rate hit 25 percent. These two numbers are not a good apples-to-apples comparison because they were prepared using two different sets of data. I believe the federal government is greatly understating the unemployment problem, as people who cannot find work are taken off the unemployment numbers as permanently unemployed. It is as if they do not count. With all the adjustments made to make the unemployment numbers look better than they are, I believe the country is already at a 12 to 15 percent unemployment rate—comparable to the numbers calculated during the Great Depression. As described in Chapter 3, the nation is already in an extremely weak and perilous economic condition, dependent on the federal government for deficit spending to keep the economy from collapsing. These unemployment figures, along with almost no economic growth, are primary indicators of a weakened state.

With respect to business activity during a depression, many bad things happen. Personal income, tax receipts, corporate profits, and virtually all prices fall. This phenomenon is known as deflation, which is not good. During the Great Depression, farm prices fell 60 percent, international trade fell over 50 percent (due mostly to a bill called the Smoot-Hawley Tariff Act), and unemployment hit 25 percent. Companies that manufactured products or provided services that were discretionary, such as cars, clothes, and appliances, were severely impacted by a significant fall in demand. These companies had to downsize, laying off more people and damaging other businesses dependent on them. Once the cycle starts, it continues until the market finds a bottom. During the first few years of the Great Depression, almost 2,300 banks were closed, manufacturing fell 46 percent, and wholesale prices fell 32 percent. Thousands of businesses and commercial farms were closed due to unavailability to borrow to fund operations. A modern-day example of life during the Great Depression is a city like Detroit, Michigan. Detroit has lost almost 25 percent of its population in the last 10 years, leaving 60,000 homes vacant; houses are very cheap. The city became bankrupt and in 2013 it filed for bankruptcy. Over 50 percent of African American males are unemployed, and almost 40 percent of Detroit's population lives below the poverty level. Luckily for these Detroit residents, there is the federal government to bail them out. Without the federal government, unemployment and welfare benefits flowing into the city would cease. That is what will happen to the entire country when the federal government gets caught in the Debt Trap; it will have little cash to give away to programs like welfare and unemployment.

Some businesses do very well during a depression, such as entertainment, debt collection, bankruptcy law, accounting, auto repair (people are not buying new cars), healthcare, law enforcement, the wine and spirits industry, and some government agencies. Those people who have a job are not affected as much as those who do not, but they will become the source for friends and family who need a handout.

Many noneconomic things happen during a depression. Family life changes in many ways. First, many people postpone marriage out of fear that economic hardship will take both of them down, while many people stay married longer, lowering the divorce rate. This is all to save money. Everyone goes into money preservation mode, so families eat at home more, make their entertainment at home, take short driving trips, drop country club memberships, and do hundreds of things a day differently in an effort to lower the cost of living. Of course, this hurts businesses by reducing the revenue many types of them receive. Some families grow closer together as they share the hardships; others fall apart. Psychologically, people who cannot find a job despite trying are hardest hit. The suicide rate increased dramatically during the Great Depression as did prostitution, alcoholism, cigarette smoking, and malnutrition. The crime rate soared, as you might expect: a man with a hungry family to feed will do anything to feed them. As we are seeing today, minorities and younger people are harder hit. It is more difficult for them to find a job. This will be the case during the coming depression.

WHAT IT ALL MEANS TO GOVERNMENT WORKERS

It is no secret that most government workers have received and are receiving very lucrative compensation and pensions. These are going to be the first things hit when the country gets caught in the Debt Trap. If you are receiving a government pension or will receive one, you should check out what the current funding for that pension looks like. Most pensions are underfunded, meaning there is not enough money in the pension fund to pay full benefits to all the pensioners. Pension funds invest the money they have taken in from contributions from the government. Federal pensions invest in a portfolio of government bonds, which over the last five years have had almost zero returns. Pension managers plan to make a return every year on the portfolio, which increases the amount of money they have to pay pensioners. The higher the returns, the more money there is available to pay pensioners. Since 2008, the United States has seen little economic growth, and returns have been smaller for pension funds: consequently, the amount in the pensions available to pay out to pensioners has not grown much at all. For federal pensioners this is not good news, as the amount of underfunding has increased.

Once the Debt Trap closes on the United States, people working for the federal government can expect to receive millions of pink slips, especially in administrations that are not essential. Even if someone is not terminated, he or she can expect a reduction in pay. During the Great Depression, government pay was not cut, but there will be a major difference between the coming depression and the previous one. In the Great Depression, the federal government had not borrowed much money and could deficit spend. That depression was a result of the Federal Reserve raising interest rates and shrinking money supply, a mistake of the times. In the coming depression, the government cannot borrow any more money and will be forced to cut dramatically. Social spending cuts are likely the last expenses to be cut, so if you work for the government, expect a significant pay cut.

If you are dependent on the government for any type of assistance, you can expect that essential programs will stay in effect but will be cut, especially with respect to qualifying. All of the thousands of programs listed in Chapter 4 will be cut, as well as grants to states. Government benefits that are not essential, such as the free cell phone program (Obamaphones), will be eliminated. The more critical the program, such as healthcare, welfare, and national defense, the more likely it will survive. But people receiving benefits from those programs, whether working for or receiving money from them, will see declines in benefits.

THE ORDINARY WORKING MEN AND WOMEN

If you are lucky enough to have a job, you will still not be immune from the effects of either a depression or hyperinflation, the two likely outcomes the country is facing. In the event of a depression, your home will become a refuge for friends and family who do not have jobs, have lost their homes, and need money to survive. Commodities such as oil, food, and any imported items will more than likely rise if we experience inflation. I think there is essentially no chance that the nation would enter the Debt Trap and a depression without the Federal Reserve doing everything it could to create money and inflate our way out. Consequently, my comments are aimed at the potential of hyperinflation as the most likely way out.

If the country enters a hyperinflation period, you can expect that prices will quickly outpace any increase in your salary or wages. There are many steps you need to take as the Debt Trap is closing. One of the smartest moves you can make is to sell your home or convert a variable-interest-rate mortgage to a fixed, long-term mortgage. The reason selling your home and leasing is smart is because when a crisis hits, whether an economic or currency one, real estate values plummet, and you will lose any equity you have in your home. In Greece, home values have fallen on average around 25 percent and in some areas over 50 percent, and that is because the Western European banks from other countries have mobilized to make mortgages available at relatively low interest rates, such as 6 to 7 percent. If these banks had not moved into Greece and made funds available, residential real estate would have fallen much farther. Without the banks making mortgages available, the only buyers would be people who could pay cash for 100 percent of the purchase price. There is no telling where prices will end up, but it will be ugly. If America enters a period of hyperinflation, there will be no loan availability for a few years until banks can determine that it is safe to lend. This will kill prices in the United States. The reason converting your mortgage to a long-term fixed rate is smart is that interest rates will soar, and you will have a low-fixed-rate mortgage.

Any capital purchases such as a car, new appliances, and the like, should be postponed to see if the country can dig itself out without a crash. These purchases chew up cash equity, and if you borrow money to buy them, you will be committing to cash payments in the future that you may not be able to afford. If you have to buy,

buy used. If we see hyperinflation, all commodities will skyrocket in price, including oil, electricity, food, healthcare, and clothing. Position yourself to minimize these expenses. Any commitments that involve long-term liabilities, such as a bank guaranty of someone else's debt, appliance purchases, purchasing a second home, and the like, should be avoided. Take out a significant portion of your investments in the stock market, if not all of it, and sit out this dance for awhile. The risk is far greater than the potential reward. Do everything you can to secure your job—that is the source of your cash flow. Borrowing costs will soar, as they did in the 1980s, with 20 percent interest rates (if not more). If you have any loans with variable interest rates, do what you can to pay them off (for example, sell the boat).

PREPPERS

Survivalists are now called "preppers" because they are preparing for an economic collapse. One website estimates that there are 3 million families who are actively preparing for a collapse. At first, I was a little unsure of their "extremist" views, but I kept studying. They are not crazy. The first analysis of theirs that I was initially dubious about turns out to be correct: it is smart to plan for no food access at grocery stores if a major crisis hits. Everyone is so used to seeing all the shelves full every time he or she goes to a store, so it is hard to imagine going to a grocery store and having every shelf empty. Here is how it happens. Today, grocery stores stock shelves to meet the everyday shopping demand. Most people shop twice a week and buy for three to four days at a time. The entire inventory of a grocery store turns over once a month, but fresh produce, milk, bread, and other perishable items turn over every two days. When a major event such as a stock market crash, hurricane, or 9/11 hit, people rush to the store and buy 30 days or more of supplies. If 100 percent of the customers buy an average of 3 days of supplies and the store can keep up with that, it takes only 10 percent of the customers to buy 30 days of supplies to clean the store out. This is exactly what happened to me in Nantucket, Massachusetts, during Hurricane Bob in 1991. Everyone knew it was coming several days in advance, and by the time I got to the grocery store two days before the storm hit, there was nothing left on the shelves, and I mean *nothing*. So, the preppers' idea is to buy large supplies of nonperishable goods and rotate them through your pantry, first in first out, at all times, keeping 180 days or whatever you like in supplies. They also like big supplies of flour, rice, and so forth, that can keep for long periods.

A second prepper concept is that banks in a major banking crisis may stop processing credit cards, especially on higher-risk cardholders. This may or may not happen, but it seems logical that everyone would borrow his or her cash limit and buy every food item possible in the event of a financial collapse. Shoppers would use their credit cards up to the limit. The credit card companies are not stupid and know that in the event of an economic collapse everyone would be doing this. Were I a credit card company, I would not let this happen to me because the chance of getting repaid when bills are sent out is not good. It would be a good idea to keep some cash around the house.

On the list of other necessary items are drinking water, an axe, matches or lighters, flashlights, batteries, radio, knives, first-aid kit, gasoline storage, sewing kit, and a backup plan for what to do in case of the need to evacuate immediately. These items are very cheap now, and it won't hurt to have them regardless of what happens. The backup plan should be where you and your family will go and how you will survive in the event it is unsafe where you are or if you are robbed of all your food and money. This is not a pleasant thought, but a little planning cannot hurt. The preppers even have a "bugout" bag packed in the event they need to leave in one minute.

The last thing that they are prepared with is self-defense items. This includes pepper spray and, of course, guns and knives ... and lots of bullets. It is difficult to think that things could ever get this bad, but if they do, a gun may keep the bad folks away from you and send them toward someone else who is not as prepared. Some people think it wise to have guns, and others laugh it off.

I don't think that we will see a significant amount of violence in the event of a depression or hyperinflation experience. Both Spain and Greece have seen riots but they were relatively short-lived. What has happened is that people have reached out to help those without food or medical support. This is a human, altruistic response that I think will be more prevalent here.

WE CAN STOP THIS FROM HAPPENING

The people in America who are aware of the financial repercussions of our government's excessive borrowing and spending have a secret weapon that is rarely used. Generally, people who are aware are not the type who speak about it. We seem to keep our thoughts to ourselves and allow others to think freely whatever they care to think without our influence. The liberal mind does not think like this at all: liberals are proselytizing their credo 24/7. We see every day that the liberals are lecturing to their audience—students, press followers, and entertainment watchers—and filling their minds with the liberal message. The liberal message is being propagated by every method available to the liberal mind, but the conservative mind does not push conservatives to proselytize.

The liberal mind is a strong creative force. The messages coming from that mind are aimed to destroy the public opinion of the conservative mind, and the public, starting in grade school, is buying it. Liberals claim conservatives are not caring about people, when in fact conservatives give more to charities, both in terms of total amount and percent of income. They claim that conservatives do not want to help the poor or minorities, when in fact that is exactly what conservatives want to do. In fact, in 1964 Republicans voted 80 percent for the Civil Rights Act while Democrats voted 60 percent for it. A Democratic senator, Robert Byrd of West Virginia, filibustered against it. Conservatives know that handing out welfare does nothing but keep the poor in poverty for their lives and for generations. Conservatives want to get them to a job where they can earn their way out. We have seen how job creation (capitalism) in India and China have brought around 600 million people out of poverty in the last 20 years. Liberals claim the conservatives want to keep poor and minorities down, when in fact it has been the conservatives who want to free them from government control when the liberals want to keep them where they are to continue getting their vote.

This whole story has to change if we are going to save the country from financial ruin, and we must pull out our secret weapon. Probably the greatest weapon we have is to use our businesses to educate employees about financial matters. Business owners and executives are generally well aware of financial issues and have to start talking with employees about what is happening to the country. I see this as the best hope.

All responsible business owners at some point in time realize the financial implications of operating their businesses and the decisions they make. Most of the time, employees are oblivious to financial matters, and this must change. Owners and managers should educate their employees on how financial matters affect their business and how they affect the salaries and benefits of the employees. They should also explain how government laws and regulations are affecting their business and what it means to each employee. They also need to educate their employees on the financial impact of government policies and spending on the economy as a whole and the impact of their individual business. Ultimately, the impact falls to the employee, and he or she should understand how the government policies ultimately impact the economy and the individual.

This book is a good place to start.

This book is intended to give the reader all the information necessary to decide for himself or herself about the events unfolding before our eyes. I encourage you to talk to others about the issue and do your own research on any follow-up issues you may have.

NOTES

CHAPTER 1: A NATION IN THE RED

1. Max Winkler, *Foreign Bonds: An Autopsy* (Philadelphia: Rowan Swain Company, 1933): 21–23.

2. Peter Lindert and Peter Morton, *Developing Country Debt and Economic Performance*, Volume 1, *The International Financial System* (Chicago: University of Chicago Press, 1989); David Beim and Charles Calomiris, *Emerging Financial Markets* (New York: McGraw-Hill/Irwin, 2001); Carmen Reinhart and Kenneth Rogoff, *This Time Is Different: Eight Centuries of Financial Follies* (Princeton, NJ: Princeton University Press, 2009).

3. Ibid.

4. "The Global Debt Clock," *The Economist,* referenced 2013,

   http://www.economist.com/content/global_debt_clock.

5. *Fiscal Year 2012 Budget of the U.S. Government* (Washington, DC: Office of Management and Budget, 2011), 22–23, historical tables, http://www.white-house.gov/sites/default/files/omb/budget/fy2012/assets/budget.pdf.

6. *Fiscal Year 2014 Budget of the U.S. Government* (Washington, DC: Office of Management and Budget, 2013), 183, summary tables, http://www.whitehouse.gov/sites/default/files/omb/budget/fy2014/assets/budget.pdf.

7. *Fiscal Year 2013 Budget of the U.S. Government* (Washington, DC: Office of Management and Budget, 2012), 244, summary tables, http://www.whitehouse.gov/sites/default/files/omb/budget/fy2013/assets/budget.pdf.

8. U.S. Department of the Treasury, TreasuryDirect website, October 2012, http://www.treasurydirect.gov/govt/reports/ir/ir_expense.htm.

CHAPTER 2: REAL NUMBERS

1. USGovernmentSpending.com.

2. *Economic Outlook Analysis and Forecasts*, OECD, Economic Outlook Annex Table 25: "General Government Net Debt Interest Payments," http://www.oecd-ilibrary.org/economics/country-statistical-profile-united-states_20752288-table-usa.

3. "2012 Census of Governments," U.S. Census Bureau, Table 2: "Organization Component Preliminary Estimates," http://www2.census.gov/govs/cog/2012/formatted_prelim_counts_23jul2012_2.pdf.

4. "Summary of Receipts, Outlays, and Surpluses or Deficits: 1789–2017" (Table 1.1) (Washington, DC: Office of Management and Budget, n.d.), retrieved 2013, http://www.whitehouse.gov/omb/budget/Historicals.

5. "Summary of Receipts, Outlays, Surpluses or Deficits as Percentages of GDP: 1930–2018" (Table 1.2) (Washington, DC: Office of Management and Budget, n.d.), retrieved 2013, http://www.whitehouse.gov/omb/budget/Historicals.

6. James Agresti, "National Debt Facts," JustFacts.com, 2012, http://www.justfacts.com/nationaldebt.asp.

   Calculated with data from:

   (a) *Government Current Expenditures by Function* (Washington, DC: U.S. Bureau of Economic Analysis, September 14, 2011), Table 3.16, http://www.bea.gov/national/nipaweb/TableView.asp?SelectedTable=119&ViewSeries=NO&Java=no&R.equest3Place=N&3Place=N&FromView=YES&Freq=Year&FirstYear=2008&LastYear=2009&3Place=N&AllYearsChk=YES&Update=Update&JavaBox=no#Mid;

   (b) *Fiscal Year 2012 Historical Tables: Budget of the U.S. Government* (Washington, DC: White House Office of Management and Budget, 2012), 47–55, Table 3.1: "Outlays by Superfunction and Function: 1940–2016," line item: "Veterans Benefits and Services," http://www.whitehouse.gov/sites/default/files/omb/budget/fy2012/assets/hist.pdf.

7. "2012 Index of Dependence on Government: No Slowdown in Sight," Heritage Foundation, February 8, 2012, http://www.heritage.org/research/factsheets/2012/02/index-of-dependence-on-government-no-slowdown-in-sight.

8. Mark S. Ludwick and Stan J. Bellotti, *NIPA Translation of the Fiscal Year 2013 Federal Budget* (Washington, DC: Bureau of Economic Analysis, March 2012), Table 10: "NIPA Federal Government Current," http://www.bea.gov/scb/pdf/2012/03%20March/0312_fed-budget.pdf.

9. *Economic and Budget Outlook: Fiscal Years 2000–2009* (Washington, DC: Congressional Budget Office, January 1999), http://www.cbo.gov/sites/default/files/cbofiles/ftpdocs/10xx/doc1059/eb0199.pdf.

10. "The Effects of Automatic Stabilizers on the Federal Budget as of 2013," Congressional Budget Office, reposted March 15, 2013, http://www.cbo.gov/sites/default/files/cbofiles/attachments/43977_AutomaticStablilizers3-2013.pdf.

11. *Updated Budget Projections: Fiscal Years 2012 to 2022* (Washington, DC: Congressional Budget Office, January 2012), http://www.cbo.gov/sites/default/files/cbofiles/attachments/March2012Baseline.pdf.

12. *The Budget and Economic Outlook: Fiscal Years 2013 to 2023* (Washington, DC: Congressional Budget Office, February 2013), http://www.cbo.gov/sites/default/files/cbofiles/attachments/43907-BudgetOutlook.pdf.

13. *The Budget and Economic Outlook: Fiscal Years 2013 to 2023* (Washington, DC: Congressional Budget Office, February 2013), 26, http://www.cbo.gov/sites/default/files/cbofiles/attachments/43907-BudgetOutlook.pdf.

14. (a) Stephen G. Cecchetti, M. S. Mohanty, and Fabrizio Zampolli, *The Real Effects of Debt* (Basel, Switzerland: Bank for International Settlements, 2011). They conclude that debt beyond 85 percent of GDP hurts economic growth.

    (b) Andreas Bergh and Magnus Henrekson, "Government Size and Growth: A Survey and Interpretation of the Evidence," *Journal of Economic Surveys*, April 2011. They concluded that the larger the government as a percentage of GDP, the slower the GDP growth rate.

    (c) Cristina Checherita and Philip Rother, *The Impact of High and Growing Government Debt on Economic Growth: An Empirical Investigation for the Euro Area*, European Central Bank, Working Paper 1237, August 2010. They concluded that as government debt grows as a percentage of GDP they negatively affect GDP growth in a nonlinear fashion. So as debt reaches higher levels, GDP growth suffers more and more as debt approaches 100 percent of GDP.

15. Preview of the Comprehensive 2013 Revision of the National Income and Product Accounts, Changes in Definitions and Presentations, Bureau of Economic Analysis, March 2013, http://www.bea.gov/scb/pdf/2013/03%20March/0313_nipa_comprehensive_revision_preview.pdf.

16. *Budget and Economic Outlook: Fiscal Years 2013 to 2023*, p. 44.

17. *Fiscal Year 2014 Budget of the U.S. Government* (Washington, DC: Office of Management and Budget, 2013), 183, Table S–1: "Budget Totals," http://www.whitehouse.gov/sites/default/files/omb/budget/fy2014/assets/budget.pdf.

18. *Budget and Economic Outlook: Fiscal Years 2013 to 2023*, p. 7.

19. *How Different Interest Rates Would Affect Budget Deficits* (Washington, DC: Congressional Budget Office, March 27, 2013), http://www.cbo.gov/publication/44024?utm_source=feedblitz&utm_medium=FeedBlitzEmail&utm_content=812526&utm_campaign=0).

20. "Historical Tables," *Budget of U.S. Government: Fiscal Year 2013* (Washington, DC: Office of Management and Budget, February 2012), Tables S-14 and S-15, http://www.whitehouse.gov/omb/budget/Historicals.

21. *The Budget and Economic Outlook: Fiscal Years 2012 to 2022* (Washington, DC: Congressional Budget Office, 2012), 14, Figure 2: "Federal Debt Held by the Public Projected in CBO's Baseline and Under an Alternative Fiscal Scenario," http://www.cbo.gov/sites/default/files/cbofiles/attachments/01-31-2012_Outlook.pdf.

22. *The Budget and Economic Outlook: Fiscal Years 2013 to 2023* (Washington, DC: Congressional Budget Office, February 5, 2013), 1, http://www.cbo.gov/sites/default/files/cbofiles/attachments/43907-BudgetOutlook.pdf.

23. *Fiscal Year 2012 Historical Tables* (Washington, DC: Office of Management and Budget, 2012), 139, http://www.whitehouse.gov/sites/default/files/omb/budget/fy2012/assets/hist.pdf.

24. *Fiscal Year 2012 Analytical Perspectives* (Washington, DC: Office of Management and Budget, 2012), 68, http://www.whitehouse.gov/sites/default/files/omb/budget/fy2012/assets/spec.pdf.

25. "Life Expectancy Graphs," University of Oregon, Mapping History Project, retrieved 2013, http://mappinghistory.uoregon.edu/english/US/US39-01.html.

26. *Coping with Demographic Challenge: Fewer Children and Living Longer* (Washington, DC: U.S. Social Security Administration, 2006), http://www.ssa.gov/policy/docs/ssb/v66n4/v66n4p37.html.

27. *Coping with Demographic Challenge.*

28. *Financial Audit. Bureau of the Public Debt's Fiscal Years 2007 and 2008* (Washington, DC: U.S. Government Accountability Office, 2008), 19, http://www.treasurydirect.gov/govt/reports/pd/feddebt/feddebt_ann2008.pdf.

29. Tevjian Pettinger, "France National Debt," www.EconomicsHelp.org, May 8, 2012, http://www.economicshelp.org/blog/3076/economics/france-national-debt/.

30. Tyler Durden, submitted by Mark Grant, "The True French Debt to GDP: 146%," ZeroHedge.com, April 2, 2012, http://www.zerohedge.com/news/true-french-debt-gdp-146.

31. *Fiscal Year 2012 Historical Tables* (Washington, DC: Office of Management and Budget, 2012), 139, http://www.whitehouse.gov/sites/default/files/omb/budget/fy2012/assets/hist.pdf.

32. *Fiscal Year 2013, Analytical Perspectives* (Washington, DC: Office of Management and Budget, 2012), 491, http://www.whitehouse.gov/sites/default/files/omb/budget/fy2013/assets/spec.pdf.

33. *Citizen's Guide to the 2012 Financial Report of the United States Government* (Washington, DC: United States Department of the Treasury, December 2012), p. iv. http://www.fms.treas.gov/fr/12frusg/12frusg.pdf.

34. *The 2012 Report of the Board of Trustees of the Federal Old-Age and Survivors Insurance and Federal Disability Insurance Trust Funds* (Washington, DC: U.S. Social Security Administration, April 25, 2012), 65.

35. *2012 Annual Report of the Board of Trustees of the Federal Hospital Insurance and Federal Supplementary Medical Insurance Trust Funds* (Washington, DC: Board of Trustees, Federal Hospital Insurance and Federal Supplementary Medical Insurance Trust Funds, April 23, 2012), http://www.cms.gov/Research-Statistics-Data-and-Systems/Statistics-Trends-and-Reports/ReportsTrustFunds/downloads/tr2012.pdf.

36. "Net Stock of Fixed Reproducible Tangible Wealth in Current and Chained (2005) Dollars" (Washington, DC: U.S. Bureau of Economic Analysis, 2010), in "Income, Expenditures, Poverty and Wealth," *Statistical Abstract of the United States: 2012* (Washington, DC: U.S. Census Bureau, 2012), http://www.census .gov/compendia/statab/2012/tables/12s0723.pdf.

37. *2012 Annual Report of the Board of Trustees of the Federal Hospital Insurance and Federal Supplementary Medical Insurance Trust Funds* (Washington, DC: Board of Trustees, Federal Hospital Insurance and Federal Supplementary Medical Insurance Trust Funds, April 23, 2012).

38. *The 2012 Long-Term Budget Outlook* (Washington, DC: Congressional Budget Office, 2012), 25, http://www.cbo.gov/sites/default/files/cbofiles/attachments/06-05-Long-Term_Budget_Outlook_2.pdf.

CHAPTER 3: THE DEBT TRAP

1. *Fiscal Year 2012: Historical Tables* (Washington, DC: Office of Management and Budget, 2012), http://www.whitehouse.gov/sites/default/files/omb/budget/fy2012/assets/hist.pdf.

2. *Historical Statistics of the United States: Colonial Times to 1970* (Washington, DC: U.S. Census Bureau, 2012), 992, http://www.census.gov/compendia/statab/past_years.html.

3. Federal Reserve Bank of St. Louis, "FRED Graph," Economic Research, 2012, https://research.stlouisfed.org/fred2/graph/?graph_id=94236&category_id=0.

4. "Dow Jones Industrial Average: (1900–Present Monthly)," Stockcharts.com, 2012, http://stockcharts.com/freecharts/historical/djia1900.html.

5. *Fiscal Year 2012: Historical Tables* (Washington, DC: Office of Management and Budget, 2012), http://www.whitehouse.gov/sites/default/files/omb/budget/fy2012/assets/hist.pdf.

6. *Historical Tables* (Washington, DC: Office of Management and Budget, n.d.), Table 1.2: "Summary of Receipts, Outlays, and Surpluses or Deficits as Percentages of GDP: 1930–2018," http://www.whitehouse.gov/omb/budget/Historicals.

7. The interview was on MSNBC news on August 16, 2011. It can be seen at http://www.youtube.com/watch?v=1HjTX0wdMW4.

8. *Fiscal Year 2012: Historical Tables* (Washington, D.C: Office of Management and Budget, 2012), http://www.whitehouse.gov/sites/default/files/omb/budget/fy2012/assets/hist.pdf.

9. *Historical Statistics of the United States, Colonial Times to 1970* (Washington, DC: U.S. Census Bureau, 2012), p. 992, http://www.census.gov/compendia/statab/past_years.html.

10. Roy Avik, "The Myth of Medicare's 'Lower Administrative Costs,'" *Forbes*, June 30, 2011, http://www.forbes.com/sites/aroy/2011/06/30/the-myth-of-medicares-low-administrative-costs/.

11. Raw data from International Monetary Fund World Economic Outlook Database, April 2012 edition. Graph prepared by Randall Hoven, American Thinker, using simple regression analysis from raw data, http://www.americanthinker .com/2012/05/in_search_of_the_dreaded_austerity.html.

12. *Federal Debt and the Risk of Financial Crisis* (Washington, DC: Congressional Budget Office, 2012), www.cbo.gov/publication/21625.

13. "Greece Government Bond 10Y," TradingEconomics.com, 2012, http://www .tradingeconomics.com/greece/government-bond-yield.

14. *Federal Debt and the Risk of Financial Crisis* (Washington, DC: Congressional Budget Office, 2012), www.cbo.gov/publication/21625.

15. Constantino Bresciani-Turroni, *The Economics of Inflation* (1937), Northampton, Great Britain: Universita Bocconi, Table IV, 441.

CHAPTER 4: THE FINANCIAL CAUSES OF THE DEBT TRAP

1. James Agresti, "National Debt Facts," JustFacts.com, April 26, 2011, http:// www.justfacts.com/nationaldebt.asp/:
Office of Management and Budget. (2012). Historical Tables. Calculated with data from:
(a) Table 3.2: "Federal Government Current Receipts and Expenditures," line items 1 and 20: "Current receipts" and "Current expenditures," U.S. Department of Commerce, Bureau of Economic Analysis, last revised February 25, 2011, http://www.bea.gov/national/nipaweb/TableView.asp?S electedTable=87&ViewSeries=NO&Java=no&Request3Place=N&3Place =N&FromView=YES&Freq=Year&FirstYear=2008&LastYear=2010&3Place =N&AllYearsChk=YES&Update=Update&JavaBox=no#Mid;
(b) Table 1.1.5: "Gross Domestic Product," U.S. Department of Commerce, Bureau of Economic Analysis, last revised February 25, 2011, http://www .bea.gov/national/nipaweb/TableView.asp?SelectedTable=5&ViewSeries =NO&Java=no&Request3Place=N&3Place=N&FromView=YES&Freq =Year&FirstYear=1929&LastYear=2010&3Place=N&AllYearsChk= YES&Update=Update&JavaBox=no#Mid.

2. *The Budget and Economic Outlook: Fiscal Years 2013 to 2023* (Washington, DC: Congressional Budget Office, February 2013), 20, http://www.cbo.gov/sites/ default/files/cbofiles/attachments/43907-BudgetOutlook.pdf.

3. "2013 Index of Economic Freedom," 2013 Macro-Economic Data, The Heritage Foundation, 2013, http://www.heritage.org/index/explore?view=by-variables.

4. Jean-Baptiste Colbert, French economist and finance minister under King Louis XIV of France (1619–1683). Retrieved from www.searchquotes.com/quotes/ author/Jean_Baptiste_Colbert/.

5. "A–Z Index of U.S. Government Departments and Agencies? USA.gov, 2012, http://www.usa.gov/directory/federal/index.shtml; also *Catalog of Federal Domestic Assistance*, 2012, https://www.cfda.gov/.

6. John B. Taylor, *First Principles: Five Keys to Restoring America's Prosperity* (New York: W.W. Norton & Company, 2012), p. 117.

7. *Catalog of Federal Domestic Assistance* (2012), https://www.cfda.gov/.

8. *The 2012 Long-Term Budget Outlook* (Washington, DC: Congressional Budget Office, 2012), 24–25, http://www.cbo.gov/sites/default/files/cbofiles/attachments/06–05 Long-Term_Budget_Outlook_2.pdf.

9. *OECD Health Data 2012*, OECD.org (The Organization for Economic Co-operation and Development), 2012, http://www.oecd.org/health/healthpoliciesanddata/ oecdhealthdata2012-frequentlyrequesteddata.htm.

CHAPTER 5: PSYCHOLOGICAL CAUSES OF THE DEBT TRAP

1. Tad DeHaven, "Corporate Welfare in the Federal Budget," *Policy Analysis*, July 25, 2012, http://www.cato.org/sites/cato.org/files/pubs/pdf/PA703.pdf. © The Cato Institute. Used by permission.

2. *Annual Report Fiscal Year 2011*, Amtrak, 2012, http://www.amtrak.com/ ccurl/677/158/2011-Amtrak-Annual-Report-Final.pdf.

3. LeBon, Gustave. *The Psychology of Socialism* (Kitchener, Ontario: Batoche Books, 2001), p.127.

4. *Catalog of Federal Domestic Assistance* (2012), https://www.cfda.gov/.

5. Ibid.

6. John B. Taylor, *First Principles: Five Ways to Restoring America's Prosperity* (New York: W.W. Norton & Company, 2007), Chapter 5.

7. Karl Marx and Friedrich Engels, *Manifesto of the Communist Party*, 1848. Translated by Samuel Moore in cooperation with Friedrich Engels (London, 1892).

8. Alexis de Tocqueville, *The Old Regime and the Revolution*, 1856. Translated by John Bonner (New York: Harper & Brothers, 1856), Chapter XV.

9. *The World Factbook*, U.S. Central Intelligence Agency, 2012, https://www.cia. gov/library/publications/the-world-factbook/.

10. *Total Outlays to GDP* (Washington, DC: U.S. Department of Commerce, Bureau of Economic Analysis, *2012)*, http://www.bea.gov/itable/.

11. *Temporary Assistance for Needy Families: Implications of Changes in Participation Rates*, GAO-10-495T (Washington, DC: U.S. Government Accountability Office, 2010), http://www.gao.gov/assets/130/124169.pdf.

12. Steven Pinker, *How the Mind Works* (New York: W.W. Norton & Company, 1997), p. 426.

13. Lyle H. Rossiter, Jr., *The Liberal Mind: The Psychological Causes of Political Madness*, 2006, p.329.

14. Pinker, Preface, x.

CHAPTER 6: THE EUROPEAN ECONOMIC AND CURRENCY CRISES

1. "Euro Indicators: Euro Area Government Debt Up to 88.2% of GDP," *Eurostat*, News Release (2012), http://europa.eu/rapid/press-release_STAT-13-114_en.htm.

2. Tyler Durden, "Spain's Real Debt to GDP Right Now: 146.6%," *Zero Hedge*, June 11, 2012, http://www.zerohedge.com/news/spains-real-debt-gdp-right-now-1466.

3. Trading Economics.com, 2012, http://www.tradingeconomics.com.

4. Interest rate data, Eurostat (2012).

5. "Monthly Statement of Treasury Securities," (Washington, DC: U.S. Department of the Treasury, September 2012).

6. Sidney Homer and Richard Sylla, *History of Interest Rates*, 4th ed. (New York: John Wiley & Sons, 2005), 1–5.

7. Moody's Investors Service, July 13, 2012. Rating Action: Moody's downgrades Italy's government bond rating to Baa2 from A3, maintains negative outlook. Retrieved from: https://www.moodys.com/research/Moodys-downgrades-Italys-government-bond-rating-to-Baa2-from-A3—PR_250567.

8. "Destitution and Hunger in Greek Prisons: 'Not Even One Grain of Rice Left in Warehouses,'" *The Daily Sheeple*, June 3, 2012, http://www.thedailysheeple.com/destitution-and-hunger-in-greek-prisons-not-even-one-grain-of-rice-left-in-warehouses_062012.

9. "Risk of Greek Blackouts Increases as Traders Cut or Halt Power Supplies," *The Telegraph*, October 26, 2012, http://www.telegraph.co.uk/finance/financialcrisis/9349980/Risk-of-Greek-blackouts-increases-as-traders-cut-or-halt-power-supplies.html.

10. "Bilateral Trade and Trade with the World," European Commission, April 2013, 10, http://trade.ec.europa.eu/doclib/docs/2006/september/tradoc_113465.pdf.

CHAPTER 7: THE 5 WAYS OUT OF THE DEBT TRAP

1. Alexander Jung, "Millions, Billions, Trillions: Germany in the Era of Hyperinflation," *Spiegel*, 2009, http://www.spiegel.de/international/germany/millions-billions-trillions-germany-in-the-era-of-hyperinflation-a–641758.html.

ACKNOWLEDGMENTS

I would like to begin by thanking all the professional business people, economists, psychiatrists, and friends who directly and indirectly contributed to my research. Thanks also to the educators at Highland Park schools in Dallas, Texas, at Washington and Lee University and School of Law, and at the University of Virginia Graduate Business School, who gave themselves to my education and the education of thousands of others. Particularly, I am grateful to the educators at Washington and Lee University for instilling in all of us a healthy work ethic, the necessity of behaving as a gentleman at all times, and the maintenance of the highest ethical standards (honor system) in all endeavors. As with all educated people, educators are at the core of your character.

I acknowledge as contributors to society those leaders who operate under high moral principles and who can see and act on the vicissitudes of the complex world in which we live. These leaders are not seduced by the power given to them as elected officials or executive management of American businesses. Their focus is on the long-term good for the most people. They are objective, do their homework before decisions are made, consider all options, and assess the impact on all who will be affected by any decision. These people are complex and caring; they must be honest, altruistic, brave, confident, understanding, moral, ethical, trustworthy, humorous, loving, hardworking, smart, clever, competitive, likeable, organized, savvy, team-oriented, authoritative, goal-oriented, flexible, level-headed, objective, concerned with the personal development of others, perseverant, respectful, self-confident, humble, accountable, jet-fueled, good under pressure, action-oriented, relationship savvy, selfless, tough, positive, willing to sacrifice, good at prioritization, accessible, balanced, capable of sharing power, rule following, and a good "poker player." These are just a few of the attributes of a leader.

A few simple events in my life brought home the importance of financial stability. During college, I dreamed of being a professional pilot, but the pilots coming out of the Vietnam War were getting these jobs. I turned my dreams to flying for a corporation until some corporate pilots explained how little they made and that I should get "a real job" and fly for fun. This I did and it has made all the difference. I encourage everyone to reach out and pass on wisdom to others: it can change their lives. The lesson I learned is true for people, businesses, and governments; if you have no money, you are limited. After this event, I turned to an education in business and law and learned how to make money. This core simple law of economics has long since been forgotten by Congress and various administrations. Before you can do anything else, you must first take care of business. It will be our downfall without leaders who know what Adam Smith knew over 200 years ago: A nation can fail in only two ways—by the sword and by debt.

I will forever be indebted to my team at McGraw-Hill, including Tom Miller and Dannalie Diaz, who professionally managed the process of taking this book to market. I am also forever indebted to Jan Miller and everyone at Dupree Miller & Associates for all they did to make this book happen. Lastly, I want to thank all those who take what they learn in this book and in their daily lives to others in an attempt to clean up the financial quagmire in which this country has descended.

INDEX

ABOUT THE AUTHOR

Murray Holland is a managing director of MHT Partners, a Dallas, Texas, based investment banking firm. He was chairman of the board and chief executive officer of Convergent Media Systems Corporation, Atlanta, Georgia, from 1992 to 2006, and chairman of the board of Convergent Group Corporation, Denver, Colorado, from 1993 through 1999. He has also served as chairman and CEO of BTI Americas, Inc., senior VP and managing director for First Boston Corporation and Kidder, Peabody & Co., respectively, and a partner in the Dallas, Texas, law firm of Akin, Gump, Strauss, Hauer & Feld.